Thieves of Book Row

TRAVIS McDADE

Thieves of Book Row

New York's Most Notorious Rare Book Ring and the Man Who Stopped It

OXFORD
UNIVERSITY PRESS

OXFORD
UNIVERSITY PRESS

Oxford University Press is a department of the
University of Oxford. It furthers the University's objective
of excellence in research, scholarship, and education
by publishing worldwide.

Oxford   New York
Auckland   Cape Town   Dar es Salaam   Hong Kong   Karachi
Kuala Lumpur   Madrid   Melbourne   Mexico City   Nairobi
New Delhi   Shanghai   Taipei   Toronto

With offices in
Argentina   Austria   Brazil   Chile   Czech Republic   France   Greece
Guatemala   Hungary   Italy   Japan   Poland   Portugal   Singapore
South Korea   Switzerland   Thailand   Turkey   Ukraine   Vietnam

Oxford is a registered trademark of Oxford University Press
in the UK and certain other countries.

Published in the United States of America by
Oxford University Press
198 Madison Avenue, New York, NY 10016

Library of Congress Cataloging-in-Publication Data
McDade, Travis.
Thieves of Book Row : New York's most notorious rare book ring
and the man who stopped it / Travis McDade.
pages   cm
Includes bibliographical references and index.
ISBN 978-0-19-992266-6 (hardcover)
1. Rare book—History—20th century.   2. Thieves—Literary collections.
3. Art thefts—New York (State)—New York.   4. Rare books—New York
(State—New York.   5. New York Public Library—History—20th century.
6. Poe, Edgar Allan, 1809–1849—Manuscripts.   7. Poe, Edgar Allan, 1809–1849—Library
resources.   I. Title.
Z1029.M33 2013   090.9'04—dc23   2012042895

Frontispiece: The New York Public Library at the corner of Fifth Avenue and 42nd Street,
a few years after its opening. The area was crowded with pedestrians and traffic,
a situation favorable to book thieves. © *The New York Public Library Archives,
The New York Public Library, Astor Lenox and Tilden Foundations.*

9 8 7 6 5 4 3 2 1

Printed in the United States of America
on acid-free paper

*To
PWM*

Ours is a world of words.

I do not believe that it will ever be possible to stop book stealing from large public libraries.

What portion of Rare Book Sales of the last 100 years do you think have been ex-library books salted into the private stacks? Clean of label, stamp and emboss and often with an "Historic Origin" tale tied to each. What portion of national dealers, largest to smallest, rarity stocks offered and sold, likewise? Some knowingly stolen and some (very few indeed) not known as such. Any given estimate would be merely a guess but that ratio very high indeed. The Public Library has been both the largest source and also the easiest and quickest.

Contents

Acknowledgments

LIKE MOST STORIES THAT HAVE NEVER BEEN TOLD, THIS ONE had to be pieced together from hundreds of parts. Court records, deposition transcripts, institutional memos, interlibrary letters, newspaper articles, magazine profiles, bookseller memoirs, and unpublished remembrances—I took sources where I could find them. This meant that aside from a great deal of research, which I like to do, I was forced to rely on the help of others, which I don't like to do. Still, I was continually surprised at how cheerfully librarians and archivists provided me sources—even if I prefaced the request with "You probably won't have anything like this." These folks did a great deal of work on my behalf—including scaring up files that had never been accessed before—when their only payment was my thanks. Through poor recordkeeping or oversight I will undoubtedly leave out people who have been of material help to me, and for that I am sorry.

Kimberly Reynolds, curator of manuscripts at the Boston Public Library, found in their collection some really terrific material that immensely helped the book. Margaret Sullivan at the Boston Police Archives was also very helpful. Sean Thibodeau at the Pollard Memorial Library in Lowell and Marcia Jakubowicz at the Thayer Memorial Library in Lancaster were extremely helpful in tracking down information at their libraries. My first visit to the New York Public Library was getting ready to be a disaster before I got some wonderful help from Ted Teodoro and Jessica Pigza. Jessica also helped me several other times after that. Susan Malsbury at the NYPL also did some great searching on my behalf.

Sue Presnell at the Lilly Library at Indiana University answered several of my questions on the physical state of its *Al Aaraaf*. Very early in the process, the Harvard University Archives sent me its file of newspaper articles on Clarke. The Ontario Archives sent me its amazing Harold Clarke file. Matt Schuler at Iowa State was able to get me an article I could not locate elsewhere. Ann Wieland at the Cleveland Public Library searched their archives on my behalf. Julie Koehne at the Hamilton (Ohio) County Law Library helped me immensely tracking down an important court case. Priscilla Gabela braved the copy machine at the New York Municipal Archives when I could not. Steven Rothman, president of the Philobiblon Club, was kind enough to send me a 1989 speech George Allen delivered to the group in Philadelphia. Sandra Stelts, curator of rare books and manuscripts at Penn State, helped me find some great information regarding its collection. Meghan Constantinou at the Grolier Club offered me both access to its wonderful library and help once I got there. Elizabeth Fuller at the Rosenbach Museum and Library was also very helpful, providing me access to its collection and helping me track down some important letters.

I teach a class called "Rare Books, Crime & Punishment." The last two times I've taught it, the students have read one part of this manuscript or another; many of them offered feedback of the sort that was very helpful. On several occasions I sought, without success, to find any living relatives of William Bergquist. My research eventually led me to Shawn Ott, a relative of Bergquist's, who was doing his own genealogical work on the family. With his help I was able to locate Jeanne Flagg, Bergquist's daughter. It was a treat to speak with Mrs. Flagg about her memories of her father and her own life in New York; I thank her for the opportunity.

I asked several people to read the manuscript at various stages. One of the things they all have in common is that they are very busy people, so it means a great deal to me that they took time to read my work. Jym Gregory, a fellow student of history, offered good advice and a careful read of the manuscript. Jeremy Dibbell, a person I know mostly through his fine blog, has always been generous with his time in reading things I've written. Thanks again to him for reading this and offering me good advice. Irene Sakellarakis has been a remarkably patient and dedicated reader of my work for many years. As usual, she gave me good and important feedback on the manuscript. Lyn Warmath has also been a tremendous supporter of my work and gave my manuscript a careful read. Tom Ulen, too, was kind enough to read and comment on an early draft of the book.

One of the best things about law school was getting to meet Emery Lee and Chris Maynard. Both one-time law review editors, they have solicitously reviewed my manuscripts. Emery looked at this book with an exacting, but generous, eye. Chris, too, offered fantastic advice in matters both large and small. Mark Mitek, a member of the Washington, DC, bar who had plenty more he could have been doing, looked at an earlier version of the manuscript with the eye of a man used to reading contracts. He gave me comprehensive and important notes, many of which guided the book toward its later incarnation. Don Krummel, a great bookman himself, taught the class that first got me interested in rare books. He was nice enough to read the manuscript and give me the sorts of advice I simply could not have gotten anywhere else.

Thanks very much to my editor, Nancy Toff. She was extremely patient with me throughout the process of getting approval for the project, and in getting the manuscript turned into a book. Her advice on my manuscript made it much better, even if I was sometimes reluctant to take it. Maybe more important, she let me keep the things I thought were necessary, even if she disagreed. I can't ask for anything more than that. Sonia Tycko, also at OUP, was equally patient in helping me with the fine details of the editing and publication process. I would also like to thank my colleagues at the University of Illinois. I have leaned on some of them for favors or advice and never been turned down. The University of Illinois in general, and the College of Law in particular, is a terrific place to work and I feel lucky to be there.

I have a really wonderful family. I have the best parents in the world and great siblings, to boot. Aside from the general love and support I get, they have also read parts of my work and offered me sound feedback. Thanks to Dick and Kay McDade, Pam Manselle, Traci Yingling, and Amy Goudschaal. I am also now doubly fortunate in that I have great in-laws—Miles, Shelley, and Jordan—that I gained by marrying my wife. Ashley Mitek has heard me talk about this story (and many others) since I first discovered it. She has always been a tireless cheerleader of my work, a ceaseless listener-to-stories and has kindly let me spend countless weekends in the office. So, thanks to her for her support—and for being altogether terrific.

Thieves of Book Row

Prologue

A WANDERING STAR

Edgar Allan Poe never lived to be as old as he looked. He was born poor and died poor, and in the forty years separating those events he knew success just often enough to know what he was missing, supporting himself in the meantime with hack writing and routine editorial work, never staying in one place long. Sixty years after his death, the *Baltimore Sun* put this sentiment more poetically: "He raised the cup of prosperity many times in his life and every time, just when he was about to place his parched lips to the draft, Fortune cast it away from him."[1] Of course, prosperity was not the only cup he raised to his lips. Poe nurtured an artist's range of vices—he also gambled with money he did not have, accrued debts he could not pay, and quarreled regularly with men in a position to do him harm. In short, he acted a great deal like a genius well before posterity bestowed that laurel upon him.

Like many artists, he comforted himself with the idea that a future age would treat his work more kindly than his own. But not even his opulent imagination could have foretold how right he was. In the century after his death, the popularity of his written work grew so much that even the physical artifacts of his publishing career would acquire the value of relics. A single faded copy of any number of his printed works took on astounding value, becoming worth several times the sum total of money he had made in his entire life. This was particularly true of his early poetry.

Tamerlane and Other Poems was published in 1827, when Poe was a teen with adult-size problems. Attributed only to "a Bostonian," this drab little book was printed in a run of no more than two hundred copies, the poems composed between bouts of gambling and drinking at the University of Virginia.[2] (An early biographer noted that while there Poe "led a very dissipated life, the manners of the college being at that time extremely dissolute."[3]) The first poems from an unhappy teen are rarely a recipe for publishing success, even in the nineteenth century, so *Tamerlane* met with predictable results. But despite the lack of popular response, this first flimsy issuance from Poe's pen did offer two things: the benefit of experience, and material he could revise.

With the optimism of youth, he set to work on his follow-up almost immediately. Half its poems were revised versions of ones that appeared in *Tamerlane*, but the title poem was new, and it was wonderful. It was called "Al Aaraaf" after a supernova astronomer Tycho Brahe discovered 250 years earlier—a wandering star, according to Poe, that "burst forth, in a moment, with a splendor surpassing that of Jupiter," and then gradually disappeared. It was also, in the Koran, a sort of purgatory "instituted for the benefit of those who, though too good for hell, are not fitted for heaven."[4] In a letter to Isaac Lea of the important publisher Carey, Lea & Carey, Poe claimed Al Aaraaf was a "medium between Heaven and Hell where men suffer no punishment, but yet do not attain that tranquil & even happiness which they suppose to be the characteristic of heavenly enjoyment."[5] He very much wanted Lea to print the collection, and so he closed his entreaty with a qualification: the work was "by a minor" and "truly written under extraordinary disadvantages." Despite this caveat, the publishing house was unwilling to take a risk on the twenty-year-old without a one-hundred-dollar guarantee against losses. Lacking anything close to this, Poe was forced to look elsewhere. In November 1829, he settled on the small Baltimore firm Hatch and Dunning.[6] *Al Aaraaf, Tamerlane and Minor Poems* was printed the next month in a run of about 250 copies.

Having learned the lessons of *Tamerlane*, Poe endeavored to make his second publishing experience—the first using his name—a success. He meant to make it available in bookstores, for one thing, and to have it reviewed in magazines and newspapers. These were good ideas, and he received a modicum of gratification on both counts. *Al Aaraaf* was sold in a few places, and it garnered several reviews. Unfortunately, the sum total of critical opinion of the work could best be described as mixed. The view of *The Ladies Magazine*, a Boston publication, is probably most representative. "It is very difficult to speak of these poems as they deserve. A part are exceedingly boyish, feeble, and altogether deficient in the common characteristics of poetry; but then we have parts, and parts too, of considerable length, which remind us of no less a poet than Shelly [*sic*].

The author, who appears to be very young, is evidently a fine genius; but he wants judgment, experience, tact."[7] Another review noted that the sheer originality of the material made the reader forget the uneven poetry read like "travelling over a pile of brick bats."[8]

Even well-reviewed books of poetry are hard to sell, so very few copies were purchased. Fewer still were kept—those that survived more than a decade were generally the ones given as gifts to friends or relatives.[9] Even Poe did not hang on to any. In an 1845 letter to James Lowell, he noted he had been "so negligent as to not preserve copies of any of my volumes of poems—nor was either worthy [of] preservation."[10] But while early commercial flops are the sorts of things that haunt writers' nightmares, they are often the stuff of booksellers' dreams. Interest in *Al Aaraaf* picked up only decades after Poe's death when, because of the success of his other works, collectors discovered his early writing; by then, there were almost no copies left.

One collector, writing in the March 1862 issue of the *The Philobiblion*, demonstrated how little was even known of Poe's early work. "I am desirous of obtaining information concerning the first volume of verse published by the late Edgar A. Poe, its date, size, contents, etc. It appears to be a scarce book—so scarce, indeed, that Dr. Griswold never saw it."[11] By this he meant Rufus Wilmot Griswold, one of Poe's rivals in life, detractors in death (announcing Poe's demise, he noted that many would be startled "but few will be grieved"[12]), and self-appointed Poe literary executor. Griswold was the author of *Poets and Poetry of America,* whose fifteenth edition, available in 1862, had a brief biography of Poe. Of his early works, Griswold wrote only that the author "had printed, while in the military academy, a small volume of poems, most of which were written in early youth."[13] More than thirty years after *Al Aaraaf* was published and more than fifteen after Poe had become world famous, the slim book of poetry, the first to bear his name, was all but unknown.

But it was not *entirely* unknown. Evert Augustus Duyckinck, in his 1856 *Cyclopedia of American Literature*, got it right, noting when, where, and how *Al Aaraaf* was published. Of course, Duyckinck had been a friend of Poe, so it is not surprising he knew of it. Also, he owned one of the few remaining copies, so getting the title right was as easy as walking to his bookshelf. In the 1870s, Duyckinck's *Al Aaraaf* made its way from that bookshelf to the terrific collection housed in James Lenox's library, on Fifth Avenue across from Central Park. There it sat, protected by Lenox's strict usage rules, until the second decade of the twentieth century, when it moved some thirty blocks south, as part of the foundational collection of the recently completed New York Public Library. It was still there on a cold Saturday in January 1931 when a young man from North Carolina, using an alias, requested it from the rare book collection.

Al Aaraaf, Tamerlane and Minor Poems—thin, delicate, and cured to the color of weak tea by the passing century—was about to make another thirty-block trip to the south. This time it came to rest in an area known to all of literary America as Book Row.

CHAPTER 1

The Antics of the
Leading Industrials

THERE WAS NOTHING QUITE LIKE MANHATTAN'S BOOK ROW.
Stretching up six blocks of Fourth Avenue from Astor Place to
Union Square, the area came by its name honestly: It was simply packed
with booksellers. They came in all shapes and sizes, these stores—large to
small, crowded to sparse, opulent to shabby. They ranged from specialty
shops to general practitioners, from highbrow to low-, from fly-by-night
concerns to near-permanent fixtures. One bookseller noted that some
"shops were impressive, specialized, antiquarian enterprises operated by
highly knowledgeable bookmen; some were clean; some were notori-
ously scruffy book caves where occasional worthwhile first editions and
elusive titles awaited searching and patient eyes, along with thousands of
unwanted volumes priced at a dollar, fifty cents, and even less."[1] If it was
printed, it was said it could be found there, somewhere, in an area that
was home to more than a million books.

Standing in the middle of a pocked and pitted Fourth Avenue in
1930, it was not hard to imagine it so. There were books everywhere—
stacked in windows, painted on awnings, in the very air people breathed:
the dusty smell of old tomes exhaled from each open door. Books even
crowded the sidewalks in front of the shops. Weighing down rickety and
overburdened tables, under handmade signs announcing their afford-
ability, these bargain-priced books were as much a part of the scenery of
Fourth Avenue as the derby hat and Model A. Even on a bleak day, the
novelist and book collector Christopher Morley recalled, when a stiff
wind "blew down the street, the pavement counters were lined with
people turning over disordered piles of volumes."[2]

In other parts of the city, crowds of men jostling for position, manners subservient to appetite, meant breadlines and apple carts. On Fourth Avenue it meant cheap books. The sidewalk stands lined the street to tempt subway riders or patrons of Wanamaker's department store with their Depression-cheap prices, and, for many booksellers these tables were as important as the in-store stock. In his novel *The Haunted Bookshop*, Morley, modeling a character on the proprietor of a Book Row business, explained the importance of the ten-cent books he set out on tables first thing every morning. To draw customers in, this bookseller noted, there was nothing like a whole bunch of cheap books right out on the sidewalk, particularly in bad weather. "When it rains I shove out an awning, which is mighty good business. Someone is sure to take shelter, and spend the time in looking over the books. A really heavy shower is often worth fifty or sixty cents. Once a week I change my pavement stock...a good deal of it is tripe, but it serves its purpose."[3] That purpose was to bring patrons close enough to the entrance that they might peek through the windows (they, too, often "opaque with books") or wander inside.[4]

Of course, for many folks, the inside of a bookstore might as well not exist. For them Book Row *was* the bargain stands—the stores were merely backdrops, awning supports, or way stations for soon-to-be-bargain books. A 1929 *New Yorker* account noted it was difficult even to *get* inside one bookstore because its doorway was "almost impassable" with stalls of cheap books.[5] The 1930s *WPA Guide to New York City*, over the course of seven hundred pages, gave exactly two sentences to Book Row. One of them was this: "The outside tables, displaying bargain items, attract browsers at all hours."[6]

In 1930 the browsers were still mostly men, dressed in starched collars and waistcoats, heads covered with hats. Some milled around Book Row with nothing much better to do, passing the time the Depression made available, avoiding their homes. Others were there with a purchase in mind. But at any distance, it was difficult to tell one from another just by looking at him. Henry Roth's 1934 novel *Call It Sleep*, about his life as an immigrant growing up near Book Row, noted of a character, "His clothes were the ordinary clothes the ordinary New Yorker wore in that period— sober and dull. A black derby accentuated the sharpness and sedentary pallor of his face; a jacket, loose on his tall spare frame, buttoned up in a V close to the throat; and above the V a tightly knotted black tie."[7] It was men of this sort who, at any random moment, comprised most of the area's population.

But there were a few women, as well. Most, to be sure, were accompanying their husbands, but some were shopping on their own. They were still largely dressed in the high fashion of the boom years: slim dresses ending a few inches below the knees. "Not yet have Mae West's curves become a national influence," wrote historian Frederick Lewis Allen in 1939 of the style at the beginning of that decade. The dresses were still slim-fitting and V-necked, the hats almost helmets with "a lock or two of hair to decorate the cheek."[8] That year was still the brackish time between the boom of the 1920s and the coming austerity of the 1930s.

But whatever people were wearing, they provided only scenery and an ever-dwindling amount of income. The personality of Book Row was in the shops, with the proprietors—the men whose fortunes rose and fell not just on what strangers deemed the quality of their stock, but the amount these people had left to spend on a luxury item. Some of these booksellers knew books and some did not, and most everyone had strong opinions on who fell into which category. Some knew little else *but* books, including the art of business: a surprising number of store owners actively discouraged patrons from their shops, treating browsers as intruders and buyers as pirates, and preferred to be left alone to read "in their littered Dickensian dust bins."[9] Other booksellers would stand in the doorways, striking up conversations to lure the sidewalk crowd inside. Some would disappear into their own stacks, browsing their collection to get to know it better or to prime the pump for men peering in. In short, there were as many kinds of sellers as there were stores. One bookman put it this way: Some "Book Row proprietors and employees would have been quite comfortable at a university faculty meeting. Others would have to skip the meeting to see their parole officers."[10] And they were all struggling to make a living "on that old street, surrounded by a ramshackle neighborhood, invaded by factory buildings and sweat-shops," battered by an unrelenting economy.[11]

Ultimately, Book Row proprietors were all working toward the same basic goal. But they were also in business to survive, and sometimes that was necessarily at the expense of others. They were alternately coopera-tive and competitive, simultaneously trying to outperform their neigh-bors while doing business with them. They had sharp elbows but held short grudges, all with the understanding that the more sellers there were on Book Row, the better it was for everyone. It was a delicate balance. "We dealers both loved and hated each other," said bookseller Harold Briggs, "but we stuck together."[12]

This was a fact that ran deeper than just good business. Many were friends simply because they had so much in common. They would gather in one shop or another after hours, gossip, swap yarns, and "sip tea from thumb-smudged cups of tin."[13] But many had come up in life together, starting out in the profession working for still other dealers. The Madison Book Store, in particular, apprenticed many future booksellers, as did the rare book department at Dodd & Mead. Most of these men had gotten their starts working for a few dollars per week, sweeping floors, washing windows, running errands, and pretty much doing whatever was asked of them by established dealers. They worked their way up to book scout, or salesman, learning lessons about the trade where they could find them.

One bookseller, Abe Shiffrin, who trained at the elbow of a predecessor, memorialized these early bookselling lessons in fiction. His novel's main character, a bookstore owner, started out as "a salaried clerk" in the place he later came to own. "[S]tudying the quaint business style of his petulant, patriarchal employer, watching the way the old man bought and sold second-hand books, listening to him coughing arguments with customers and salesman, imitating his mannerisms and chuckling at his embarrassments, he arrived at the conclusion that all a bookseller required in order to make a comfortable living was an abundance of books on every subject and in nearly every language."[14] It was a tough, unforgiving business that required what one antiquarian bookseller called "certain indispensable characteristics."[15] One of these characteristics was fierce loyalty.

Another was proximity to other dealers. The idea behind this concentration of bookstores in a single area was that it was a boon to business—it was the one place where book buyers would travel in search of books, knowing that if one of a dozen shops did not have a particular item, it might be found in another. Guido Bruno, in his 1922 book, *Adventures in American Bookshops*, noted that no "matter how large and complete the stock of a secondhand bookdealer may be, his neighbor's collection will be quite different. The clients of secondhand bookshops like 'to browse about.'"[16] And the more such neighbors, the better it was for shoppers. For a half century, that idea was just about right. For book lovers of all kinds—from bargain hunters to browsers to bibliophiles—Book Row was a kind of heaven. But for libraries, it was a kind of a hell.

Used books had to come from somewhere, and by far the cheapest and most plentiful source were the public institutions whose role it was to lend them. As one book dealer and thief put it, American libraries were "perpetual springs, always filling and always overflowing…the eternal well…with cracked walls."[17] Some of the former contents of that well, by 1930, were commonly found on Fourth Avenue bookshelves.

"Not too many people were completely pure in the book business," Book Row dealer Walter Goldwater reminisced euphemistically from a distance of sixty years. In fact, a great many dealers were absolutely *im*pure, particularly during the Depression, when a difficult industry was made nearly impossible. Booksellers did what they could to survive, ranging from the mildly unethical to the outright criminal. And most dealers, in one way or another, benefited from it.

One of the minor crimes, practiced with astonishing regularity, was called "sophisticating," which meant "improving" a copy of a book before selling it. A bookseller would take apart an incomplete version of a first edition and substitute the important "points" (the peculiar features of a book that distinguish it from other copies) into a much nicer version of a later edition. If done skillfully enough, this created a high-value book from low-value scraps. Many sellers did the work, and still more abetted it. The protagonist of the 1936 novel *Murder in the Bookshop* put it this

Fourth Avenue bookstall browsers trying to find a bargain. Mosk's Book Store, 1935. *Photograph by George Herlick, Museum of the City of New York, Federal Arts Project Collection.*

way: "The fact that the rare book trade is largely confined to scholars and literary men doesn't necessarily make it immune to tricks of the trade known to other lines of business. Indeed, it's one of the easiest fields in which to practice fraud. Often the buyer knows nothing of the fine points of a rare book save what the dealer tells him."[18] In other words, buyers with more money than sense got what they deserved.

The most infamous sophisticator on Book Row was Whitman Bennett (which is why sophisticated books were known locally as Bennett copies). He was known to think that if a rich collector wanted a first-edition *Tom Sawyer* in mint condition, he should have it—whether it was available or not. So Bennett would take a fine copy of a second or third edition, remove the binding, and put it inside the covers of a first edition. He was so good at it, almost no one could tell the difference.[19]

One of the most imaginative sophistications involved *The Ebb-Tide*, a book written by Robert Louis Stevenson and his stepson Lloyd Osbourne. It was published in serial form in *McClure's* magazine, so Samuel McClure had the manuscript—but he had only the Stevenson chapters. Gabriel Wells, one of the most well-known rare book dealers in New York, paid $1,500 for the incomplete manuscript. Then he contacted Osbourne, who was still alive, and gave him $500 to write in longhand the parts he originally contributed to the book. He packaged this combined manuscript as a complete copy and sold it for $10,000.[20]

Of course, sophisticating books and overcharging ignorant buyers were relatively minor crimes, especially in terms of their impact on libraries. But trafficking in stolen books—a crime practiced throughout Book Row—was another matter altogether. Regardless of what they later said on the subject, a great many dealers on Book Row had at least some part in the book theft trade. While few actively stole (or caused the theft of) library books, a great many more aided the practice. And almost everyone eventually benefitted from the act when they bought high-quality books at steeply discounted prices—either from book scouts traveling door to door, or from other dealers with reputations for dishonesty.

This was not a situation unique to either Book Row or the time period. Almost any book dealer specializing in antiquarian or rare books who has been in the business for more than a few years has dealt in stolen items; it is simply inevitable.[21] Although most of these dealers get these books when they have been laundered sufficiently enough not to be sold at suspiciously low prices—and can therefore be acquitted of responsibility—a good many purchase directly from the people who have done the stealing, buying very nice books with meager provenance at cheap prices. But the period of the Book Row theft ring, starting in roughly 1926 and covering the entire Northeast for a half decade, was the worst time for library theft in American history.

While the makeup of the Book Row theft ring that compelled the flow of stolen books into New York was amorphous and ever changing, it was led by a triumvirate of ostensibly honest booksellers. The old man of the group was a Russian immigrant with the face and temperament of Al Capone. Charles Romm, forty-eight years old in 1930, was savvy, tough, and built like a bulldog. He was also a man with a long track record of success in the book business, particularly with American first editions—and this success did not come by accident, or solely by hard work.[22] He had come up in the business the way many on Book Row had, paying his dues in the lean years and learning from other bookmen and bibliophiles. "The university which I attended, and still attend," he noted in the 1920s, "is every approachable book shelf within my knowledge."[23] It was Romm who, with a taste for the value of books, spearheaded the change from the run-of-the-mill thefts that took place all the time to supply Book Row to the coordinated theft ring that was as intricate as it was comprehensive.[24]

Ben Harris, a Danish immigrant and dealer in erotica (or pornography, according to the State of New York) was another of these dealers. He worked in an area of bookselling that was still subject to police raids, so he had cut his teeth on back-channel deals and the avoidance of law enforcement. In fact, in the 1920s and 1930s, while the threat of legal trouble for dealing in stolen or forged books was remote, the threat of agents from the New York Society for the Suppression of Vice was palpable. Some dealers kept afloat in rough times by selling pornography in their stores after regular hours, and these "bookleggers" and "Fourth Avenue pirates," as they were called, operated under the very real risk of immediate store closure.[25] So, they had to be savvy, and unafraid of danger. It helped to be young, too. Harris fit that bill perfectly. He had just the right combination of recklessness and ambition to take risks—and aside from his comfort with lawlessness, he also had good connections in Europe, so he was an important bridge to the Old Country market.

But the third figure, Harry Gold, was the most important of all. Young, without scruples, and approaching the book theft industry with the zeal of the recently converted, Gold was the primary recruiter and trainer of new talent.[26] For him, the jumbled bookstands and milling crowds—"book browsers and bowery bums," he called them—of Fourth Avenue were a paradise, a deliverance from the circumstances of his early life. He had grown up poor, as he later put it, in an immigrant-packed slum on the Lower East Side, "beneath the quivering shadow of the

Elevated."[27] (The "gaunt trestle-work" of this train, the *WPA Guide* noted, "brought twilight to miles of streets" around Gold's neighborhood and left an indelible mark on most everyone who lived there.)[28]

In the early twentieth century, the Lower East Side of Manhattan was, simply, an awful place to grow up. The *WPA Guide* recorded its "inhuman conditions" and how its "two square miles of tenements and crowded streets magnify all the problems and conflicts of big city life.... Crowded, noisy, squalid in many of its aspects, no other section of the city is more typical of New York."[29] Gold grew up as what was then known as a street urchin—or what he called a "gutter gamin." While he had a home and, at least, a mother, he spent most of his time at loose ends, wandering the broken and bruised streets of lower Manhattan, getting what education he could in the "rat-infested rows" of the "cemented wild."[30] And however overwrought his memories later proved ("Trees are few to obstruct Hell's view of Cancer slums that Time forgot"), there is no question he had a horrible childhood. But Gold discovered early on an escape from this waking nightmare: fiction. Books provided him his aforementioned early education, sparking both his imagination and his ambition, and gave him hope for what he could become. And when it was revealed to him that hope and ambition were not enough—he wanted to be a doctor, but that was just not possible—books were there for him again. He soon discovered he could make a living selling them.

In the May 1922 issue of *The Bookseller and Stationer*, New York dealer Harry Barton wrote, in one of his regular columns, a rags-to-riches story of the sort suddenly gaining purchase in the New York book world. In the piece, Barton told of a well-known (though unnamed) real estate magnate who had gotten his start in secondhand books. Just before the turn of the century, this man had only ten dollars to his name but "the true book instinct." When the man happened upon a small auction of personal effects, he took note of a group of books. "Having been a reader," Barton wrote, the man "knew of a few books the original editions of which were much sought for." Finding some in one particular auction lot, he spent $6.50 buying it. He promptly sold these books to dealers for $225. It was the start of a business that, when sold twenty-five years later, had afforded the man a great deal of money, including ownership of his building and "several houses."[31]

Whether the story was apocryphal or not, it was the sort of thing believable in the early 1920s, when success in the book trade seemed like it could be had by anyone with a bit of know-how and a very small stake of money. For Harry Gold, who had exactly that, the idea was particularly beguiling. So in 1925, after getting his start in a way remarkably similar to the man in Barton's article, Gold opened the first of his Book Row stores at 95 Fourth Avenue and called it the Aberdeen Book Company.[32] He furnished the inside himself, constructing bookshelves with new Maine lumber and stocking them with old used books, whatever he could afford to buy in bulk. He once bought a carload of books for a dollar. None of it was very impressive, but as far as niche selling areas go, "very cheap" at least had the quality of being plentiful. Gold even pioneered the paperback trade, "assembling a large concentration" well before they surged to prominence. But it was amidst Aberdeen's rows of space-filling brown that a few profitable shoots of green could be found. Some—a rare Eugene Field poetry book, or an old letter or daguerreotype—had been discovered by the dealer quite legitimately in his purchased stock. But most had been pulled from quiet resting places on various public library shelves and transported to Book Row. These were important, because despite the fact that the 1920s was as good a time as any to start a book business, even in the best of times it was a hard living. Publishers were always raising rates, competitors undercutting him and, Gold lamented, "Customers demand price cuts." That combination had a way of turning stolen books from a luxury to a necessity.

Recruiting book thief talent was remarkably easy on Depression-era Book Row. Manhattan was teeming with legions of itinerant men looking for work who often went from store to store to ask after jobs or milled around on street corners. And Gold was almost preternaturally aware of them. He had a terrific fear of the "quick-eyed and nimble-fingered book thieves that infested the trade, much in the same way as mice molest the grocer," and he watched them like a hawk.[33] "Creatures-consuming-soft-goods" was a popular way to describe these men at the time. One contemporaneous author noted that these "sneak thieves" occupied in bookmen "the same place as the Japanese beetle in the hearts of the New Jersey gardener."[34] Legendary Boston bookseller Charles Goodspeed called thieves "the crow in the cornfield, but with this difference—the farmer is protected in a measure by shot-gun and scarecrow."[35] And in an 1893 practical guide to men entering the bookselling trade, in a paragraph giving advice on how to get rid of "rats, mice, worms and other vermin," the author noted that "against the two-legged pest, the book thief, eternal vigilance is the only remedy."[36]

Perched on a tall chair at the entrance to his store, Gold sized up every person who walked in—and a good many prowling the bargain tables on the sidewalk out front.[37] But instead of waiting to catch these thieves and turn them over to police, he acted as a talent scout. Men who showed both an interest in books and a fluid set of morals were perfect candidates for the brand of work Gold offered.

These men he gathered were the ever-changing, ever-hunting backbone of the theft ring. Described variously as "young intellectuals from Greenwich Village, iconoclastic, daring and desperate" or "intellectual-looking young bibliophiles with glib tongues" or in some other manner indicating their age, their attitudes, and their lineage, they were men of dubious moral standing who were also clean-cut and well-dressed enough to pose as students.[38] This was particularly important in the jobless early thirties when, Gold said, "Holes took over clothes."[39] The men were not all from Greenwich Village, of course, or of scholarly bearing. In fact, before the Depression, the racket was composed mostly of those living in New York parks or in various other manners "on the bum." But after the market crash, the pool of out-of-work recruits became much more impressive than it had been before.

These were the foot soldiers of the operation. Trained by Gold or men like him, they were not taught a great deal about the business—and they rarely developed the ability to independently tell a valuable book from a useless one. They were often referred to as "book scouts," though that was a slander against an otherwise reputable profession. Legitimate book scouts were (and remain) an important part of the secondhand and rare book business. They were, according to dealer Charles Everitt, the "footloose book-hunters who actually dig in people's attics, paw over other dealers ten-cent counters," and go to the hinterlands to discover unclaimed treasures.[40] Traveling on the cheap, they scoured book sales of all types—from garages to Goodwill, estates to thrift shops—all in search of valuable, in-demand, or otherwise overlooked books. They were "a small and ill-faring group, like the one-horned Javan rhinoceros," with a particular set of skills and knowledge, willing to spend their days on the road in search of books.[41]

The Romm Gang scouts took this small, difficult profession and twisted it. They still had to travel in search of treasures, but they scoured library shelves instead of book sales or ten-cent tables. They did not pay anything for their acquisitions, and they usually could not independently determine the value of a book. These crooked book scouts were given a basic list of high-value products, taught how to recognize them on library shelves, and shown how to get them. "Once trained and deemed competent they are armed with this [list] and go forth on the perpetual Library Pick-Up Route," said Harold Clarke, a Boston thief handler.[42] There was none of the glamour that fiction (and some nonfiction) attaches to book thieves. They were not suave or debonair, and they certainly were not in it because they loved books too much.

A well-trained and experienced scout could eventually identify fifty to one hundred books of value on a library's shelves and, after some practice, manage to steal from as many as three libraries in a day. None of it required much aptitude or talent—Clarke referred to them as "the mental children of this world. No brains whatsoever"—it came down to gall, confidence, and oversized coats.[43] And, every once in a while, an ability to outrun a pursuer. With that, they were sent out into the world, traveling from town to town in search of particular items. "The pause is only the distance between libraries. These trained lads are in with lifted hats and out with lifted books before you can even recall if they are the mayor's children or strangers. By the time [librarians] go into a cautious corner and meditate the matter they are not merely gone but entering another library ten miles away and repeating elevation of the respectful fedora."[44] Besides this hat, the other major wardrobe piece designed to aid the thief was the large coat, described in the 1930s by writer Harry Kurnitz as "a loose raglan coat, so artfully fitted with hooks, slings and pockets that the works of Charles Dickens, on large paper, could nestle under it without showing a bulge."[45]

None of this was exactly secret. Booksellers and librarians alike had known for decades what to look for. Thieves were known to hide books in all manner of clothing, or between the pages of a folded newspaper. They would bring in dummy books and substitute them for good ones. They would even bring with them twine and wrapping paper, creating a parcel that would attract no attention when the thief left the library with it.[46] Here is a warning to nineteenth-century booksellers from Adolf Growoll, a man with many years of experience in the business: "Strangers with bundles, 'grips,' dress suit cases and other receptacles, and those with cloaks or loose coats with capacious packets should be closely watched. It would always be well, as a matter of courtesy, to relieve visitors of their impedimenta and temporarily care for these until they depart. This would prevent a dishonest caller from filling bogus bundles or these 'grips' and suit cases with books that the bookseller can ill afford to lose. An honest man would take no offence, and as for the dishonest man—his feelings need not be considered."[47] The argument that "strangers with bundles" comprised a great deal of the patronage of public libraries and would make watching them impractical was of little moment. Strangers with bundles comprised at least as much of the visiting population of bookstores, and booksellers somehow managed to watch *them* very closely.

These thieves usually earned a flat fee for particular books or a standard rate of two dollars, though they got up to 5 percent of the ultimate sales price on certain books. For new books, the percentage could be even higher. Of course, price was rarely an issue for them. Not only was it all profit, but there were few better options. And library theft was so much gentler than what the men were generally willing to do for money that it was practically considered honest labor.

By 1875, there were nearly 2,000 libraries in the Northeast. While most of these institutions were not libraries by today's standards, they were certainly collections of books, maps, papers, and ephemera. Massachusetts, in particular, was library rich. By the end of the nineteenth century, the Bay State had hundreds of small institutions, including more than two hundred "public libraries"—collections of more than a thousand volumes supported by taxpayer money. This was at a time when more than half the states in the Union had fewer than five such libraries.[48] The most important thing for booksellers was that these libraries had largely built their collections at the height of the production of what was later called Americana. This collecting specialty had long been popular, but became enormous in the 1920s—and so, too, then the bookseller appetite for its steady supply.

Around 1900, according to its most important early purveyor, Charles Everitt, the term *Americana* was limited to a small class of rarities sold "by a few slightly eccentric booksellers."[49] But with popularization, the definition came to mean "anything showing how and why people came here, and how they lived after they got here." One important collector described his Americana library this way: "I have *the* story."[50] In short, Americana was any material—printed or written—that had anything to do with the founding, settling, and exploration of the United States. A 1927 book titled *Buying and Selling Rare Books* noted that for would-be booksellers, Americana was the can't-miss area. It was both popular and plentiful. The author confided that, in particular, the "following classes of Americana are, always have been, and always will be in demand": personal narratives of early explorers and overland trips to the Far West, histories of Indian wars and tales of Indian captivity, material about great Americans, and "Town, county and state histories."[51] As it rose in popularity, Americana came to mean a great many things to a great many people, but what it unequivocally meant for northeast libraries was trouble.

Because funding had been so varied and inconsistent in the nineteenth century, libraries had been happy to take donations of almost anything. This included family histories, manuscripts, and various unique printed items of the sort public libraries would never think to purchase. It was items of that type that, by 1930, were especially valuable pieces of Americana. So, too, then was the Romm Gang's connection to Boston—a city in the heart of this Americana orchard. The gang's allies there served as sorts of independent contractors, working in a loose, mutually beneficial alliance with the men on Book Row. These men in Boston handled the thieves, coordinated the Massachusetts area thefts, gathered the loot, and readied it to send to Book Row. By 1930, the two men most responsible for this were Harold Borden Clarke and William "Babyface" Mahoney. These two recruited the young men, trained them, and set them to work "touring through Massachusetts by bus, rail or shank's mare."[52] But they were also dealers in their own right, and they did their fair share of thieving and selling to a client base outside New York. In some industries this might cause friction; in book theft, the getting was so good it was hard to complain about much of anything. One particular theft demonstrates this collegiality perfectly.

On a blustery day in late February 1929, Charles Romm—a man who, regardless of his later career, was an early and astute collector of Americana—made the trip up to Cambridge to browse the Harvard collection.[53] The school's libraries had long been a particular target for thieves. Alfred Potter, head of the Widener Library, had been an assistant at Harvard some twenty years earlier when he wrote that the "collection is strong in the eighteenth century authors; the poets, novelists, and playwrights of the early nineteenth century are fairly well represented. It is also rich in the first editions of such writers as Lowell, Longfellow, Emerson and Holmes."[54] This was like catnip for thieves, and never more so than in 1929.

Going through the stacks that February day, Romm did not want for choices. He indicated his selections to Clarke and Mahoney by simply tipping the books forward on the shelf. (This is a standard book theft technique. Experienced thieves rarely just slip items into their coats as they go. Even those working without a partner very often separate the "browse" from the "harvest," preferring to concentrate on one thing at a time.) After he left, the thieves then set about the minor task of collecting the hundred or so books. Once outside Harvard's grounds, the books were scrubbed of visible markings and readied for the trip south.

One of these books was John Roque's *A Set of Plans and Forts in America*, from 1763—a collection of maps "reduced from actual surveys." Any book with old maps was valuable, but this one included maps of locations (Albany, New York, for instance) that, by the early twentieth century, had become prominent. Roque's work was a rare and important piece of Americana, and Romm knew it had significant value in Manhattan. So once it was stolen, scrubbed, and delivered to him in New York—he paid two dollars, all told, for this particular volume—he added one more link to the fence by selling it to another Book Row dealer, Theodore Schulte.

Schulte was the éminence grise of the book trade, one of the sellers who first staked out the Fourth Avenue location and the one who coined the term *Book Row*.[55] His shop at 80 Fourth Avenue was legendary. Like the other bookstores, it had a large sidewalk stock out front, "where you can choose for your pennies, tomes in old-fashioned binding and printing." But inside, behind front windows that proclaimed it LARGEST SECOND HAND BOOKSTORE IN NY, it was uniquely impressive with a huge main floor, tall balconies, and a cavernous basement. It was also well stocked. "Inside," according to Guido Bruno's *Adventures*, "are shelves laden with books in delightful disorder left by the book-hunter who looked through them before you."[56] So large was the place that the staff could not keep up with all the action: shoppers were responsible for switching on and off the bare bulbs that lighted the alcoves and labyrinthine paths of the store.

The property was owned by the nearby Grace Church, for which Schulte was a vestryman, so it was no coincidence that his expertise was theology and religion, not Americana.[57] But having a lot of stock in one area did not mean he was not in the market for items from another—and Schulte crowded his store with books of all types, "hack love stories, children's books, the latest Huxley or Maugham, expensive limited editions, detective stories, or technical expositions."[58] Some of what he had in stock was quite nice and worth a great deal of money. Romm brought the stolen $1,500 book to Schulte with confidence, and offered it to him for a third of that price. The former president of the Booksellers' League—an otherwise reputable dealer whose client list ranged from the Rockefellers to small public libraries—snapped it up.[59]

In 1937, bookseller Charles Goodspeed noted with regret, "Some dealers have been known to buy books, either with the knowledge that they have been stolen, or at least with such neglect to assure themselves that this is not the case as amounts to the same thing."[60] Schulte demonstrated that neglect. He almost certainly was not aware of the theft that precipitated the sale, but it would have been difficult not to at least suspect the item was stolen.[61] Book dealers were not ignorant of the Romm Gang. The theft ring, and who was in on it, was common knowledge among the Fourth Avenue sellers. Everyone knew. Bookseller Charles Heartman described the situation in a 1935 *American Book Collector* editorial:

The few of us who have made an effort to bring cases before the authorities, or to help in the prosecution, know that any serious effort to stamp
out the evil is always hampered by a number of others who will not sign
a complaint or help prosecute them. Is it because they are ashamed to
admit in court that they were the victim…or are they afraid that a skillful
cross-examination may bring out unsavory details?

The piece went on to say that "thieves and forgers and their ambassadors"
do not come to all shops, because they know better. "They do not go to
Drake or to Harper to Edgar Wells or Madigan or to Rosenbach, nor will
they visit the Brick Row Book Shop anymore."[62]

"Prudence dictates," Goodspeed wrote two years later, "that at all time
great caution must be observed in dealing with unknown persons. Volumes
offered must be examined for erasure of ownership marks—removal of
bookplates, eradication of rubber stamps or smoothing out of embossed
markings. Crooks are clever, and despoilers of public libraries are skilful in
the art of removing protective devices."[63] Three decades into the twentieth century, this was old news to any honest bookseller. In fact, it was
axiomatic forty years earlier when Adolf Growoll wrote the same sentiment. He cautioned bookmen that, when buying books from someone
they were not entirely sure about, they should "try to discover how he
came into possession of whatever of value he may be offering. A little tact
and knowledge of human nature may help the bookseller in such cases to
protect himself" and the bookseller community against fraud and theft.
"It need hardly be pointed out that no honest bookseller would be so
foolish as to entertain an offer to buy from an unresponsible person for
two dollars a work which he knows is worth five times as much."[64]

Growoll would have been chagrined to find out that, for the bulk of
New York booksellers, it not only needed to be pointed out, it should
have been stamped on their cash registers. There were plenty of men on
Book Row to whom the Romm Gang felt perfectly fine going; dealers
who very rarely asked questions about the origins of the largesse and
certainly never reported anything to authorities. In the case of *A Set of
Plans*, Schulte was one of these. Guido Bruno noted of Schulte's store
that a "narrow passageway becomes narrower on each visit you pay to
the shop because of newly-arrived books and pamphlets." But Roque's
book did not contribute an inch of width to the hall because, in silent
testimony to knowledge of its acquisition, Schulte did not add it to his
stock. As soon as he got it, he turned around and sold the book to the
New-York Historical Society for $850 in a quiet transaction involving
few people and no publicity.

This little crime produced several beneficiaries—Clarke, Mahoney, Romm, Schulte, and the New-York Historical Society—and one loser: Harvard. For tens of thousands of library books, this was the economic reality of the Book Row theft ring. With the personal courage of the average bookseller sapped by financial forecasts, and very little chance that any of them would have to pay a legal price, there was absolutely nothing standing between the locust-like appetite of the Romm Gang and tens of thousands of books sitting on library shelves throughout the American Northeast.

One of the real assets of a theft ring on Book Row was the simple variety of customers. There was no area of bookselling that was not covered by the stores on Fourth Avenue, or in Midtown between Park and Fifth. That made the list of books and documents the scouts could steal from distant libraries almost endless. It contained not only the obvious American and English first editions but also a group of books so varied that no librarian would think them at risk. This meant a surprising number of works published within twenty or even ten years of the thefts, including books by Theodore Dreiser, Christopher Morley, John Galsworthy, and James Branch Cabell—authors who might have been familiar to librarians but not thought particularly valuable.[65] The handlers developed a list of items both wanted from, and available in, most East Coast libraries. It was comprehensive, inclusive, and broad enough that each trained scout, on a first pass through a library, could come away with something. Harold Clarke, the Boston thief, had a list with dozens of paragraphs describing unobvious items libraries had in abundance. For example, paragraphs 65 and 66:

> Old Magazines before 1850; Newspapers before 1840. Early Western-Sleuth Blood-Thunder Thrillers. Early Color Plate Books of all nature. All Erotica; Example Fanny Hill or Dolly Morton, etc. (Open any as found and will readily see WHY they are wanted.)
>
> All FINE Bindings, elegant covers. Tooled Leathers. By Sangorski, Riviere, etc. etc. Specialized books on any One subjects such as Pistols; Weapons; Whales; Poisons; Herbs; Pirates; Mines; Railroads; Antiques; Cookeries; Trials; Precious Stones; Juvenile; Birds; Alchemy; Small Colonies of Newfoundland, Nova Scotia, Hudson Bay, etc. etc. Early Law, sciences, art, genealogies, bibliographies, plays, songsters, costumes, circus, etc. etc.
>
> All books illustrated by Great Artists or Unknown ones. From Remington, Whistler, Pennell, Frost, Dore, Hogarth, Baxter, Cruickshank, Leech, etc. English, American, French, etc. Classics and Illustrations if

early. All Letterpress books (Beautiful hand type and paper) by Grolier, Dove, Falstaff, Kelmscott, Mosher, etc. etc.

Many of these items may have seemed safe to librarians simply because they were thought worthless to booksellers. Newspapers, for instance, were almost completely without resale value, even if they were very old and rare, unless they came in a complete run. But if it was free, it did not hurt Clarke's scouts to be over-inclusive. And there were always exceptions, even with newspapers because, "As in everything else about the rare book business, the rules are like French irregular verbs—an inch of rule and a yard of exception."[66]

One of Clarke's pages simply gave a list of authors—in no particular order except what dawned on him as he was typing—whose "firsts" were ripe for stealing: "Scott; Carlyle; Conrad; Caxton; Rosetti; Gray; Johnston; Johnson; Jonson; Voltaire; Hugo; Daudet; Dumas; Heine; Tolstoi; Mencken; Stevenson; Bangs; Andersen; Grimm; Burnett; Strachey; Cobb; Bronte; Alger; Henty; Tennysen; Masefield; Bridges; Defoe; Lesage; Jane Austen; Henry Adams; Aldrich; Bierce..." These were the first thirty-five of a list that included nearly 250 and ended with "etc. etc. etc. These are about 5 percent of the wanted Authors." Harry Gold, for his own store, was known to simply type up a copy of book titles from the latest version of *Book Prices Current* and give this out to his men. Sometimes he simply tore out pages of booksellers' catalogs, circled particular items, and handed them to scouts.

Most of these books, regardless of condition or value, were sitting on the open stacks. At this time in America, few libraries had areas set aside for rare books, let alone first editions that were less than fifty years old. (And even in those libraries that did have closed stacks, it was fairly easy for an experienced scout to get to them—sometimes with the approval of the librarians.) In state after state, according to Clarke, libraries had "their open stacks stuffed with First Editions running $40 to $1,000 . . . and all the smaller [libraries] were just wide open." This was the low-hanging fruit of the book trade, and it was almost without exception, "no matter where you went . . . Maine to Florida to Seattle."[67] His travels "both with the Mobs and also privately on my own, revealed these books at every turn, every step, every shelf, without fail in large city or small town across our lands."[68] Not that Manhattan libraries were immune. Columbia University, Hunter College, NYU, and a half-dozen other New York colleges with libraries were routine victims of the thieves, particularly during bouts of inclement weather that made traveling difficult. As were, of course, the city's public libraries. Almost no one was spared.

The men at the top of the book theft ring ultimately had one job: to turn these stolen books into cash. In any ordinary theft ring, this was usually no problem. Books came in so infrequently that making them ready for sale and getting them out on shelves could be done without much difficulty—as an adjunct, really, to the normal course of acquisitions. But with the Book Row operation, books came in regularly and in such volume that an ad hoc approach just would not work.

The first major problem was library marks. These usually came in the form of one of three different kinds of stamps: ink, embossing, or perforation. Library marks were not always a fatal flaw—there were plenty of legitimate reasons (then as now) why a library stamp would be in a book for sale in a shop. Libraries regularly deaccessioned books, selling discarded stock to the public or directly to dealers. When that happened, the library stamp rarely got any treatment other than perhaps another stamp reading "Withdrawn." But the Romm Gang did not want stamps in its books. For one thing, these were high-value items of the sort libraries did not usually deaccession, and a stamp raised suspicions. But more important, any stamp or mark on a high-price book was a value killer, library stamps most of all. Not only was the mark indelible, but it was an indication to the buyer that the book had been handled roughly. So before they got to Book Row, library stamps usually had to go.

A simple ink stamp was by far the most common, and it was easily eradicated with various kinds of bleach, often referred to as "Javelle water." In a pinch, a scout could use something like tobacco juice or any of a dozen different recipes favored by men on the road. Regardless of what substance was used, getting rid of a stamp using any chemical was far from foolproof. If not done skillfully, the eradication itself left a telltale clean spot on a page, which was as recognizable as the stamp. Harry Gold was particularly sensitive about bad erase jobs, and he counseled his young scouts not to even attempt it until they knew what they were doing.[69]

Embossed stamps could be smoothed out in a slow and tedious process using a hot iron. Many men on the road, who did not carry that tool with them, used a candle to heat a spoon. But this, too, left a mark for a discerning book inspector, so a hasty job was often not worth the effort. Most surprising, even perforations could be repaired. The holes could be filled in with a painstaking process or the whole area fitted with a sort of patch. But this "bright little trick" was difficult enough that the task was often farmed out to experts in England, which was rarely worth the expense.[70] (Filled-in holes could be easily detected, too. If the page was bent a certain way, they popped right out.) If the stamp was too difficult,

THE ANTICS OF THE LEADING INDUSTRIALS   25

or somehow impossible to remove without damaging the text, or the seller just did not want to bother, the page could simply be removed and replaced by a surrogate from a cheaper edition. It was in this way that a competent sophisticator could aid the theft business.

But whatever was done with the stamp, it took time. And while a book dealer might not object to scrubbing a mark or two, a steady stream of marked books was a real impediment to business. For obvious reasons, he might not want to spend hours scrubbing books—nor did he want to keep in his own shop materials of the sort needed to clean lots of books. So the Romm Gang generally had the books cleaned by the scouts, or the men who handled the scouts, before they came back to Book Row.

Quantity was another major problem. At first the fence was done in the traditional way: the dealers simply added the stolen items to their inventories, or the inventories of Book Row confederates. But soon enough, the flood of quality books was just too much for Book Row to handle and the Romm Gang looked to spread out. While it was certainly true that a lot of high-quality rare material stayed on Fourth Avenue to be sold, the most natural outlet for better items was higher up the island of Manhattan, in Midtown.

Part of the history of antiquarian bookselling in New York was the split between general secondhand booksellers and those in the rare book trade. In most cities this was a separation that happened from store to store, or street to street. In New York, the distinction was less subtle: forty-five city blocks. While the Book Row area housed plenty of book-stores that sold antiquarian items (particularly by 1930, when these things seemed to grow on trees), the upper-tier market of high-priced rare books was located mostly in Midtown around 58th Street, in closer proximity to Central Park and, as it happened, the New York Public Library (NYPL). This was only natural. By the 1920s, the city had been transformed into the financial heart of the world. And its commercial engine was Midtown where, by mid-decade, the skyscrapers were rising almost in time with the value of companies listed on the New York Stock Exchange.[71]

Filled with taller and taller buildings—in the summer of 1930 the Chrysler Building was the world's tallest; by October, construction of the Empire State Building had surpassed it—Midtown was packed with everything a roaring economy provided: shoppers, cars, lights, and the many targets of conspicuous consumption. Fifth Avenue north of 34th Street was jammed with things to buy and people to buy them. Lord & Taylor, Bergdorf Goodman, B. Altman, and Saks were surrounded by smaller department stores, jewelry stores (Tiffany & Co. was on the corner of 37th Street and Fifth Avenue), and specialty stores (even the high-end grocery store Park & Tilford had a Fifth Avenue address), as thousands of people meandered up and down sidewalks, looking for somewhere to point their money. The only significant difference in the amount of traffic from then to now, save for the style of cars, was that in 1930 Fifth Avenue traffic moved in both directions. If anything, that gave the street an even more congested feel.

Several of the men who ran bookstores in this area had once owned shops in Book Row. One of the more famous of these graduates was the Argosy's Louis Cohen. As a young man, Cohen cut his teeth at the high-end Madison Book Store on 59th Street. After he scraped together enough money and experience, he opened the Argosy Bookstore on Book Row in 1925. A few years there and he became successful enough to make the move back north to Midtown, near the Madison. Of this move he later noted, "I didn't like Fourth Avenue anymore.... My stock was getting better, and I lovingly thought of Fifty-Ninth Street."[72] (The Argosy is still there.) This was not an uncommon practice among successful Book Row alums. Though not every Fourth Avenue dealer longed to decamp farther up the island, it was far from rare.

And for the same reason people with an interest in regular secondhand books came to Book Row—volume—the tony book traffic came to that part of Manhattan. The area was home to a dozen antiquarian dealers, including Arthur Swann (598 Madison Avenue, between 57th and 58th Streets), Thomas Madigan (54th Street), the Ritter-Hopson Galleries (57th Street), and Gabriel Wells (57th Street). The area was also home to the New York store of A. S. W. Rosenbach, the most important bookseller of the twentieth century, and, soon enough, another major dealer, Hans P. Kraus. Appropriately, the Anderson Galleries, site of many of the most important book auctions of the twentieth century, was located at 59th and Park Avenue. (The Trump Park Avenue, on the corner of these two streets today, describes this address, in typically understated fashion, as "the city's most coveted address.")[73]

But by the second winter of the Great Depression, even these successful antiquarian book dealers were in trouble, right along with many of the other businesses on Fifth Avenue. "Buyers for five figure books were as scarce as the books themselves," wrote dealer George Goodspeed of the early 1930s.[74] The Argosy's Regina Cohen conveyed the same sentiment a bit more gravely: "Cold cash was rarer than blood in a bloodstone."[75] This was not a surprise. As one member of the trade explained, the "market for rare books is remarkably sensitive to the rise and fall of listed stocks, and follows the antics of the leading industrials with a precision which delighted bookdealers in the boom years, but which they found disheartening in the depression."[76] While the market crash had hit everyone, it hurt none more so than those who dealt in luxury items. Worse yet, the 1920s bull market had coerced many of these dealers to buy books—sometimes whole libraries—at top-drawer prices. A 1923 *New York Times* article explained what had been the prevailing attitude this way:

> Literary property is selling at boom prices in the markets of the world. Old books and old manuscripts are being offered not only for their literary and sentimental value but as a high type of "gilt edge" security to the prospective investor. Even in financial panics, it is pointed out, their values continue to climb and, according to experts, the limit is not yet in sight. Prices which today seem to be beyond all reason will be regarded in future as ridiculously cheap, it is predicted.... Attics, cellars, closets, old trunks and other abandoned repositories in the Old World and the New are being rummaged for hidden literary treasures to supply the demand.[77]

This was an attitude that brought predictable results when the business climate went south. The *American Book Collector* noted a few years into the downturn that the only people with money left to spend were the stock market "short-sellers," and they "are usually not persons with a cultural background or inclined to spend money on a literary or artistic property."[78] (What the article did not state was that it had been a very long time since it had been simply attics, cellars, trunks, and "abandoned repositories" that were rummaged for their goods.)

It is difficult to overstate how large the trade in rare books was, or how many people depended on it. The antiquarian book trade now is a niche industry that caters to a very small percentage of the American buying public. But in 1930, the trade, particularly in Manhattan, did a lot of business—and received a corresponding amount of press coverage. The *New York Times Book Review* had a section in each issue called "Notes on Rare Books." More than just "notes," this regular column was roughly 1,500 words of rare book boosterism, reporting on auctions, major acquisitions, the state of the trade, and the health of individual businesses. (Even at the height of the book theft ring, the column rarely mentioned the seedier side of the trade, eschewing coverage of any crime but forgery, the only crime that threatened to actually do harm to the industry.) And in addition to the display advertisements throughout each issue, the *Book Review* had a full page of classified advertisements for dozens of local booksellers, buying and selling rare and antiquarian books. *Publishers Weekly* also offered excellent coverage of the antiquarian book trade, to include the dark parts the *Book Review* steered clear of. (The journal *Antiquarian Bookman* began in 1948 as an offshoot of a *PW* feature.) The *American Book Collector* was a monthly journal dedicated to the trade, with substantial articles on collecting and collectors. And then there was *The Colophon; a book collector's quarterly*. Started in 1929, this journal was remarkably opulent, featuring terrific articles by first-class writers (including Sherwood Anderson, H. L. Mencken, Edith Wharton, and Christopher Morley) in a design format that changed with each issue.

With all this coverage, some rare book dealers were even famous outside the book industry. Chief among these was A. S. W. Rosenbach. An interesting mix of showman and scholar—his PhD was so well known that many people in the business referred to him simply as "The Doctor"—he was author of regular articles in magazines such as the *Saturday Evening Post*. He was also frequently the subject of features and profiles in other publications; in fact, the Philadelphian appeared so often in the *New Yorker*'s "Talk of the Town" section that the magazine seemed to have a person stationed in his office. Rosenbach's lifestyle, spending habits, and personal connections were well known to readers of newspapers and general magazines and to other regular folks in the know. In fact, Rosenbach was "so well known that those best appraisers of fame in all its shapes of family, fortune, or notoriety, the headwaiters of speak-easies, always found a table for him in the crowded peepholed caverns."[79]

There were a lot of people with a personal financial stake in the continued success of the rare and antiquarian book industry (not least, headwaiters at Manhattan speakeasies), and many of these men had their hands on the reins of power. With every month of recession, these booksellers' reliance on high-quality books at suspiciously cheap prices only grew. As it turned out, the only thing that drove the looting of libraries more than a really good rare book market was a really bad rare book market.

But even this Midtown outlet was not enough to relieve the pressure of all those books, coming in as regular as mail. What distinguished the Romm Gang from earlier such groups was not that its size and scope were larger, but they were an order of magnitude larger. Regular book theft rings (and individual book dealers who employed thieves) ordered what they could sell. The law of supply and demand dictated, to a large extent, what was stolen. But the Book Row theft ring was practically an industry. Books came in constantly, regardless of demand. This meant the ability to move product soon became secondary to the ability to store it. By 1930, Romm's group sat on thousands and thousands of books not yet ready to be sold—either because they had not been scrubbed or because the group was in possession of so many copies of the item there just was not a market. If library security ever put a stop to the wholesale looting—a remote possibility, to be sure—the ring had enough stored inventory to live off for a decade.[80]

Milwaukee bookseller Harry Schwartz witnessed this surplus first-hand. In a 1930 book-buying trip to New York, he met up with his old friend Charles Romm. He had known the man as an acquaintance and chess foe years earlier when Romm had worked in a small, undistinguished store in lower Manhattan. While poking around some Book Row stores in 1930, Schwartz discovered, quite by accident, that Romm had moved to a much larger space. Seeing his old friend returned from Milwaukee, Romm invited Schwartz in, escorted him through the main store, and into a very large back room. Schwartz found himself "in a veritable treasure house of rarities. I looked to Romm to ask him where he got the money to bring together this fine lot. He had left me alone so I began to go through the books carefully. Frequently I found three and four copies of the books in the first edition then being sought for by most dealers. There were the early Cabells, Byrnes, Hearns, Dreisers, Morleys, James', Robinsons', etc. I picked out a group of thirty or forty and told Romm to keep them for me until the following day, as I did not have enough money with me then. As I left his shop the thought struck me, Why do not other dealers know of this cache? Moreover, I thought that his prices were extremely reasonable, and wondered why other dealers had not snapped them up."[81] (Schwartz never did go back. After he left, he ran into another book dealer friend of his who told him where Romm got the books.) Romm's "back room" was just the start. The gang had piles of books stashed in similar rooms all over the place. They eventually filled a large building just off Fourth Avenue with tons more. One insider estimated these to have a value of more than $5 million.

The group accumulated all these books by casting a wide net. There was no collection of books too small to escape the attention of the gang. From archives to athenaeums, from local libraries to historical societies, the men in the ring scouted, indexed, and pilfered them all.[82] While other, earlier gangs targeted large and well-heeled libraries, the Romm Gang understood that the real treasures were in institutions in backwater towns throughout the Northeast and as far west as Ohio.

But there was one library they never hit, and it was just up the street from Gold's store: the New York Public Library. The stacks there were, of course, lined with items of terrific value rivaling any library in America. But they were nearly impossible for thieves (unless they worked for the library) to access. And the best items—including an unrivaled collection of Americana—were housed in something called the Reserve Book Room, an area that might as well have been on the moon as far as thieves were concerned.[83] The NYPL was one of America's few libraries that were fastidious about security. In the grand tradition of library theft, it had learned its lesson the hard way. But it had learned it nonetheless.

CHAPTER 2

The Accumulated Wisdom

IN 1899, THE STRUCTURE ON FIFTH AVENUE BETWEEN 40TH AND 42nd Streets looked like a fortress—a walled city designed to keep people out. It was, in fact, designed to keep water in. The distributing reservoir of the Croton Aqueduct System was an impressive edifice that had the look of something that might last a millennium. In actuality, it disappeared in less than a year. Powerful men had designs on the location and planned to replace the reservoir with an equally impressive building whose contents, they hoped, would become more important to locals than even water: the New York Public Library.

The Astor Library, the major antecedent of the NYPL, was, like the Croton reservoir, dying. But its death was natural, and gradual. Started fifty years earlier with a $400,000 grant from the estate of John Jacob Astor, it was located in a spot in the heart of Manhattan adjacent to what became Book Row. When it opened, it had more than 80,000 volumes in a large, airy hall of gilded balconies and double-height alcoves.[1] Many of these were books purchased in Europe during the 1840s, a time of unrest (generally the best time to buy good books on the cheap).

Aside from being large and opulent, the Astor was, upon its opening, one of only six libraries in the United States with holdings of fifty thousand volumes or more. (Harvard, Yale, the Library of Congress, the Boston Athenaeum, and the Library Company of Philadelphia were the others. The Boston Public Library, another very large institution with a similar mission, opened a few years after the Astor.) It was founded with a specific purpose: to be a public resource for scholars and researchers.[2] Still, the Astor was not exactly a public library by today's standards. It had limited hours, inaccessible stacks, and a cool attitude toward users—librarians there had a "reputation for churlishness and indifference" to patrons.[3] A *New York Times* article from around the time of the library's opening noted a rather strict rule about usage: "No volumes can be taken from the building. No one is allowed to remove a book from its place unless accompanied by an officer of the library."[4] In fact, the Astor seemed more like a private book museum than a public library.

"It would have crazed me," said Joseph Green Cogswell, Astor librarian, "to have seen a crowd ranging among the books, and throwing everything into confusion."[5] So while the reading room was open to the public, the stacks were closed: patrons could not merely browse the shelves; they had to apply to librarians to fetch books for them. This was particularly difficult since the Astor had no reliable catalogue. Because patrons had to rely on the benevolence of librarians with a reputation for incivility, a lot of people came once and never returned.[6] One scholar, writing in the *New York Times* of his only trip to the Astor, noted an experience that was simultaneously coarse, disappointing, and typical. If women, in particular, he wrote, wished to avoid the "insults of officials and underlings," he "would sooner recommend them to go, unattended, to the Bowery Theatre, than to the Astor Library."[7]

But even rude librarians and closed stacks (which, next to an iron chain, is still the most simple and effective policy for theft prevention in existence) could not keep the Astor completely safe from thieves. The men who wanted books managed to get them out, no matter the barrier.

Astor librarian Frederick Saunders learned this in early April 1881. A Bleecker Street bookseller named John Duggan offered the librarian a copy of Robert Bentley's *Medicinal Plants*, a four-volume set of books containing some three hundred hand-colored plates. Saunders declined the purchase, telling Duggan that the library already owned the sixty-dollar set. In fact, what the library owned were the very books offered by Duggan. Saunders discovered this fact a few days later and returned to the bookseller. He asked Duggan where he got them and was told of a man who fit the description of "Irishman" Samuel Watt, a man Saunders recognized as a regular visitor to the library.[8] (The mention of Watt's nationality was no accident. The Irish were not well thought of, particularly among the literate classes. One Philadelphia bookseller of that era noted of another, John Campbell, that he had the "characteristics of his

Irish countrymen" in that he "acted first and thought afterwards."[9]) Records indicated that Watt had last looked at the books shortly before they were offered by Duggan to Saunders.

After Watt's theft was discovered, Saunders scrutinized Watt's other borrowings. Convinced that Watt was regularly stealing from the library, Saunders, along with fellow librarian Carl Bjerregaard, revisited Duggan's bookstand. Bjerregaard was a Danish immigrant who had been working at the library for less than two years. Still in his early thirties, he was a soldier and scholar—a graduate of both the University of Copenhagen and the Military Academy of Denmark—and, after an early lifetime of political intrigue and espionage, had recently become an American citizen.[10] Ideally suited to battling thieves, he was in many ways the precursor to the NYPL's book crime–fighting legends, and he had ample occasion to deal with thieves over the course of his more than forty years with the Astor and the NYPL. On that April day in 1881, Saunders and Bjerregaard discovered eight more of their books, all with markings erased. With Duggan's help, the two men tracked Watt down and later testified against him at trial.

For the Astor, the only thing atypical about this experience was that the thief was caught and jailed. Over the course of its existence, the library was routinely victimized by its readers, despite the precautions taken by the institution and its librarians. Like most major American public libraries, the only question in theft was how much and how often. But along with the regular and mundane book thieves that beset every library, the Astor also had the distinction of hosting one of the true originals of American book crime, a man who set the standard for rare book theft while the crime was still in its infancy: Theodorus Olynthus Douglas.

In many ways a larger-than-life figure, he put the lie to the idea—particularly popular in the nineteenth century, but still with us today—that people stole books simply because they loved possessing them. Even sitting in the police dock, Douglas made no bones about why he stole: "to make a living."[11]

A tall, sallow, dark-haired young man who had the bearing and appearance of a distinguished scholar, Douglas was an almost daily patron at the Astor and Columbia College (then on 49th Street) libraries. It is difficult to know how much of his backstory is true and how much invented, but it is clear that one newspaper's description of Douglas as "the orphan son of an Englishman married to a native of Greece, [later] adopted and educated by a charitable American" hardly told it all.[12] There were several stories about his childhood floating around, all of which had the same basic facts. He was born in Greece to a Greek woman and English father—an architect working in Athens—and orphaned at seven years old. According to Douglas, Cornelius Bliss, a wealthy resident of New Jersey, found the boy as he was traveling through Greece and brought him back to the United States. Also according to Douglas, he lived with the Bliss family until he was twelve, when his benefactors died and he was sent to live with a member of the family in Philadelphia. After a couple of years there, he was turned loose and made his way to Chicago. There he started working for a shoe manufacturer who took interest in the young man and, eventually, sent him to Yale College.[13] This part was not only true but also believable: By the 1890s, Yale was practically a finishing school for book thieves. Frederick Bullard, later charged with thefts from several important Boston antiquarian booksellers, including Goodspeed's and Lauriat's, was an 1893 Yale graduate.[14] An 1894 Yale man, James Brittain Miller, was even more prolific. Four years after graduating, he was caught stealing books by slipping them into an overcoat "fitted with pockets such as professional thieves wear."[15] Police later found thousands of stolen books in his home. Harvard, Brown, and the University of Pennsylvania educated their fair share of these thieves, but for some reason Yale seemed to attract the most.

Whatever the actual facts of his upbringing, Douglas lived a somewhat charmed life. Possessing a great deal of personal magnetism, he made friends easily and enjoyed the company of many wealthy and well-placed members of society in New Jersey, New York, New Haven, Chicago, and Washington, DC. At Yale, he was known for showing off his fantastic rare book collection, most of it culled from the college's library. When he moved to Washington, DC, and later, New York, his reputation as a book connoisseur only grew. But this reputation got him more than just prestige and money—it got him access to more books. At Columbia, he was given special access to the collection thanks to an introduction by Professor John Newberry—a man who knew Douglas's love of books and thought he saw a lot of potential in him. This connection got him an audience with George Baker, the librarian, who, along with his son, soon became close friends with Douglas and allowed him access to the stacks. With that, Douglas worked constantly—and alone—in the recessed alcoves of the library, selecting the books he wanted and carefully secreting them in his large coat.[16]

Over the course of about six months, Douglas visited either Columbia or the Astor each day—he lived at Broadway and 23rd Street, a location convenient to both libraries. His residence was also relatively close to nineteenth-century New York's major bookselling area. The cluster of secondhand bookshops that came to populate Fourth Avenue in the 1920s had its antecedent farther downtown, around Ann and Nassau Streets, in the 1850s. Bookshops slowly migrated northward over the next half century, most populating the area near Astor Place. But in the 1890s, this was still a work in progress, so there were a number of shops spread over lower Manhattan, south of 23rd Street.[17] If anything, this space between stores gave Douglas a better opportunity to spread his sales around without raising suspicions. In this way, after scrubbing them of their marks, he sold hundreds of books to stores within walking distance of his home or across the river in Brooklyn. This income continued to fuel the opulent lifestyle that, in turn, got him access to even more people with books.[18]

This, in a strange way, is what distinguished Douglas from so many in this criminal fraternity. Wearing a large coat and pretending to be a scholar was not exactly an inspired ruse, even in the infancy of American library theft. Douglas was good at the hard part of the crime—the selling. Unlike many of his book theft heirs, who dropped the student/scholar identity as soon as they had the books out the door, he incorporated it into his fence, selling books to many of the people who were closest to him. This included, most notably, George Baker, librarian at Columbia College. And the way he pulled it off was remarkable.

Douglas, as Baker's friend, first offered the librarian a gift of several rare books from what Baker thought was Douglas's collection. These books, as it turned out, had been stolen from the Astor. Most other library thieves would sacrifice a finger before they would give away—to another library, no less—the valuable books they had worked hard to steal. But Douglas was working the long con, a particularly sophisticated fence for a young man, and one almost never seen in book thievery. After setting Baker up with the donations, Douglas eventually came back to the librarian and told him that he was interested in donating *more* books but, due to some financial mix-ups, he was forced to sell them instead. The best he could do for the library was to sell them at a very deep discount. What made this fence so effective was not just that it insinuated him into a buyer with large pockets, but that it made a library thief's greatest weakness—the necessity, due to lack of provenance, to sell books at a deep discount—into an asset. As predicted, the librarian was completely taken in by it.

At the same time, Douglas was selling other books for more immediate profit. With the quality of material he was getting, he found himself welcomed in all of the city's best stores. He sold to a range of booksellers,

including a who's who of late-nineteenth-century New York men:
A. J. Bowden, W. R. Benjamin, Dodd, Mead & Co., and Richmond &
Crossup among them.[19] He also sold to Charles L. Woodward, an early
and important dealer in Americana. But unfortunately for Douglas,
Woodward was a particularly astute bookman and noticed something
amiss with the young man. The dealer became convinced that Douglas
was selling items that he had not inherited or purchased, but rather stolen
from somebody. Still, without more to go on, there were not a whole lot
of ways to identify the true owners of the books Douglas was selling. But
Woodward would not let his hunch go. He decided to take out an advertisement in an early February edition of *Publishers Weekly*:

> To whom it may concern. Having recently purchased from a man who
> I have since learned is unreliable and irresponsible certain valuable
> books—Swedberg's America Illuminata, Originals of Aurelius and
> Campanius Holm's New Sweden, vols. 1 and 3 of Backus' Church
> History, Brickell's Carolina, Beverley's Virginia, and other not so
> valuable, I am desirous to meet as soon as possible any adverse claimants,
> if such there be.[20]

What made this act particularly notable—and rare in the history of
library/bookseller relations—is that Woodward placed the ad *after* he had
already purchased the books. That meant that if Douglas was crooked,
Woodward would have to give the books back to their true owners
without remuneration. Essentially, he was spending money on an advertisement to most likely lose more money on books. Not exactly a wise
business practice, but he did it anyway. And it worked.

With the help of this ad, it soon became clear to local librarians—
particularly those at the Astor and Columbia—that Douglas was stealing
from them. Still, he was not arrested right away. Columbia's George
Baker, in particular, was reluctant to believe the young man was the culprit and less willing to see him thrown in jail. But as the evidence against
Douglas started adding up—including the fact that Douglas had, without
permission, drawn money on Baker's account—even the librarian came
around. About a month after the ad was placed, Douglas was arrested
shortly after stealing from the Astor Library two volumes of the 1761
book *Journal of a Voyage to North America: Undertaken by order of the French
King*.[21] He was held on $5,000 bail—which he could not make—and
charged with grand larceny. When police went to his room, they discovered thirty books from the Astor and 113 from Columbia. Douglas was
later tried for the theft of just two works, valued at $150, *History of Peru*
and *History of the Indies*.[22] He pleaded guilty to grand larceny in the

first degree and was sentenced to a short prison term at the Elmira Reformatory.[23]

Charles Woodward, it should be noted, was neither reimbursed for the books he gave back to the libraries or the ad he took out in *Publishers Weekly,* nor sent so much as a thank-you note from the librarians. He was not at all surprised by this, knowing "enough of both institutions to know that getting anything out of either, except by theft, would be like drawing teeth."[24] Of course, if this was one instance where major libraries acted to the financial disadvantage of a bookseller, the favor was paid back a thousandfold over the course of the next century.

By the time of Theodorus Olynthus Douglas, the notion of the Astor as a stand-alone institution was fading. Thanks largely to local press, the opulently unfriendly downtown institution had given way in the local imagination to the idea of a unified public library for the people of New York, somewhere in the middle of the city. In an 1892 *Scribner's* article, politician, lawyer, and executor of the Samuel Tilden estate, John Bigelow, set out a plan for such a library, between Fifth and Sixth Avenues and 40th and 42nd Streets.[25] His plan called for a building provided at the site by the city and comprising the existing collections of the Lenox and Astor Libraries along with $2 million from the Tilden trust (down, thanks to his family, from $5 million). Among the many reasons Bigelow offered the city for the acceptance of the idea was one of public good:

> The appetite for [books] grows by what it feeds on. They displace meaner tastes and recreations. By bringing within our reach the accumulated wisdom of our race, they put us in stronger sympathy with all its members; thereby making better citizens and more harmonious families, with a constant tendency to the elevation of national character. They make life sweeter and better. They furnish the most effective antidote to the allurements of the drinking saloon, and they can do more than any available substitute to purify the ballot, to quench the unhallowed fires of political partisanship, and to make statesmen of politicians.

In 1895, a consolidation agreement formed a new corporation, called the New York Public Library, Astor, Lenox and Tilden Foundations, to "establish and maintain a free public library and reading form in the City of New York."[26] Once the site was secured in 1897, a competition was held for the design. The winning firm, Carrere & Hastings, was awarded the project in November 1897. In its description of their plans, Thomas Hastings wrote, it "has been the desire of all those connected with the Library to have a simple and dignified design, not depending on an over

amount of ornamentation, Renaissance in style, based on classic princi-
ples, and modern in character."[27]

But though the Astor was soon to become part of the New York
Public Library, it remained vulnerable to thieves. It also remained vulnerable to something even more disheartening—the whims of the American
judiciary. The seriousness with which judges take rare book theft has
always been as important as it is unpredictable. For weighty evidence of
this, the Astor needed look no further than the book theft cases handled
by two New York judges, both appointed to the bench the same year the
consolidation agreement was created.

In 1895, despite lack of judicial experience, H. A. Brann was appointed
magistrate at the Tombs Police Court by Mayor William Strong. He came
to the bench with a fairly high opinion of working men and very little
good to say about anyone in power—and his generous attitude toward
defendants, at the expense of the state, became legendary. The first person
ever arraigned before Magistrate Brann was Albert Smith, arrested in the
Bowery for intoxication. Smith told the judge that he had worked hard
all day and merely had a couple of drinks. Brann discharged him. The
next man before him was Thomas Shea, who had been arrested for
attempting to free prisoners being escorted to jail by an Officer Sheehan.
Sheehan, in court to testify against Shea, told Brann that the defendant
had assaulted him and then ran away only to be caught after a long chase.
Brann discharged Shea, too.[28]

It was a trend that did not go unremarked upon. The magistrate
quickly developed a reputation for treating leniently anyone of humble
background while at the same time treating anyone of means with a
harsh hand. Henry L. Wilson, an editor at *Puck*, was held in jail overnight
by Brann on a minor charge (which later proved bogus). Magistrate
Brann justified keeping the well-spoken and obviously wealthy man by
saying it was not his duty to free well-dressed "and well appearing prisoners and holding others not possessed of those advantages."[29] This
preference against the powerful in favor of the defenseless took a peculiar
turn in the case of a student pretending to be named Jacob Friedman. He
was caught stealing books from a library, an institution of the sort, most
felt, would fall into the "defenseless" category. Magistrate Brann was not
among these, largely because this particular library had the name Astor
attached to it.

After the boy, in tears, admitted he stole the books because without
them he would have been unable to keep up with his class, as his parents were too poor to buy him books, Brann urged librarian Ferris
Lockwood to drop the charges.[30] When Lockwood refused, Magistrate

Brann badgered him, saying that this was the boy's first offense, he did not intend any wrong, and that "his whole life will be ruined in consequence."

"Don't you think this boy has been sufficiently punished?" the magistrate continued. "Don't you think that the great Astor Library could make a little concession in this case, where it might mean the ruin of a boy's life?"[31] When Lockwood continued to insist on prosecution, telling Brann that he was not acting on his own behalf but rather the policy of the executive committee of the library, Brann said, "The world is right; corporations are soulless, heartless."[32] He then reluctantly fined the boy the least amount he could—a sum that was quickly paid by local philanthropist Jacob Schiff.[33]

The truth—as it only sometimes does in library theft cases—came out a little more than a week later. The young man had not been arrested in the midst of some sort of misunderstanding, but rather thanks to some theft-prevention work done by the librarians. The Astor staff had noticed over the course of a couple of months that in areas with open access, certain books had gone missing. They also noticed that similar books in the closed stacks had gone missing but by a different method: A young man would request a book using a false name and then simply not return it. Friedman was recognized as this man. When he was arrested, he initially denied the scheme but eventually confessed. When police went to his room, they found books stolen from the Astor, with their marks torn out. None of this, of course, mattered to Magistrate Brann.

Despite clearly being in the right, the library felt it had to defend its actions in prosecuting the boy by saying that Friedman was not robbing the Astor but the other schoolboys who made use of the Astor Library to help them in their studies. When "one boy carried away books that were in demand, he deprived all the other boys of [that] opportunity.... It is not the value of the books that may be stolen which they regard as important, but the fact that the community at large is defrauded of its rights whenever a book is taken which a hundred or a thousand visitors ought to have the privilege of consulting."[34]

If there was anything good that came out of the notoriety of this case—thanks largely to the rants of Magistrate Brann—it is that the executive committee of the library, now part of the trust that formed the New York Public, had a chance to think on this subject. In the aftermath of the Friedman thefts, they decided to act, approving the hiring of an attendant to patrol the reading room and look after readers. In 1901, notices were placed around the library offering a reward for evidence resulting in the conviction of people cutting up books. The library also started using perforated stamps, instead of simply ink, for marking.[35] Like a great many libraries after them, they acted only in the aftermath of thefts. But they did act.

It is tempting to think that Brann's blasé attitude toward library theft was typical in *fin de siècle* America, and that we now have a more evolved understanding of the nature of this crime. The truth, in fact, is the opposite. The Friedman case was more of an exception to the rule of its time than it would be today. The attitude then toward library thieves was far more negative, even openly hostile.

In 1907, a *Dallas Morning News* editorial ranked the "Library Book Thief" as "probably the meanest thief God ever let live" on Earth. "The person who takes advantage of a collection of books maintained by the decent people of a city, under universal tax for the benefit of all, and steals a volume that better people need" is enough "to make fallen angels weep." It went on to note that "God is supposed to know everything, maybe he knows why such people exist—but no one else does. Perhaps these people—like the dog poisoners, whom they resemble—cumber the earth merely to teach humility to those of us who are apt sometimes to think too complacently of human nature as she degenerates in the crowd."[36]

An April 1904 article in the *New York Daily Tribune* spent a thousand words expressing a similar sentiment, but began with a quote from a judge sentencing a library thief to jail: "Stealing books from the libraries of the public is one of the unspeakable crimes—like stealing coins from the eyes of dead men or robbing the poor box that hangs in the church entrance. I take pleasure in sentencing you to the full penalty prescribed by the law. I am sorry I can give you no greater punishment."[37] An editorial from around the same time appeared in the *Lowell Citizen*, and was reprinted in the *Boston Globe*. It noted that it is "a wonder Boston does not rise in wrath and lynch its alleged book thief to the nearest post! To steal books from the Boston public library must seem to the average Bostonian like laying violent hands on the ark in the holy of holies."[38]

This idea of vigilantism in the service of the public good was also not new. In an 1891 issue of *The Newsman* ("A Journal for Newsdealers, Publishers, Booksellers and Kindred Trades"), one editorial noted that book thieves are "a species of humanity floating on the earth, lice in human form." The "miserable, sneakish book fiend is utterly wanting in every trait that proclaims human kindred. Will an enterprising bookseller make an example of one, cut his ears off, or in some other manner denote his base perfidy? Ten thousand booksellers should each buy a gun, and as a victim is lassoed, shoot him on the spot." Such action, the article noted, would end the present generation of book thieves.[39]

This was the attitude that was brought to the next major Astor thief. And that fact, again, was thanks only to the judge assigned to the case. In January 1895, John W. Goff was installed as New York's "Recorder," a magistrate judge for criminal trials in the city. It was an important and distinguished job, and by the time Goff took over, the Recorder was the oldest judicial office in the United States. An Irish immigrant and former prosecutor, Goff took the job very seriously. He was sober and straight-forward and aware that his position on the bench was among the most important criminal law appointments in the state. His greatest ambition, he said, was "to endeavor by application, by assiduous attention to my duties, and, above all, by a conscientious desire to do what is right" to follow in the footsteps of his predecessors.[40] What that meant, in practice, was that he was a much tougher law enforcer than Magistrate Brann.

He was not known to be eloquent or much of an orator, but the "master of the colloquial method." He spoke, according to an attorney who practiced before him, "without hesitation; deliberately, yet by no means prosily; is magnetic in voice and look when addressing a jury; conversationally logical, never attempting persuasion, avoiding even implications of personal views when marshalling facts, and preferring simple Saxon words to those of Latin or Norman origin."[41]

Compare his very first day on the job—after a feting that included the present of a chair made of roses and lilies from the Hungarian citizens of New York—with Brann's. Goff oversaw the case of a woman, Ella Washington, who was convicted of larceny. The Recorder promptly sentenced her to six months in prison.[42] Starting immediately—and continuing for the next twelve years—he oversaw some of the most interesting and contentious cases in New York history, right up until he left to become a justice of the New York Supreme Court. As with Brann, one of those dealt with an Astor thief.

Twenty-eight-year-old Leon Gomberg was the leader of a book theft ring prowling the boroughs of Manhattan and Brooklyn, and unlike the men later based on Fourth Avenue, he was not exactly a working-behind-the-scenes type of boss—Gomberg took an active part in the process. By 1904, that meant he did most of the fencing of the items stolen for him by his employees. But he also skulked around libraries, scouting out potential thefts. If he found a book he liked, he would check it out from the library and examine it more closely. This inspection was designed to see what kind of shape the book was in, what edition it was, and whether it was marked.

Gomberg's theft ring was, in many ways, his generation's version of the Romm ring. It was much smaller and less complex, to be sure, but so was the bookselling business. The gang Gomberg was a part of stole from libraries all over, right the way up to Boston, and focused on high-value books that could be sold to New York dealers.

The gang did most of its best work in 1903, though it was not until February 1904 that it caught the attention of the Astor Library's Carl Bjerregaard. It was then that a copy of Nathaniel Hawthorne's *Grandfather's Chair* was reported missing. When a letter was sent to the address of the person who had checked it out (for use in the reading room, of course, since books did not circulate from the Astor), it was returned by the postal service as undelivered: there was no such person at the address. The loss of rare books from his library in this or similar manners was becoming routine, so Bjerregaard decided to do something about it. He gave orders that the next time someone asked for a rare book, he was to be notified.

It did not take long. A few days later, a "man with an undershot jaw, and looking and talking like a Russian" came to the desk and asked for the most recent issue of *Book Prices Current*. Accompanied by another man, he also asked specifically for a publication that listed the names of rare books, and the shops that were in the market to buy them. Suspicious of these men, Bjerregaard put himself in a position to watch them for a good long while, committing their faces to memory.[43]

Within a couple of days of this, a librarian at the Lenox, Victor Hugo Paltsits, acted in a similar fashion. (Paltsits, as it happened, was a major contributor to Poe scholarship, discovering several theretofore unknown Poe manuscripts in the Lenox collection.) He, too, had taken note of a recent theft from his library. Theft was particularly rare and difficult (and therefore quickly noticed) at the Lenox because it had only a small collection that was, for all intents, closed to the public. What had happened was that a man had come in and requested a book; after looking at it, he returned it unharmed. Days later, the book came up missing. Suspicious of one man in particular—a fellow who gave the name W. Agar when requesting books—Paltsits waited for him to come in again. Just as Bjerregaard had done, Paltsits got a good look at the man while he patronized the library. But the Lenox librarian went one step further: he made a pencil sketch of the man's face.

On April 5, 1904, Gomberg went to the Astor and requested a copy of George Bancroft's *Poems*, from 1823. He returned the book as usual, but the following day it came up missing, along with several other Americana titles. (Gomberg received the thirty-dollar *Poems* from the man who stole it and promptly sold it to Brentano's for $7.50.)[44] The librarians then circulated the pencil sketch of Gomberg at local stores.

Their efforts paid off. On April 18, a man fitting the image of the Gomberg sketch was caught selling one of the Astor's Hawthorne books, worth roughly forty dollars, at a secondhand bookshop in New York.[45] Gomberg was arrested at another bookstore nearby, Everett & Francis; he was found with a list of books, with prices after the names, all under either the rubric "A" or "L."[46] He was arraigned the next day in New York. District Attorney Smyth requested substantial bail, which was set at $1,500, a sum large enough that Gomberg was unable to post. Three days after his arrest, still in jail, he was indicted by the grand jury for larceny.

He did not offer much of a defense. Unlike most thieves, who claimed absentmindedness or lunacy, Gomberg claimed the book he was caught with, along with the many others from the Astor and Lenox libraries he was found to have, was given to him to sell by a friend.[47] It was the first indication that he was part of an organized group of men who stole from libraries and sold to (often complicit) secondhand bookshops. On May 5, 1904, Gomberg pleaded guilty to petit larceny and two days later was sentenced by Goff. After hearing pleas for leniency, Goff told Gomberg straight: "You are the leader of a gang of book thieves"[48] preying on Brooklyn and Manhattan libraries. Goff found Gomberg had "conducted a system of continual thefts from the public libraries of the city" and sentenced him to one year in the penitentiary, the maximum allowed by law.[49]

The sentence was an important one not because it was overly severe but because it was recognition of a problem. Book thieves were now organized, systematic, and willing to travel in search of books. For some, stealing from libraries had even become a profession—and these men were undoubtedly watching with great interest the construction of a particularly large building in Midtown.

After more than a decade of planning and construction, the magisterial New York Public Library opened its doors on Fifth Avenue, between 40th and 42nd Streets. A slew of local and national celebrities presided over the event, including President William Howard Taft. In a long review of the monumental building for the March 1911 issue of *Harper's*, David Gray gushed about the structure, writing that "surrounded by the towers of commerce, swept by the tides of traffic and tumult, its long sculptured façade, its low, abiding mass, its marble whiteness, proclaim a new note in the life of New York."[50]

The Fifth Avenue entrance to the NYPL, a uniformed guard at the front door. The hard surfaces and airy nature of the lobby, formally Astor Hall, meant that the sound of commotion—a man running down the steps, for instance—could be heard at a distance. © *The New York Public Library Archives, The New York Public Library, Astor, Lenox and Tilden Foundations.*

Unfortunately, the beauty of the place could not entirely overcome the old notes. In the spring of 1913, NYPL director Edwin Anderson submitted a report to the board of trustees detailing the rising problem of theft. He noted what had taken place in the previous ten years (mostly at the Astor and branch libraries since the NYPL building had not yet been finished) and how important it was to stop the losses. Like most major proclamations of the sort, this one came after the problem had gotten too large to ignore. The small measures taken to remedy book crime had been largely ineffective—and the one large measure had, if anything, backfired.

Three years earlier, in the summer of 1910, then-director John Shaw Billings, realizing library theft was becoming rampant in the city, sent around a circular as a direct appeal to secondhand bookstores. Titled *Book*

Thieves, it promised twenty-five dollars "to any second-hand book seller for evidence which results in the arrest and conviction of a book thief who has stolen books from any of [our] Branches."[51] The circular spent seven paragraphs explaining to booksellers exactly how to recognize an NYPL book, including how to determine if an embossed stamp had been ironed out, an ink stamp had been bleached, or a perforated stamp had been filled in. It also included some very specific identifications:

> In the Astor and Lenox Branches, books are numbered on the 99th pages, lower margin, with a numbering stamp. In the Circulation Branches books are numbered on the 97th pages, in the margin, inner, top, or bottom; other pages with numbers ending in 97, i.e., 197, 297, 397, and so on, are usually stamped with a rubber stamp. Pages used in former times and occasionally found bearing numbers written in ink, or stamped, are: 17, 51, 99, and 101.

This was a remarkable paragraph, essentially giving away to book dealers all of the NYPL's marking secrets. Billings must have assumed that booksellers were men of goodwill (though not *too* much goodwill, hence the twenty-five dollars) who would steer clear, if possible, of buying library books. They just lacked the right information to contribute to the effort. This philosophy was, at best, naïve. At worst, it only added fuel to the fire. In any event, it had little obvious effect in the short term. So a shorter version of the circular, with most of the description trimmed out, appeared seven months later. This version's most important sentence, aside from the one offering money, was this: "Dealers are especially cautioned against the purchase of a book with title page, or page 97 or 99 missing, mutilated, or supplied from another copy of the same book, not bearing an identification mark."

Billings certainly thought this was just one of many ways to help keep the books safe. But by the time his successor Edwin Anderson addressed the board in 1913, he knew that nothing tried to date had been effective. Not extra patrols, not better marking, and certainly not asking for the help of book dealers. If anything, things had gotten worse with the new building—despite the fact that it, like the Astor, had closed stacks. "During the past three years it has been found necessary to delegate one person to give a large part of his time to the work of investigating cases of book thefts, and the recovery of books missing in circulation," Anderson said. For anyone in the book theft business, the name of this "one person" was already familiar. For several years, he had been a library security advocate, spearheading a move to petition the state legislature to provide for better protection from library thieves.[52] His name, Edwin White Gaillard, had even appeared at the bottom of Billings's 1910 circular, to be contacted if a dealer discovered a stolen book. By 1913, his regular library duties had been consumed by trying to keep the books safe, and Anderson wanted to make this job official.

"It is believed that it will be to the interest of the Library to employ a competent man to give his entire time to this work. Cases are constantly arising which need careful investigation, not only in connection with actual thefts of books, but with the sale of stolen books through second-hand dealers and also in connection with the recovery of books taken out by readers and not returned. The persistent following up of all these cases would not only effect a large financial saving in reducing the actual loss of books, but the moral effect of such persistence would be of even greater importance."[53]

Authorized the next month, the inaugural position of special investigator called for particular qualifications—"a combination of librarian of wide experience and detailed information, police officer (with detective specialization), expert in criminal law, and humanitarian." Edwin White Gaillard was just the man for the job. The son of a famous Confederate physician—himself "descended from highly honored Huguenot ancestry"—Gaillard had spent his life in libraries, becoming the champion of a number of causes.[54] One of these was the idea of lending libraries, particularly in immigrant communities. He was also an early advocate of libraries in schools. But along with Gaillard's standard library experience, he had also proven himself very much committed to preventing book theft. Anyone who spent any time at all with Gaillard knew he was dogged in pursuit of thieves—or, as one reporter put it, he had exhibited "skill and ingenuity in catching the rogues" of the library theft trade.[55] Still, despite his knack for it, he was reluctant to accept the special investigator job. He liked what he was doing and was "disinclined to lose a librarian's contact with the books and the public."[56]

His first taste of book theft had come the way it does to most librarians: He was a victim. It was 1904, and Gaillard was the librarian at a "settlement house" on Manhattan's Upper East Side, whose aim was to integrate and commingle social and economic classes. The library there was in the market for a copy of Francis Marsh's *A Thesaurus Dictionary of the English Language*, so he placed an advertisement in local papers. One response was from a fellow librarian who had been the victim of a theft. The man asked that if Gaillard was offered a copy of the book, he look on a particular page for an accession number. "If you find one, the copy is mine."[57] Over the course of the next few weeks, Gaillard was offered several copies of the book and checked each one for the particular number, but none matched the one that had been stolen. The copy he ultimately bought was from a young man who claimed to have purchased the book in Canada and used it in newspaper work. But, according to the seller, since he needed money, he said he could afford to use other, inferior sources instead. Gaillard was glad to have the book and completed the transaction.

A week later, that same man returned to Gaillard's library in the late afternoon, claiming to have come across another copy of Marsh, this one in a very fine shape. Gaillard thought this a nice gesture but told the young man that he had no more funds for an additional purchase. When the man insisted Gaillard would like this copy, "politeness combined with curiosity, tinged with caution and a shade of mistrust" prompted the librarian to take a closer look. He then discovered, on the appointed page, the accession number mentioned weeks earlier by the victim librarian. Gaillard had a colleague stall the seller while he left the library to get a policeman. Then, according to the report, he "turned over to the police [the] courteous, affable, and apparently engenuous man."[58]

The possession of the book was not enough to prosecute the man, who claimed ignorance of the theft, but the local magistrate agreed to hold him for forty-eight hours pending more evidence. What followed was a hasty, unplanned two-day investigation during which Gaillard discovered from several librarians that copies of the book had been stolen from their collections. At the end of his work, Gaillard came to believe that at least three men were operating together as a sort of book theft team. One man did the initial investigating of the library, another did the stealing, and a third sold the books. The territory the little gang covered seemed to stretch from Boston to Washington, DC—and maybe farther still. Worse yet, the stealing itself was just the beginning. The men covered their tracks by erasing stamps—or removing the page upon which it was impressed—and by removing the catalogue card, too, if possible. In short, it was a well-oiled library theft machine of the sort no one had seen before.

Gaillard went on to note that in "consequence of my investigations I am convinced that there is an organized body of men who know book values, library methods and who are skilled in book alteration, who prey upon public and semi-public libraries."[59] It was the same conclusion that Recorder Goff, Carl Bjerregaard, and Victor Paltsits had come to around the same time in their dealing with Gomberg. After *his* run-in with the same gang, library security became first an interest and then almost an obsession with Gaillard.

Once he became the NYPL's investigator, Gaillard was immediately enrolled with the police department as a "Special Patrolman." This was not just an honorary position—he was a functioning police officer in the 23rd Precinct who made monthly reports and registered as a plainclothes officer.[60] After being sworn in, he teamed up with two veteran detectives so he could be shown how to run an investigation, perform an arrest, and how to behave in court. Gaillard quickly learned that it was all necessary if he was going to do the job right. "It soon became evident," he wrote, that "familiarity with the Penal Law, law of arrest and the Code of Criminal Procedure was absolutely essential." This was in addition to his existing training as a librarian. He noted that "with librarians [I] must be a librarian, yet with police officers [I] must accept the rough and tumble of police courts, upon occasion the physical difficulties of arrest, registering prisoners at police station, police back-room camaraderie, the rough work with patrol wagons, insane prisoners and the prison pens in the courts."[61] The job turned out to have a steep learning curve—the sort of thing that, if he had known what he was in for, he would not have agreed to do. It took him nearly two years to fully understand everything he needed to be successful. But he learned. For the bulk of the worst decades in American book theft—from an office filled with files on book crimes and images of known thieves—Gaillard kept safe one of America's most prestigious collections.[62] One of the most important, if indirect, ways he did this was by consistently securing the conviction of the offenders.

A library official later noted that he "acquired an adequate, precise knowledge of the legal enactments relating to libraries, of court procedure, of the nature of evidence. When Mr. Gaillard brought to court a case involving the Library's interests, many of the court officials came to realize that sufficient evidence, of an admissible kind, would be produced in support of the action. In no case so brought to trial by Mr. Gaillard has there been a failure to convict the offending person."[63] Gaillard later reluctantly admitted that not every person he arrested was convicted. "One man committed suicide when his name appeared on the calendar. One forfeited his bail and disappeared," and about 10 percent were sent to the mental health ward at Bellvue Hospital or other similar institutions.[64] This proficiency was not by accident. As Gaillard explained, "in order successfully to prosecute a case or a number of cases involving larceny, it is necessary to understand something of court proceedings, of the law, and of the nature of evidence."[65] As he would also demonstrate, right from the beginning of his career, it was also sometimes necessary to go to great lengths.

For instance, shortly after he began his job, Gaillard discovered that a suspected thief had decamped with a number of books from the address the NYPL had on file for him. The false address gambit was a fairly standard technique in the years before picture IDs, and was a plague on libraries all over the country. (Gaillard's successor eventually added to checkout cards this line:"Use of false name or address may mean exclusion from use of the Library.")[66] For most librarians, if it was not obvious who had committed the crime, the book was simply considered lost. But Gaillard did not give up that easily. In the case of this one man, he had taken out the library card with his real address, but simply kept the books when he moved to a new one. In order to track him down, Gaillard approached the postmaster in the New Jersey town the man lived in and asked for his forwarding address. When the postmaster refused, the special investigator devised another plan. He sent a registered letter to the thief's old address and hid inside the envelope a piece of carbon paper. Gaillard assumed that once the letter reached the New Jersey post office, it would be readdressed.

His plan was this: He would wait until after the envelope was given the forwarding address, but before it was sent out, to recall the letter. Then, even if the postman crossed out the new address, he would have a carbon copy of it within the envelope. Gaillard's idea, however, didn't quite go according to plan. The postman never got a chance to write down the new address and Gaillard never found the thief. But it was a perfect example of both Gaillard's dedication to the job and his creativity in pursuit of thieves.[67]

He was tireless in the role of special investigator and, at least in the opinion of Keyes Metcalf, chief of the stacks at NYPL, sometimes overzealous. He was quick to accuse those he merely suspected of theft, particularly library employees, and sometimes treated people roughly. (In Gaillard's defense, Metcalf, by his own admission, treated insider thieves with kid gloves. On several occasions when he caught "page boys" stealing from the library, Metcalf, in lieu of prosecution, merely fired them. In one instance, he told a boy the library would not prosecute if "he would return the pamphlet and promise to go to his priest and confess."[68] Having hired the boys, Metcalf had a special affinity for them and almost certainly felt that mercy was the best option. That is a nice trait to have in a normal person, but not one to be encouraged in a special investigator.) As the main security enforcer for one of the country's premier libraries—one that was during his tenure second in size only to the Library of Congress—Gaillard felt it was his job to be thorough.[69] He understood human nature and knew that even the visitors to the NYPL, while perhaps a better class of person, were still, as one article put it, "a thoroughly human body [that] furnishes illustrations of some of the frailties to which human nature is subject."[70]

He also understood that the whims of the judiciary could let him down, no matter how complete the case against a guilty man was. Recognizing this, he felt the best thing he could do was to be dogged in his preparation and follow-up. Early on in his new job, Gaillard wrote of these frustrations to Edwin Anderson. Gaillard said he was in the courtroom when Judge Warren Foster noted to a book thief who had pleaded guilty, "You can take what you want and if you prove to the jury that you did not intend to keep it forever you are not guilty of the crime of larceny. . . . The appellate division has ruled that property taken with the intention of using it and returning it is no larceny." Gaillard told Anderson, "I am giving you these rulings from the Bench verbatim to show you one of the difficulties which we ourselves must face in making the charge of larceny."[71]

Another problem was arresting men of means. In the case of Joseph Bernstein, charged with disorderly conduct and book mutilation and "suspected of various irregularities in the Circulation department," Gaillard reported that the "affair was taken up by his family with the utmost seriousness; they engaged two lawyers and went to considerable expense in the matter."[72] In addition, they sent to Austria for their father; the man was asked to come to New York and take charge of their household.

But one of these judicial disappointments stung worse than the rest. It was the case of Italian newspaper correspondent Franco Frusci, and Gaillard later said it was the worst he dealt with in his time at the NYPL. Just before Christmas 1924, a janitor at 27 East 22nd Street happened to look at some books that were being moved, along with some other effects, from the office of Domenico Marino of the Italian consulate. The janitor noticed that some of the books appeared to bear the stamp of the NYPL, so he took two of them and delivered them to the local police station.[73] The matter was then referred to Gaillard who, in a subsequent interview with Marino, learned that Frusci worked in the space where the books were found. Frusci was promptly arrested and admitted to having another big stash of books in a cellar at 101 East 16th Street. Despite their clear markings as NYPL books, Frusci said he had not stolen them but rather bought them all from a library employee some twelve years earlier.

That was certainly possible, but Gaillard just did not believe it. With a little effort, he determined that some of the books in question had been in the library's possession much more recently than that and pressed

Frusci for the truth. The Italian, under pressure, admitted only that he had, in fact, purchased *more* books from this source—and they were in his home on 181st Street. So Gaillard went there, too, and found a lot more books. Three carloads later, Gaillard got all 407 of them back to the library.[74] Still, Frusci would not admit any of them were stolen.

That was a problem. Even if Frusci was in possession of stolen books—in fact, even if he admitted to stealing them—if Gaillard could not prove any of the thefts were recent, the district attorney said he could not prosecute. Frusci, who Gaillard knew to be as guilty as a man could be, looked to be about to wiggle off the hook. So Gaillard got back to work. He continued to go through the books, meticulously trying to figure out when they had last been in the library. He just needed to find one he could prove with certainty had been stolen in the past four years; after a great deal of effort, he found three. After another meeting with Frusci in Marino's office—it consisted of "two hours' conversation"— Frusci finally admitted he had stolen two of the books in question.

He was arraigned and subsequently pleaded guilty to the theft of one of the books. But one of the conditions of his plea was that, to protect his reputation, he would not admit to the crime as Franco Frusci. Instead, he substituted the name Joseph Vestiglia. (This was the name the *New York Times* reported in its article on the subject, so it appears his reputation indeed remained intact.) He was sentenced to several years in the penitentiary, a term that was suspended contingent upon three years of good behavior.[75] After his sentence was handed down, Frusci privately admitted to Gaillard that he had stolen all of the books in his possession and more besides, including some from the Boston Public Library. But he never saw the inside of a prison cell for any of it.

In 1925, Gaillard called this the "most serious case of book stealing in the history of the Library." But though he was not wrong about much, he was wrong about that. He had, in fact, discovered the most serious case of book stealing in NYPL history some ten years earlier.

Charles P. Cox had been in the book business for three decades when he and Edwin Gaillard had their first run-in. Cox's first business, at 42nd Street and Third Avenue, was a well-known literary headquarters—until it burned to the ground. (His house, too, later burned down when his dog supposedly knocked over a lantern. If anyone thought these fires suspicious, history does not record the fact. In a more cynical age, the 1980s, it was the second fire to strike Texas book dealer John Jenkins that convinced many doubters that the bigger-than-life Austin bookman was crooked.) By 1914, Cox had relocated to 125th Street and Eighth Avenue, a spot that, as it happened, was nicely situated near Columbia University.[76]

By that point, not only had he been trafficking in stolen goods almost as long as he had been in business, but he had also passed the habit on to his son.

Carol Cox was just a boy the first time his father, Charles, came to police attention for dealing in stolen books. In 1902, a Brentano's clerk named Fred Evans was found to have taken more than $2,000 worth of books and sold them to several secondhand dealers. When detectives visited Charles Cox's store, they found a number of the books in question. Cox told police that Evans had offered him the books at less than market prices and he could not pass up the bargain.[77] It was a practice that had been going on for at least eight months. Other book dealers purchased books from Evans, too, but Cox seemed to be the one who did so the most, and for the longest. He told police he was just a stooge who had made a mistake, and, lacking any other evidence, the police did not charge him.[78] Fourteen years later, Gaillard was not as easily fooled as the police had been. Of course, by that point Cox had learned the lesson that most crooked book dealers usually learn: no one cares when you steal from libraries. That meant Cox had become reckless, confident that no one was paying attention.

But by 1916, someone was. In January of that year, investigating the sales of other libraries' books in local stores, Gaillard became "more intimately than ever before brought into touch with a portion of the secondhand book trade in this city."[79] It might be difficult to believe that a man who had been dealing with thefts as long as Gaillard had was surprised by the almost systematic participation by secondhand book dealers, but apparently he was. This was *after* his first dealing with the Gomberg gang. It was also well after NYPL director Billings's circular to book dealers, sent in the full knowledge that they were selling stolen books. And it was after three solid years on the job, during which any illusions about the innate honesty of library users had been shattered. Still, Gaillard's investigation into the Cox affair seemed to open his eyes in a way nothing had before.

During the course of his investigation, he was told by one soon-to-be-famous book dealer, Charles Heartman, that men in the book business were "obliged to buy stolen books." And after spending a lot more time peeking behind the curtain of the book trade, he had become "more than ever convinced that it is exceedingly difficult for a dealer in secondhand books to conduct a legitimate business." Worse still, it appeared that part of the problem was internal. Gaillard discovered that a number of people employed by the NYPL, many of them as stack boys, sold books to secondhand dealers in their free time. "The opportunities for sale of the books in their care are enormous," Gaillard told Anderson, while the

THE ACCUMULATED WISDOM 53

"chances of detection . . . are very few." One NYPL employee in particular, William Gough, was known to frequently sell to Harry Barton—a book dealer who was, in turn, known to be crooked. This led Gaillard to tell Anderson, "I should like to go on record as saying that the petty purchase and sale, soliciting orders and peddling books by librarians employed in this Library is thoroughly improper and seems to me contrary to the ethics of the library profession."

Despite the amount of circumstantial evidence Gaillard gathered attesting to the fact that there was an almost systematic effort on the part of local booksellers, Cox being chief among them, to sell library books, nothing ever came of it. The only thing Gaillard got from the episode was knowledge of the bookselling trade, and a newly hard bark.

But even with a few failures undercutting his many successes, Gaillard ultimately created a culture at the NYPL that was hostile to book thievery. Aside from a staff whose job it was to help him prosecute book thieves, he instituted a uniformed service of men in the library, many of them former police officers, who patrolled the building and guarded the exits. He also instilled in regular employees the ability to recognize suspicious behavior.[80] One Friday in the middle of July 1920, it paid off.

On that day, two stack boys were reporting to work through the Fifth Avenue entrance to the library when they noticed a man walking out who seemed to have a distinct bulge in his coat. Rudolph Bade and Irving Newmark, the stack boys, turned to follow him. They suspected they knew what the bulge was from. The man walked south on Fifth Avenue for two blocks before stopping to pull two secreted books from under his coat. He tore the book card holder and date slip from the inside cover of one and threw it in the garbage before proceeding south. At the next corner, he did the same thing with the other book. On both occasions, the slips of paper were retrieved by the boys. While he walked, the man "gnawed with his teeth the library seal and the classification number from the back of both books."[81]

The boys eventually followed him all the way to 35th Street, where they saw him go into Best & Co., an upscale retail clothing store. Newmark followed him in while Bade went to get a police officer. The police officer told the boys that since he had not seen the man steal anything he could not arrest him, but he would watch as they did. Newmark went over and placed the man—Julius Sandberg—under arrest. The four then went to Sandberg's store locker, where he produced the two books in question. From there, they proceeded to the local police station and he was locked up.

Gaillard met the boys there shortly thereafter to question Sandberg. The man assured the special investigator that he had never stolen any other books from the library and had only stolen these two because he did not think he could get them from a lending library. Gaillard did not believe him, particularly since the man had ripped out any indications that they were library books. He went immediately to Sandberg's house, where he discovered forty-six other stolen library books. Sandberg eventually pleaded guilty.

As he liked to do, Gaillard attended court during as many parts of the legal process as he could. He particularly liked to be there during the trial and sentencing portions of his cases. In the Sandberg case, that was a good thing. During the sentencing hearing, the judge was inclined, after the testimony of the probation officer, to merely fine him twenty-five dollars. Instead, Gaillard took the stand and contradicted several aspects of the probation officer's report. As a result, the judge sentenced Sandberg to the penitentiary for up to a year.[82]

Of course, many of the things Gaillard did had nothing to do with keeping the book collection safe. The NYPL was a large, people-filled building, open to the general public. Much of his job involved merely keeping these people in line. In December 1914, for instance, he reported to Edwin Anderson that "one hundred and forty-nine men were politely invited to leave the building. (A month ago I would have said 'ejected,' but in the meantime all of the uniformed force have been especially coached in politeness and courtesy.)"[83] The reasons for these polite invitations varied. Two men were sent out for boxing, twelve for disorderly conduct, seven for drunkenness, four for "malicious mischief (boys)," seventy-four for sleeping, three for smoking, five for spitting, twenty for "war discussion," and twenty more were simply "tramps." (The Great War was much on the minds of people in New York in the autumn of 1914. On November 19, Otto Lippolt was arrested in the NYPL newspaper room for tearing from the *Manchester Guardian* a caricature of Kaiser Wilhelm. Lippolt did not deny the charge but thought the image an insult to Germany and that it was his "duty as a German to protect the interests of the Fatherland.")[84] The large numbers of people sent out of the building was thanks to Gaillard's insistence that the uniformed men make hourly patrols of the building.

Perhaps Gaillard's greatest legacy came from his zeal to proselytize and help prevent crimes in the first place. A tireless speaker, he appeared at all manner of gatherings to speak about his work. In 1921, he wrote down his thoughts on the matter in a two-part article called "The Book Larceny Problem," published in *Library Journal*; he was just finishing a longer work on the subject when he died in 1928. In addition to his more public efforts, he also privately offered his help to any libraries that needed it.[85] The job of special investigator, starting with Gaillard and continuing with his successor, was seen to encompass more than just the NYPL. Other libraries—even bookstores—called the NYPL for advice on how to prevent, or for particular help with solving, book crimes. The special investigator was always willing to pitch in for the capture and prosecution of thieves, wherever they operated.

Gaillard performed the role of special investigator with both vigor and seriousness. During his tenure, the library implemented measures that severely cut down on thefts, including not only posting guards at the doors to check bags but also giving the rare book collection its own separate area. No one could have kept all the books in the NYPL safe, but by the time Gaillard died in 1928, the library was about as secure as could be hoped. While libraries everywhere were leaking books at a torrent, the large building on Fifth Avenue was keeping it to a trickle—and those that got out were generally of modest value.

Gaillard's most important contribution to book security at the NYPL was the *idea* that the books were safe. By being very public about the fact that he took security—and prosecution—seriously, Gaillard scared away many would-be thieves. There were plenty of other libraries with little or no security; thieves often just took the path of least resistance. Still, a state of détente between the theft community and the NYPL did not sit well with everyone; the very fact that the library's collection was so off limits inspired a unique type of covetousness. For some people, library shelves had become little more than storage racks for their own personal book business—and there did not seem to be any reason at all why the big building on Fifth Avenue between 40th and 42nd Streets should be different.

CHAPTER 3

A Purloined Poe

SAMUEL RAYNOR DUPREE WAS NOT FROM GREENWICH VILLAGE, or anything like it. In fact, if that area of Manhattan had a direct geographical and social opposite, it might have been Pinetown, North Carolina. It was in this small farm hamlet that Dupree was living in September 1925, awash in the large-seeming problems of early adulthood: he did not get along with his father, work was scarce, and small-town life offered little excitement. So he decided to light out for cities up north where his father did not live and opportunities were said to abound. Like many such boys, he was in for a rude awakening. While he did manage to find some work, a few weeks of Philadelphia winter was as much northern opportunity as he could stand and so the ragged Southerner made his way back home after his very first December above the Mason-Dixon line. He tried again the next year, finding odd jobs this time in the New York service industry and, at one point, steady work as a busboy at O'Reilly's Coffee Pot. But that was just until winter set in again and he again headed south.[1] The Scylla of Pinetown and the Charybdis of points north bounced the teenager back and forth in that manner for several more years before he finally found himself, in the summer of 1930, in New York City for good.

Dupree was much like the men Stephen Crane described for the *New York Press*, wandering around "slowly, without enthusiasm, with his hands buried deep in his trousers' pockets, toward the downtown places where beds can be hired" for pennies. "He was clothed in an aged and tattered suit, and his derby was a marvel of dust-covered crown and torn rim. He was going forth to eat as a wanderer may eat, and sleep as the homeless sleep."[2] Living in the city's various parks, Dupree met many other men like him: immigrants who had come to town for jobs and been disappointed.

The city, like most of America, was a mess. New York had more than eighty breadlines, and landlords were evicting New Yorkers from their homes by the tens of thousands.[3] Some of these people took to living full time in Central Park, where chimneyed shacks complete with beds and chairs were a regular sight. Far from being a city in which to find a job, New York had become a gathering place for the unemployed. But steady work in a legitimate field was only one option for Dupree, and among the teeming masses and their floating craps games there was always someone with word of one-off jobs that paid a great deal of money. Some of these stories were even true.

Two who seemed to be in the know on this underground economy were men Dupree knew only as Paul and Swede. He had met them on several occasions during his trips in and out of the city, and he made their acquaintance again when he moved to New York permanently. Despite the big talk that always seemed to fly around gamblers and park camp-fires, these two men seemed believable, mostly because they dressed well and always seemed to be flush with cash. Dollar bills had a way of adding credibility to a man's talk, and so Dupree sidled up to them. What he discovered was that their racket was not a secret at all: they were book thieves, and they did not care much who knew it.

They stole books from everywhere—libraries, bookstores, residences—and sold them up and down the island of Manhattan. They had regular customers on Book Row, but they also sold to plenty of people in higher-class stores. One proprietor Paul and Swede worked for at the time was Jascha Giller, the gnome-like owner of a nice shop—"the best books intelligently selected, charmingly displayed, courteously presented"—on 59th Street.[4] According to Paul, he had stolen a first edition of *The Scarlet Letter* from the nearby Brick Row Book Shop and sold it to Giller for $150. But such a thing seemed beyond the realm of possibility to Dupree. That was an obscene amount of money—and nothing worth that much should be so easy to steal. So even after Paul showed him the wad of cash that had come from the transaction, Paul and Swede knew it would take more to make a believer out of Dupree. They decided to take him under their wing and let him tour the area for a few weeks. If their talk could not convince him, watching them steal and then counting the money as dealers put it in their hands surely would.

It did. The trade, to Dupree, seemed to have absolutely no downside. The victims were hapless, the crooked book dealers generous, and no one at all seemed to be after them. After weeks of learning from the men, Dupree got his book theft feet wet, swiping cheap books here and there and handing them over to the men. It was nothing big; just enough to convince him that he had found the job of a lifetime. But even as he suddenly had a chance to make a steady income—a state of affairs almost impossibly rare during the Depression and certainly one he had never known—winter loomed on the horizon. It terrified him. He knew he could handle being hungry, dirty, and uncomfortable, but he could not be cold. Even if he could afford a warm place to live, it was not going to do him any good if he could not go out to work. So he finally came to a compromise: he would spend the winter in New York, but he would get a really warm overcoat. The right garment might even improve his odds as a thief.

Unfortunately, book theft had taught him that stealing items of value was not difficult—and he naturally assumed this applied to all manner of goods. When he got pinched trying to steal a winter coat, he learned the truth.[5] Overcoat theft, strangely, was one of the great petty crime scourges of New York at the time. In fact, coat theft was easily the biggest problem Edwin White Gaillard had to deal with during his time as special investigator. He was constantly arresting men for stealing unattended overcoats in the reading room. Library employees, from janitors to reference librarians, were told to be on the lookout for men acting suspiciously in relation to these garments. In February 1914, Gaillard's men nabbed one thief whose pockets contained the tickets for five coats he had already stolen and pawned. This required the special investigator to write letters with the description of each of the coats to the twenty-three people who had recently reported losing their coats at the NYPL.[6] Nine months later, Gaillard even ran a sting operation, using his own coat as bait. They nabbed a forty-year-old waiter—a man who admitted he had come to the library to steal coats.[7]

Dupree became another statistic in the coat theft epidemic. After being arraigned on petit larceny charges and released on his own recognizance, Paul and Swede recommended to the man without a fixed address that he simply not show up for his court date. Since they had not led him astray so far, Dupree decided to follow their advice and, by December, was officially an outlaw. He was also still coatless as the cold set in. And though he did not know it, his life was about to take a turn for the worse.

As the 1930 Christmas holiday approached and business picked up, Paul and Swede brought Dupree to the man who had introduced them to the book thief game and was still one of their best customers: Harry Gold. ("I'll take you down town and introduce you to the fence," was how Swede put it.)[8] At that point, the dealer was in the market for all sorts of books. He liked rare and antiquarian, to be sure, but he also liked new books—they were easier to get and much more difficult to trace back to him. Besides, he was getting plenty of really terrific rare items from Massachusetts. For Gold, Paul and Swede's specialty was obtaining recently printed books. They did most of their work stealing from Womrath's, Doubleday Doran, and the Gotham Book Mart, often going straight to Gold's as soon as they grabbed the books. He paid as generous a rate as they were likely to get, and he was reliable. On that first day when Gold met Dupree, Swede got several dollars from the dealer for some new books he had brought in. Paul, on the other hand, got seven bucks for a single book, a work of poetry he'd stolen from Drake's bookstore on West Fortieth Street. As Gold was inspecting the item, Paul told them the story of how he had almost gotten caught by the proprietor. He had been seen just after he had slipped the book into his coat pocket and was terrified when the owner hurried over to accost him. Bluffing his way out of it, he had somehow managed to scamper from the store.[9] He said it was the closest he had come to getting in trouble and he could not believe he had made it out.

They all had a laugh about the whole thing, and then, as Gold was settling accounts with the two men, he noticed Dupree, standing there watching him dole out the cash. He looked up from the transaction and asked, "Don't you have anything?" Dupree said that he did not, but that he might later. He had made a commitment to start stealing full time.

Gold, sensing a new recruit, motioned for him to come closer. As long as he was going to start stealing, Gold thought he should at least know what to get. If he followed his advice, Gold told Dupree, they would make a lot of money together. Then, pulling out a catalog from a Midtown dealer, he pointed to John Galsworthy's *The Man of Property* and told Dupree that it would bring in a lot of money. He proceeded to point out a number of other books he was in the market for, before handing the issue over. He suggested Dupree use the catalog as a guide as he toured the shops of Midtown dealers—he noted, in particular, Dutton's and the Brick Row as good places to get fine material. Other stores that had proven to be reliable victim bookshops were Drake's, the Chaucer Head, the Madison, and St. Mark's.

Gold also handed Dupree two dollars. He told the Southerner if he got anything good in Midtown—whenever he got it—he was not to walk it back to Book Row, or even take the subway; he was to take a cab. This was not the gesture of a benevolent man, but merely good business. They were in the thick of Prohibition, when there were roughly twice as many places to buy liquor in New York as there had been before ratification of the 18th Amendment, and so there were many distractions between 59th Street and Book Row. This was particularly true of Midtown, where one would, according to Frederick Lewis Allen, often "notice well-dressed men and women descending the steps to the basement entrances of certain brownstone houses. They are not calling on the cook, but making a routine entrance to a speakeasy: standing patiently at the door till Tony or Mino, within, has appraised them through a little barred window and decided to unbolt the door."[10] Gold did not like the idea of his scouts, their coats filled with treasures, stopping for a drink. Or, worse yet, deciding that other book dealers—ones closer to Midtown speakeasies—might give them a more immediate offer for their books.

Dupree agreed to bring whatever he stole back to Gold and, with guide in hand, left the store. He headed up Fifth Avenue, knowing it would not be long before he would be back on Fourth Avenue.

A 1917 survey of Edgar Allan Poe's works could locate just ten copies of *Al Aaraaf, Tamerlane and Minor Poems*: "One is in the New York Public Library, another in the Peabody Institute, Baltimore, and the others mainly in private libraries—five in New York City, one in Chicago, one in Washington, and one in Pittsburgh."[11] The NYPL's version looked a lot like the rest: flimsy and thin, with a greenish-blue

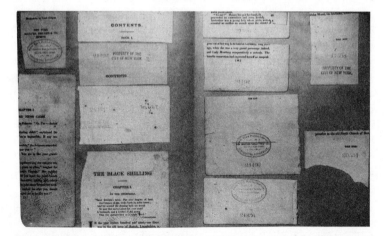

Examples of ways to mark library books hung in the special investigator's office. Accession numbers and a variety of types of stamps used by the NYPL were meant to be a warning to thieves and a tipoff to book dealers. © *The New York Public Library Archives, The New York Public Library, Astor, Lenox and Tilden Foundations.*

cover over seventy-one pages the color of dry sand. It was eight inches by five inches with minor tears on several pages and the sort of creases that come from use. But the main thing that separated this version from the rest of the extant copies was that the "Tamerlane" on the title page appeared haloed in light blue ink, just slightly less visible than the black. The Lenox Library stamp had been impressed on the reverse of the page decades before when the book came to the library from the collection of Poe's friend Evert Duyckinck. By 1931, the blue had bled through to the other side.

But that was less obvious protection than it might have seemed. The problem with stamps in general, and a Lenox stamp in particular, was that they were not always a sign of library ownership. Many books with library stamps came and went from the market all the time, most quite legitimately. A glance at any edition of *American Book Prices Current* (*ABPC*) at the time demonstrated that fact adequately enough. Dozens of books per year listed, in their description of condition, some such stamp. Often the description gave the name of the library (a fall 1906 edition of *ABPC* noted, in its catalogue description of Edward Boynton's 1864 *History of West Point*, that the book had a "Lenox Library stamp on the back of title") or sometimes it merely read "library stamp." Dealer catalogues were the same way. Most of these books had been sold by the library in question as a duplicate copy and no one had bothered to remove the stamp. The Lenox, like many libraries, did this with a number of books. On top of that, though most people in the book trade knew the Lenox Library had become the NYPL, it was at least plausible for a dealer to feel that the stamp of a defunct library meant nothing.

A. S. W. Rosenbach was nine years old in 1885 when he heard his uncle Moses—the man from whom he inherited his bookselling spirit—predict that fifty years after Poe's death, his works would be the most valuable of all American author first editions.[12] Poe died in 1849, and, right on cue at the turn of the century, privately owned copies of *Al Aaraaf* started becoming consistent high sellers whenever they were offered in New York. This was a spot-on fulfillment of Moses's prediction, too, because just a decade earlier Poe's works had not been nearly so popular. For a good example of the *fin de siècle* skyrocketing of Poe prices, we need look no further than the experience of George D. Smith, Rosenbach's early rival for the title of greatest American bookman. At one point Smith paid sixty cents for a copy of *The Murders in the Rue Morgue*. He sold it in the early 1890s to a dealer for an entirely reasonable sixty dollars; that dealer sold it to Frederick French in 1896, for ninety dollars. Five years later, it sold at French's auction for $1,000.[13]

Al Aaraaf, like most other Poes, benefitted from this rally. In 1894, a copy of *Al Aaraaf* sold at an Americana auction for $150.[14] But auctions of the slim book of poetry in 1900 and 1901 brought $1,100 and $1,300 respectively; a couple years later an autographed copy sold for $1,825. In 1906, *Al Aaraaf* fetched the highest price for any single volume that season: $1,500.[15] George Smith paid $1,460 for an *Al Aaraaf* in 1909, and a New York sale four years later brought in $2,000.[16] The story of one particular copy of *Al Aaraaf*—it, too, eventually given to the New York Public Library—offers a perfect microcosm of the book's rapidly rising value. In 1894, George Henry Moore's copy of the book was sold at auction for seventy-five dollars. It was sold again nine years later, by William Nelson, for $1,825. A mere six years after that, in 1909, Stephen Wakeman bought it for $2,900.[17] In a decade and a half, it gained nearly forty times its value.

Poe works, and *Al Aaraaf* in particular, seemed to have no ceiling, or anything to inhibit their upward rise. The *Washington Post* noted in 1909 that Poe works were so in demand "and of such excessive rarity that the appearance of one of them in the auction rooms is in itself a bibliographical event."[18] So popular had *Al Aaraaf* become that just about the only thing that could have sustained its steady upward tick in value was a long dry spell. After the Wakeman purchase, that is exactly what happened.[19] The absence of *Al Aaraaf* auctions was so long, in fact, that by 1932 *The American Book Collector* (*ABC*) editor Charles Heartman, himself a long-time Americana dealer, opined that *Al Aaraaf* was the rarest Poe. According to him, *Tamerlane*, Poe's first, unattributed book, came on the market more than did *Al Aaraaf*—and "even three new *Murders in the Rue Morgue* were found within five years."[20] *Al Aaraaf*, on the other hand, proved to be the most elusive; it could not be found anywhere. And Heartman was in a position to know—he had just done a complete census, spread out over four issues of *ABC*, of all Poe first editions.

In the meantime, since the early twentieth-century flurry of *Al Aaraaf* sales, the prices for Americana had exploded.[21] By 1931, very few people knew exactly what *Al Aaraaf* could fetch on the market, but most knew it would be a great deal. One who knew for sure was Rosenbach. In 1928, he had purchased, in a private sale, a presentation copy (Poe had given it to his cousin) for $10,000. The next year, he sold it for $33,000.[22] Of course, that was the sort of gaudy business that could be had in the 1920s and almost certainly did not represent the value in 1931. Still, in September 1930, a year after the start of the Depression, Charles Goodspeed said he would pay $5,000 for an *Al Aaraaf*—"or more if in *very fine* condition."[23] Whatever the exact sum a collector was willing to pay for it, a Book Row dealer could be forgiven for thinking that monetary value, above almost everything else, inhered in this early Poe work.★

But aside from monetary value, early Poe books had something else going for them: lore. More than the works of any other American author, Poe's seemed destined to turn up in bundles of trash, recognized only by a savvy dealer, and subsequently sold for breathtaking prices. This was a uniquely useful trait for purveyors of stolen books, as it tended to offer good cover for lack of provenance. Some of this lore could be chalked up to a *Saturday Evening Post* article written in 1925 by Vincent Starrett. Titled "Have you a *Tamerlane* in Your Attic?" the article was the impetus for the discovery of several copies of the book. The most popular of these stories was that of Ada Dodd, of Worcester, Massachusetts, who lived "in two poor rooms with her elderly sister."[27] Dodd, after reading the Starrett article, did look in her attic for a *Tamerlane* and was very surprised to find one. On the advice of a Worcester librarian, Dodd wrote to Boston dealer Charles Goodspeed: "I understand this is a very rare book. I should like to sell it." After a visit to confirm its authenticity, Goodspeed eventually sold the slim volume to Owen D. Young. Young, a former utilities lawyer, had by then become chairman of General Electric and the founder of RCA. He was not only very wealthy but also quite a collector of Poe works. For her part, Dodd earned about $14,000.

But many of these Poe discoveries had nothing to do with the Starrett article. For instance, another Poe find that benefitted Owen Young did not come from an attic at all, but rather from the random luck of a book dealer buying in bulk. The proprietors of the storied Dauber & Pine bookstore at 66 Fifth Avenue used to buy "odd-lot bundles" of books and pamphlets at various auctions. "Whenever books or collections or pamphlets turned up in various auction rooms, it had been our practice to examine them individually," Sam Dauber said, "but when they were tied up in bundles or large containers so as to prevent close inspection, we just

---

★ It is impossible to know the current value of one of the eighteen known existing copies of *Al Aaraaf*. All but one are in institutional libraries, so there will not be much of a chance to find out. Still, the rapid increase in monetary value has found no plateau—and, if anything, is rising at an ever-faster rate. The penultimate privately owned copy, subsequently donated to the University of Chicago, brought $40,000 at a 1974 auction.[24] The remaining privately owned copy of *Al Aaraaf* was listed in a catalog, eighteen years later, for $120,000. While it has not appeared at auction since, the price has undoubtedly ballooned. For a comparison, look at the still-escalating value of *Tamerlane*. One copy was purchased at auction in 1990 for $165,000.[25] Not quite twenty years later, that same copy sold at auction for $662,500, a 400 percent increase over an already high price.[26] A sale of *Al Aaraaf* in the near future would likely fetch somewhere in the neighborhood of half a million dollars.

followed our flair and gambled heavily on them."[28] These stacks of
material accumulated in the store until someone had a chance to go
through them, sifting the wheat from the considerable chaff. In 1926,
Dauber happened to knock over a pile that had been sitting around for
years. A quick look and he knew he had discovered something great.[29]
One of the uncovered pamphlets was the first separate printing—outside
of *Graham's Magazine*—of *The Murders in the Rue Morgue*. The proprietor
soon sold it to Owen Young for $25,000; sadly, the Second Avenue junk
dealer who had sold the pile of "discards" in the first place committed
suicide over having lost the treasure.[30] (Young later donated his Poe collection to the NYPL.)

One story of a Poe find from 1913, reported in New York, came out
of Washington, DC—a city whose proximity to Baltimore added an
interesting personal wrinkle. An old woman, living "in poverty in the
attic of a house three blocks from the United States Treasury," the
Washington Post reported, was saved by the chance discovery of an *Al
Aaraaf*.[31] The woman had sent word to local bookseller John Loomis
that she had some fine old books she wanted to sell so she could get
money to eat. But Loomis found what the woman offered nearly worthless and was on his way out the door when he stumbled over a slim
volume used to balance a bureau that had lost a caster. The woman had
assumed it was her least valuable possession. She explained to Loomis
that Poe used to visit Adeline and Elvina Wolf, two Baltimore residents,
and gifted them this book; because it was not very successful, no one
thought much of it. It was later given to the woman's mother by relatives of the Wolf sisters. The old woman offered it to the dealer for five
dollars, but he instead, offered to sell it for its full value and take only
the standard commission.

These accounts, between them, have most of the elements of a good
Poe discovery story: a poor widow, a dusty attic, a chance discovery, a
book dealer, and a wealthy industrialist. They share these facts with an
even earlier Poe discovery story whose account was printed in the *New
York Times*. This one, too, came complete with these hackneyed details,
though it also had the other elements of a good Poe story: loss and
duplicity. The 1909 article told of the country origins of a pamphlet for
which J. Pierpont Morgan paid $3,800 at an auction. What the *Times*
described as a "wide-awake commercial traveler" but what was, in fact,
a book scout named Louis B. Cole, was roaming through Dutchess
County, New York, in 1906, trying to find books and pamphlets on the
cheap. In one village, he bought for twenty-five cents from an elderly
widow a stack of miscellaneous items. One of these, of course, was the

rare pamphlet containing Poe's most famous detective story. Cole sent the work to a book dealer on 23rd Street with whom he had an arrangement. The dealer, who agreed to split his profits with Cole, told him the book was worth twenty dollars and sent him half that much.

Upon returning to the city, however, Cole discovered that the dealer had sold the work to a 56th Street dealer for $950. Cole, demanding satisfaction "with both a gun and an officer of the law," eventually got his $475. The widow was not so lucky. She, too, came to the city to protest that she had been mistreated, but her "arguments and tears, it is believed, were unavailing, and she returned home a wiser if not a richer woman."[32]

The elements of these fact-based stories became so familiar to everyone in the trade that they were mixed and conflated, tarted up and fictionalized, taking on the life of urban legend. By the 1930s, Poe-find stories abounded on Book Row, and if a dealer did not claim to have had personal involvement with one of the finds, then he knew a dealer who did.

Harry Gold's version of the Poe discovery story was interesting in that it involved not just serendipity and great fortune but a tragic loser. In Gold's case the loser in question was not some poor widow, but a man named Schwartz with an obscure little bookshop on Third Avenue. The villain, to the extent one existed, was a Midtown bookseller. According to Gold, this Third Avenue dealer received from an elderly Brooklyn Heights woman an old book with no date and no name but "A Bostonian"—so, *Tamerlane*. Schwartz bought the book from her for a pittance, thinking it a fake or facsimile. Then he left the book at his store with a younger employee in charge while he traveled to the NYPL to do some research. When he discovered that what he had was genuine, he returned to his shop only to find that the book had been sold to an unnamed Fifth Avenue dealer. At some point after that discovery, distraught and broken, Schwartz died.[33]

Another fictional version of a Poe-find story was told by Harry Kurnitz (writing as Marco Page) in his 1938 novel, *Fast Company*. This hard-boiled detective story surrounded the murder of a crooked rare book dealer and a couple of book scouts. The Poe story, told by an honest book dealer, was meant to explain why the death of the crooked dealer (Abe Selig) was unlamented. The story is told to the murdered man's comely secretary:

> Selig was a young man, already fairly successful, and with a reputation for being a fast man in a trade or a swap. At just about this time there was a book dealer over in Brooklyn—on the Heights, somewhere—who was friendly with Selig. This fellow was located near a school, did most of his

business in second-hand textbooks, and did not know much about rarities. He just about managed to stay above starvation level, had a wife and a kid and another one on the way when he brought a bunch of books over to Abe to ask his opinion on them. He used to do that frequently and sometimes Abe would take the books and give him a few dollars. This time he had bought a lot of books from an old home in Brooklyn and picked out what he thought might be worth rent money and left them with Abe. Abe snickered over them, chided the guy for wasting his time and gave him five or ten dollars. Doc Dolan was working for Abe Selig at that time and he told me the story. One of the books was an immaculate first edition of "The Murders in the Rue Morgue" with an inscription in Poe's handwriting. The finest copy ever known. Abe got around thirty thousand dollars for it from some utility king and a ream of publicity.[34]

The honest dealer, so the story went, was distraught enough by being cheated that he shot himself. His wife, almost ready to give birth, died from shock. "Do you wonder why I can take Selig's murder in my stride?" the storyteller concludes. (Followed shortly by: "You make the drinks this time. That speech parched me.")

Stories like these were part of the tradition of the New York bookselling business. They romanticized the act of discovery, while also being cautionary tales about whom to trust. The details changed on the margins, but the essential elements were almost always there. For this reason, the idea that a theretofore unknown copy of a Poe rarity might just show up in the hands of a random book dealer was not peculiar. While other very rare books might draw scrutiny, a Poe work from out of the blue would, at least on the face of it, seem as natural as the change of seasons. Better still, it would inspire in most booksellers an almost visceral feeling to not be left out of the jackpot. No one knew this better than Harry Gold. Nor did anyone know better than Gold from exactly where the next "discovery" was going to come.

The Reserve Book Room (RBR) was actually four rooms on the south side of the top floor of the NYPL. Most of the rare material in the library had originally been organized under the American History Division, overseen since the opening of the NYPL by Wilberforce Eames. A former Lenox librarian, prolific book collector, and writer, Eames was, in the words of the *New York Times*, "the greatest living scholar of books in America."[35] This echoed a sentiment Rosenbach had made six months earlier: "Probably the greatest student of books in the whole history of scholarship and book collecting lives quietly in New York, worshiped by every collector and scholar and unknown to the world in general—Wilberforce Eames."[36]

Harry Lydenberg, director of the NYPL, put it more succinctly: "His knowledge was comprehensive, accurate, final."[37]

It was that knowledge and reputation that was part of what made the RBR among the best rare book destinations in the world. The core collection was the other part. Much of this material came to the NYPL from the two source libraries of the 1895 agreement. The Lenox Library, in particular, contributed an astounding collection of tens of thousands of volumes, many of them impossible to find anywhere else. This included the very highest lights of printing, from the most important early Bibles (including not only a Gutenberg but also the first Bible with a printed date, 1462) to notable books from the first printing presses in Germany, France, Italy, Holland, England, and North America. The Shakespeare collection was composed of a thousand volumes, including several early quartos, two first folios, and seven second folios. The John Milton collection included, along with most editions of his written works, margin-noted books from his own library. In short, the Lenox collection had every major item a rare book collection could hope to have, and it had them in spades. But maybe the most impressive part was its comprehensive Americana—an area many nineteenth-century bookmen had not seen a need to collect. Wilberforce Eames summed it up this way: "So successful was [Lenox] in obtaining not only every important book relating to this subject and period, but also nearly every edition of every important book, that I feel safe in claiming that nine-tenths of the existing literature can be found on our shelves."[38]

Not that the NYPL collection had been resting on its laurels. Since its founding, the library had continued to acquire fine material at a high rate. This included items that were purchased with dedicated money, and many more that were donated. Eames knew that if the library had a strong reputation, people would be happy to donate their material—and the collection would grow in ways it could not through sheer purchase power. (This was also library policy. Lewis Cass Ledyard, president of the board of trustees, refused to permit fund-raising campaigns, predicting that the library would gain more money from large donations than it would from a more public approach. In the 1920s, he was proved right.)[39]

Unfortunately for people who coveted this collection, the NYPL took book security seriously. This was a distinct rarity at the time and was thanks largely to efforts of Edwin White Gaillard, who had made protecting the collection routine. Even books in its regular stacks were well guarded. The rare books, as many dealers noticed, were particularly difficult to get at. (Local dealers used the NYPL's rare collection as a reference source, and so were very familiar with the setup.) The rare collection was protected both actively and passively, with nested levels of security. For one thing, the doors to the rooms housing rare books were metal, and were kept locked even when the library was open.[40] Patrons were not allowed access to the stacks—they had to request what they wanted either from the main circulation desk or one of the RBR librarians. There were two librarians on duty in the RBR at any given time so that if one left to fetch a book from the rare books stacks— located in one of three adjacent rooms—the other stayed and watched over the patrons. There was not then (and is not now) a more effective means of discouraging theft than an attentive librarian. And the RBR employed two.

This meant that simply slipping a book into a large coat was not going to work. But neither was the other method favored by Gold's men: the dead sprint. In most American libraries, a quick dash for the exit with a few books in hand was a fine option. Libraries were generally fairly small—and crammed with books, shelves, and other barriers of the sort that allowed a thief to creep within a few yards of an exit without raising the slightest alarm. From there, a few fast steps to the door were all the head start a thief needed. Sometimes, the same thing could be achieved with a hurried walk out an unprotected door. But escape from the third floor of the NYPL was altogether different. It was less a sprint than a stee- plechase, requiring planning, commitment, and more than a little luck. The circumstances for success were largely outside the thief's control.

To start, he had to scramble out of the RBR, pivot east, and run a quick thirty yards to the main hallway. This was on uncarpeted floors in the worn soles of a man without a lot of extra money for shoe repair. From there, he had the distance of half a football field ahead of him—a straight shot, but one that might require him to dodge other patrons, particularly if it was crowded. At the end of this run, he was merely at the top of the stairs. In the thief's favor was that the rest of the trip was downhill: two flights leading almost directly to the exit. But the steps between the second and third floor had a tendency to get bottlenecked even with only a few people present, so that part of the journey could be exceedingly slow. And even when fast, the steps were slick at a run. Also going against the successful grab-and-dash was the architectural demeanor of the building. The hard marble and open spaces meant that the sound of commotion carried—hurried footfalls and shouts echoing off walls tended to attract attention. As would a harried man in a place normally reserved for quiet study. The running man would draw a great deal of attention, particularly if pursued. All of which would alert the security guards stationed at each exit to prevent exactly this sort of theft. From their vantage point, the guards could see the thief coming even before he had reached the landing on the second floor. This was if they had not already been alerted by a telephone call from an RBR librarian, who had a direct line to the exit.

Gold knew all of this. If the task was not impossible, it was certainly daunting—and that is why very few people tried it. To the extent that people successfully stole from the NYPL, it was from the main stacks, reference area, or various departmental libraries. But Gold knew the value of the books in the RBR might be worth the chance, particularly if it was not him taking it.

The Southerner Dupree had proved an eager student, willing to do almost anything for a few dollars. And he was certainly expendable. A few years earlier, training a book scout was almost an investment. By late 1930, these men were in and out of his store almost more often than customers, so one less thief was not that big a deal. And if Dupree was caught and named the dealer who had put him up to theft—so what? Book theft, and Gold's participation in it, was an open secret. The authorities could not touch him.

This is what had occupied Gold's thoughts since the first day he fixed eyes on Dupree. He had been grooming him, in fact, giving him guidance on technique and ways to increase his chances of success in this gambit. That meant not only how to plausibly request books, but also how to scout a place—to know its exits and the routines of the employees. Essentially, Dupree did a short apprenticeship with Gold in the early winter of 1930, learning "the dates of the books, respective publishers, color, cover and papers" and various other characteristics Gold thought it important for his well-trained scouts to know.[41] Gold also told the zealous Southerner never to attempt, under any circumstances, to erase library stamps on his own.

And just like that, it was time to make it happen. By late December, Gold felt he had suitably prepared the Southerner for the work—at some point, he just had to turn him loose on the RBR. Well, to a certain extent. Dupree was the point man—the one to show his face, the one to take the risks, and the one to take the fall, if need be. But he was not going in alone. It was not that Gold did not trust Dupree; he just did not trust the man's nerve. He had worked with enough of these guys to know who could handle a milk run at a backwater library and who could stand up to the security of the NYPL. He did not figure Dupree for the latter, so he decided to gird him with Swede and Paul. These men, he knew, would rip the cover off a book, knock a man down, or jump through a window if they had to. Not that any of this was likely to be necessary—Dupree was almost certainly going to get turned away or captured with the first move he made—but having experienced men willing to go the distance provided a measure of comfort in any caper.

One snowy afternoon in late December, Gold gathered the men at a local coffee shop. They had only one shot at this, and he wanted them to do it right. The NYPL catalog marked the cards for the rare books in a way that made them recognizable to the browser. This, according to Gold, was the "cream." In a pinch, anything with this marking was worth stealing. But he also knew *exactly* what he wanted—he had been to the library and seen the books in person. Dupree was to aim for three works. The first two came, via the Lenox Library, from the Evert Duyckinck collection. These were *Al Aaraaf, Tamerlane and Minor Poems*—the NYPL had no *Tamerlane*, so this was the earliest Poe work in their collection—and a first edition of Nathaniel Hawthorne's *The Scarlet Letter*, from 1850. Duyckinck, a publisher and writer, knew Hawthorne personally and, in fact, was responsible for introducing his fiction to Herman Melville.[42] Anything from Duyckinck's library had the added value of association with a man who was friendly with many of America's greatest authors. The third book in Harry Gold's sights was a *Moby-Dick* that had come to the library from the collection of Admiral Franklin Hanford, a major collector of Melville works. This, too, was a first edition, in its dark olive-green original cloth, complete with six pages of publisher's advertisements. These were all in great demand, and the Poe book, in particular, was extremely hard to come by. Gold made sure his men knew it. Then he sketched out a plan.

As it happened, Poe himself had been to the approximate location at which his books then resided, though not even he could have imagined the machinations that would make it so. In the 1840s, the Croton Reservoir's forty-one-foot-high walls were a popular destination for New Yorkers to survey the city at a great height. Writing in the *The Broadway Journal*, Poe recommended the trip: "When you visit Gotham, you should ride out the Fifth Avenue, or as far as the distributing reservoir.... The prospect from the walk around the reservoir is particularly beautiful. You can see from this elevation, the north reservoir at Yorkville, the whole city to the Battery, with a large portion of the harbor, and long reaches of the Hudson and East rivers."[43]

Dupree was ready for the job. When he was not hanging out in Gold's shop, he had been accompanying Swede and Paul on theft runs to Midtown stores. He had embraced the outlaw lifestyle with vigor, and the prospect of stealing from the NYPL did not scare him at all. The edifice of the place, not to mention the stone lions out front, might have struck fear into the heart of any regular thief. But Dupree had the confidence of youth and the motivation the New York winter provided a man from a warm climate. So after his meeting with Gold he started spending a lot of time in the RBR. Not only was he figuring out the best theft method, and egress, but he was also warming up to the librarians. In countless thefts throughout the course of American history, the seemingly small fact of becoming familiar to the librarian has made a great deal of difference. So Dupree did exactly that, spending hours and hours on that upper floor, getting to know the environment and its weaknesses and earning a measure of the librarians' trust. (This technique remains a thief staple, present in many library and archive thefts in the eighty years since Dupree's job. For example, Barry Landau, a presidential historian who pleaded guilty in 2012 to stealing thousands of historical documents, was known to woo librarians and archivists by bringing them sugared confections and flattering them about the richness of their collections.)

For a succession of days in early January, Dupree called for the use of a number of different rare books, signing in with the name Lloyd Hoffman. Many of his requests were for first-edition American works only a few of which he was planning on stealing. This allowed him to establish himself as a student of these sorts of works and to see the routine of the library. One interesting thing he discovered was that he could request the books from two different places. The main catalog was along the wall in "the great rustling oaken silence of the reading room," and he could fill out a request card for rare books there—then simply meet the book in the RBR.[44] But he also saw that, once in the RBR, he could make another request and one of the librarians would leave the room to get it. With a pencil, paper, and feigned interest, he "studied" for a little while each day, paying close attention to everything but the books.[45] This included not only who was where when, but also the nature of the crowds.

The setup of the place was easy to discern: bronze grille doors protecting three locked rooms with bookshelves and a small reading room.[46] The weakness took a bit longer. Watching the two-librarian system in practice, he noted that even during the lunch hour, another librarian from a different part of the NYPL came up to lend a hand.[47] The patrons were not left alone with their requested books, and under no circumstances were they allowed to browse the shelves.

But there was one exception: Saturdays at lunchtime. Because of limited weekend staffing, the RBR was patrolled by only one librarian between 1:00 and 1:30 while the other one took his break. As far as windows of opportunity, this one would have to do. Still, the plan was not without its drawbacks. The library was usually crowded on Saturday afternoons, making the escape route more harrowing than normal. On the other hand, one of the librarians who worked on Saturdays was John Elliot, a stout, elderly man who was a holdover from the Lenox. While he was smart and good at his job, he was not the sort of man who could give chase. It was Elliot who was working that lone half hour on Saturday, January 10, 1931.

This was, in many ways, an entirely appropriate date for the theft: the second anniversary of the Kern sale, the high-water mark of early twentieth-century antiquarian bookselling. It seemed impossible to believe it had only been two years since Jerome Kern, composer of a number of entries in the American songbook, including "Ol' Man River" and "The Way You Look Tonight," had proceeded to sell off his considerable library. As it happened, book theft was part of the impetus. Kern, who had been collecting for about fifteen years, refused to lock his treasures away in a vault, claiming that owning the books was no good if he could not see them. But by 1928, they had become so valuable that it was no longer tenable for him to have them just sitting on his shelves, "possible prey to desperate booklovers in Bronxville."[48] Besides, Kern was the perfect example of a man for whom the search to acquire a book was almost more important than the joy of owning it. So, in conjunction with Mitchell Kennerley at Anderson Galleries, he decided to sell.[49] And he picked just the right time.

With men like Kern more and more inclined to donate their collections to a library or university, auctions of this sort seemed to be disappearing. So while it was neither the largest, nor even best, book auction of the century, it looked increasingly like it might be the last really good one. There were enough high-quality Kern books that it took ten different sessions over the course of two weeks in January 1929 to get the job done. "The catalogue, in two parts, came out with its superlatives like raisins in a fruitcake and was circulated everywhere auction catalogues had gone before," noted Rosenbach's biographers.[50] But despite the pre-sale hype and the number and quality of people expected to attend the sale, no one was prepared for what happened at the auction.

With the exception of A. S. W. Rosenbach, "who owed his doctorate to drama" and acted accordingly in the bidding process, rare book auctions were polite affairs. Small movements or even minor sartorial motions—a finger clutching a lapel or brushing an ear—could serve as indications of a bookman's desire to bid. James Drake once sat next to his friend, Chicago dealer Walter Hill, and draped his arm across the back of Hill's chair. After Drake won a particularly vigorous bidding war, Hill was surprised to find his friend had even been in the running. That's because to bid, Drake had merely lifted his right thumb, situated only inches from Hill's ear.[51] Henry Huntington, an early twentieth-century supernova of book buying, was separated from the rest of the rare book kingdom by a similar opposable digit—this one belonging to George D. Smith. At the Robert Hoe book sale in the spring of 1911, Smith, with only a series of "hardly noticeable" thumb movements, took down lot after lot after lot on behalf of Huntington.[52]

But despite the staid level of decorum that prevailed at the Kern auction, the bids themselves were to cause a stir. Before it began, Kennerley asked the composer what he would like to get from the sale. Kern replied he would be happy to take $650,000 to $700,000 for the entire collection. They passed that figure by the time the auction reached the letter G in the catalog.

The generous bidding was due to a confluence of events. The stock market seemed to be on a limitless climb (Owen Young's RCA stock, for example, had risen from a purchase price of $1.50 to $420). The newspapers were routinely filled with the stories of men who had bought books for a pittance and sold them for a mint. At the time of the Kern sale, the *New York Times* even editorialized that soon "no doubt, there will be a Book and Manuscript Exchange, where a seat may cost as much as it now costs on the Stock Exchange."[53] With that in mind, Kennerley persuaded Kern to extend credit to purchasers much beyond what was customary—up to two years, even. With a steady confidence in the rise of book prices, there seemed little risk.[54] So there was plenty of money, hype, and that peculiar 1920s attitude of record breaking. But there was also a fair amount of ego. Since the death of George D. Smith some ten years earlier, Rosenbach had assumed the mantle of America's greatest rare book dealer. But there were plenty of rivals to that throne, most of all Gabriel Wells, who had become to Rosenbach America's greatest underbidder. (Whatever his limitations in the auction room, Wells was certainly more popular with his fellow bookmen. As book dealer David Randall put it, "G.W. could be very generous—a character flaw the Doctor never exhibited to me.")[55] The two had clashed many times at auctions, most recently at a couple of epic bouts in 1928 that resulted in record-breaking prices. Rosenbach won them both with *Alice's Adventures Under Ground* going to him for a shade more than $75,000, and an autograph by Button Gwinnett, the elusive Declaration of Independence

signer, for $51,000.[56] The Kern sale seemed like as good a time as any for
the men to flex some more financial muscle.

The auction had the atmosphere of a feeding frenzy right from the
beginning: One passing witness to the Kern mayhem noted that a "copy
of Goldsmith's 'Vida's Sacchis, or Chess,' starting at ten thousand dollars
as we prepared to go, reached twenty-five thousand before we found our
gloves."[57] At the end of the first night of bidding, Kern telegrammed
Kennerley, "My God, what is going on."[58] What was going on was a dem-
onstration of just how valuable books had become in a short time. It was
the eighty-fourth item (of 1,842 up for bid) that set the tone for what
was to come. Kern had purchased *The Battle of Marathon* by Elizabeth
Barrett (Browning) in 1924 at $1,650; for Rosenbach, the hammer finally
fell that first night at $17,500. The book had been projected to bring
between $4,000 and $7,000, and probably only reached as high as it did
because of a mistake: both Rosenbach and Barnet Beyer (the underbidder) thought they were bidding on behalf of Owen Young. Whatever
the truth, the die was cast—and prices subsequently soared. Rosenbach
paid $29,000 for what later proved to be a sophisticated copy of *Tom Jones*
that had cost Kern $3,500. A Charles Dickens *Pickwick Papers*, which
Kern bought for $3,500, went for $28,000. Barnet Beyer took a *Jude the
Obscure*, which Kern paid $47.50 for in 1914, for $4,100.

Of course, it was not just books whose values had skyrocketed in the
1920s. A twenty-two-line fragment of John Keats "I Stood Tip-toe upon
a Little Hill," sold to Kern by George D. Smith some fifteen years earlier
for $500, went to Rosenbach (over Beyer) for $17,000. A signed, four-
page letter written by Poe quoting Elizabeth Barrett Browning's praise
of "The Raven" fetched $19,000. An American literary correspondence
record that outlasted the lifetimes of everyone at the sale, it had been sold
to Kern by Gabriel Wells for $1,250.[59] A single page of Samuel Johnson's
Dictionary manuscript was the subject of a heated bidding war. Rosenbach,
bidding on behalf of Young, finally acquiesced to a fellow Philadelphian
at $11,000. (Rosenbach later told Young that because he had sold the very
thing to Kern less than a year earlier for $1,750, he did not have the
conscience to bid higher. And his conscience on such matters, according
to one who knew, ordinarily "had a lot of stretch.")

For lot after lot, day after day, this price inflation was typical. But the
surprise glamour piece did not come until late in the sale. It was Percy
Bysshe Shelley's revised copy of "Queen Mab." It was one of only two
known extant copies of the 1813 poem, and Kern had spent $9,500 for it
in 1920. At this 1929 sale, it was the subject of a furious bidding war between, of course, Wells and Rosenbach. A *New Yorker* correspondent later

wondered whether Wells "had not been bidding out of an explicable desire to annoy his rival," and a range of other opinions suggested Wells was egged on by Mitchell Kennerley.[60] Whatever his motivation, he finally earned the Shelley work at $68,000.

All told, James Drake spent $125,000, Wells $185,000, Beyer $230,000, and Rosenbach a $410,000. The per-lot average blew away anything in existence and stood as the record for more than fifty years. This auction was later credited with the demise of many booksellers who, in the coming years, took heavy losses on the books they had paid so much for. (Wells, for instance, never did unload "Queen Mab." This, the single highest-priced item at the Kern sale, was sold in 1951, after Wells's death, for $8,000.)

Even for people who had not overspent at the Kern, the sale mattered. It gave dealers yet another excuse to reprice parts of their stock, with estimations of value moving increasingly upward. (One story of such routine repricing had Rosenbach noting to a collector that he made $1 million in one day. "In what stock?" the collector inquired. "In my own," Rosenbach replied. "I went through it today and marked it up."[61]) And the press coverage was comprehensive enough to let anyone with the slightest interest in books know exactly how valuable they were. But the Kern sale was the crest of a wave that would not rise appreciably again for twenty-five years, the trough starting almost immediately and lasting through the Depression, World War II, and the Korean War.[62] When none of those prices could be paid in the coming years, the hangover from the sale very much contributed to the atmosphere of Midtown dealers' appetites for Kern-quality books at bargain-basement prices. In that small way, the Kern sale might have even contributed to Dupree's being at the NYPL that day.

The Southerner knew none of this, of course. As he approached the entrance from Fifth Avenue, up the short flight of granite steps flanked by sculptured lions, he knew only that, aside from everything else, January 10, 1931, was a perfect day for stealing: cold enough to warrant a large coat but no snow or ice on the ground to hinder his escape.[63]

In a 1962 *Harper's* article, Marion Sanders noted that if you wanted to read in the British Library you had to provide a recommendation from "a responsible person not a hotel or innkeeper."[64] The Library of Congress and the Bodleian Library at Oxford University, two of the world's other great collections, offered their own impediments. But "to take your fill of the four million volumes in the New York Public Library you need merely be an adult member of the human race." At half past noon, Harry

Gold's three minions presented this credential to the hive of activity known as Central Circulation.

The area was packed with people, as the men knew it would be.[65] Crowds were a perennial problem in the NYPL, and the Reading Room, in particular, was often filled to more than capacity. A 1920 library report noted that a "serious difficulty affecting the service has been the increasing frequency with which the reading rooms of the Library have come to be used by people who have no legitimate reason for coming to them."[66] Dental, medical, and other students, in addition to people just trying to stay warm, were crowding out other patrons. This was particularly true on weekends when other libraries in town were closed. "On many Saturday and Sunday afternoons during the winter months, there have been hundreds more readers than seats in the Main Reading Room for hours at a time." It was a situation, Gaillard had warned, that made book security more difficult.

But it was not just the Reading Room that was crowded—the halls, departmental libraries, and exhibition spaces had their fair share of people, too. The library routinely put on displays and exhibits of many of its own collections (often supplemented by the collections of benefactors) and items borrowed from other institutions, highlighting acquisitions or celebrating one event or another. One such exhibition, six years earlier, comprised manuscript items borrowed from the Morgan Library; over the course of its run, the show brought to the echoing halls of the library 180,000 people.[67]

In January 1931, there were four exhibits going on, each one aimed at a certain constituency. The first floor housed an exhibit of Russian icons, an event designed to appeal to many of New York's immigrants, but popular with a whole lot of other people besides. On the third floor there was an exhibition of woodcut book illustration, "specially arranged to show the progress of woodcut art and technique from the earliest times up to the present day."[68] Also on the third floor—located in a large room adjacent to the top of the stairs—was a display of lithographs by Vernon Howe Bailey, meant to illustrate the city fifty years earlier. And most popular of all was a general display—housed in some thirty cases and various hung frames—of Currier & Ives prints. These were placed all over the library, contributing not only to the sense but also the fact of a crowd. It was this state of affairs that allowed the three men to go completely unnoticed on the way in—but it also hampered their escape.

At Central Circulation, Dupree filled in three checkout cards that called for a few very rare items: Edgar Allan Poe's *Al Aaraaf, Tamerlane, and*

Minor Poems along with first editions of Nathaniel Hawthorne's *The Scarlet Letter* and Herman Melville's *Moby-Dick.*[69] All of these had originally been part of the Lenox Library. (The Astor had more books *about* Poe than by him.) The requests were processed and brought to librarian John Elliot while Dupree ambled, separately, the same distance. He arrived at the grated door of the RBR some minutes later, trailed at a distance by Paul and Swede. Dupree walked into the RBR and stood next to Elliot's tall desk, waiting for the librarian to return with the books. This delay did not help his nerves any, but he was calmed by the thought that he could still call off the heist. So far he had not done anything other than what he had done a dozen times before. He looked at the telephone, just on the other side of the desk—it was not exactly a rarity in New York, but it was still novel to the boy from Pinetown. Had he known it was connected directly to the guards at the exits, he might have left the room right then, but the idea never occurred to him.

When Elliot brought the books in and set them on the table in front of Dupree, the Southerner thanked the librarian, then, apologizing, pulled two more cards from his pocket. He had filled out these book requests the day before and when he presented them to Elliot, he pretended he had simply forgotten to give them to the main circulation desk. This was Swede's idea for getting Elliot out of the room—and it came very close to not working. The librarian was loath to leave without another librarian around, but he eventually decided it was okay to do so. He had come to know, at least a little bit, the young man named Hoffman who had lately spent so much time at the library—and he seemed like a fine person. Also, Elliot knew he could watch the door from the other rooms. So he looked Dupree in the eye and told him to stay right where he was, then left the room to get the books.

Dupree, as willing to take direction as the next man, stood stock-still and watched as Elliot walked out. Much to the chagrin of Swede and Paul, waiting in the hall, he remained standing there even when Elliot was out of sight. Dupree simply was not prepared for the immediate success of the plan; his heart was pounding in his throat and he did not know quite how to react. But the two other thieves, old hands at the trade, were not surprised at all. Looking in the room after Elliot left, Swede whispered insistently for Dupree to get the books and go. He knew they should have been halfway out of the library by now. But Dupree would not move. Swede called out more loudly to the Southerner; he knew he could not yell or make a big commotion for fear of attracting more attention, but he had to get Dupree moving. Their time was running out. After a few more fruitless seconds, Swede simply walked into the room, grabbed at once Dupree and the top book off the pile—*Al Aaraaf*—and made for the door. Dupree, snapping out of his reverie, scooped up the other two books and followed Swede.

Once in the hall, Paul grabbed another of the books from Dupree: *Moby-Dick*. He knew the Melville work well, having stolen a copy from the English Bookshop on 55th Street a few weeks earlier, and he was glad to have this one. Then they all started hurrying down the hall together, made a sharp left, and fast-walked toward the stairs. Dupree noticed that both men had already put the books they had grabbed into their coats and decided to do the same. Up ahead was a crowd of men at the main third-floor intersection. The throng of people would slow them down, but it could also offer protection if anyone was following. Dupree glanced back to see if, in fact, anyone *was* in pursuit. Miraculously, no one was—it was beginning to look like they might get away with it. But when he turned back around, Swede and Paul were gone, absorbed by the milling jostle of brown hats and coats ahead of him. It was eighteen months before he would see them again.

His momentum carried him forward and Dupree reached the stairs without his associates, a little panicked that he was now suddenly on his own. He took the steps two at a time, getting closer to the guards at the front entrance with every stride. Elliot, by this time, was in action, too. As soon as he noticed Dupree had left the room, he had resisted his first impulse to give chase. He knew he could not catch up. Nor did he particularly want to leave the room unattended. Anyway, there was a better alternative: he picked up the telephone to call the guards at the public exits.[70] This was exactly why they had the direct line. Unfortunately for the NYPL, both of the exit lines were engaged. All of a sudden, everything was going wrong for the NYPL's vaunted security apparatus and everything was going right for Harry Gold.

Elliot, frustrated, knew he had one more shot. He phoned Keyes Metcalf in his office and told him what had happened. He thought maybe the chief could do something. By 1931, Metcalf had been at the NYPL for twenty years. He had arrived as a student in 1911—turning down Harvard in the bargain—to study under Mary Wright Plummer. In 1913, he was appointed chief of the stacks by Harry Lydenberg, a job that allowed him to become well acquainted with the books in the large collection. Because of that, he knew the library, its collection, and its weaknesses very well. He was not always in on Saturdays—and never during the college football season. But the Rose Bowl, the final game of the season, had been played nine days earlier, so he just happened to be in the office that day. He responded to Elliot's call immediately, running from his office down to the entrance, the normally calm and docile man creating a ruckus to get the attention of the guards. But he was too late. By the time he reached the door, the thieves were out onto Fifth Avenue. Metcalf arrived at the top of the entrance stairs just in time to see Dupree running down the street in the direction of Book Row, the back flaps of his overcoat kicking up with each stride.

In extolling the uniqueness of the city, New Yorker E.B. White wrote that "it can destroy an individual, or it can fulfill him, depending a good deal on luck. No one should be willing to come to New York to live unless he is willing to be lucky."[71] In January 1931, Dupree certainly thought he was one of the fortunate few upon whom a benevolent city had smiled. But New York soon gave him a chance to reconsider.

An hour after he had made his escape, Dupree met Harry Gold at a restaurant called Foltis-Fischer. The dealer was very happy to see the thief and happier still to hear what he had to say. Gold had not heard from either Paul or Swede, but after he talked to Dupree, he knew they would be at his store soon enough. Dupree, coming down from his adrenaline rush, was starting to feel remorse. And the more time he spent with Gold, the worse it got. He felt used—and sorry for the way he had treated John Elliot. Gold's mood, on the other hand, was headed in a different direction. He slipped Dupree twenty-five dollars for his *Scarlet Letter* and thanked him for the transaction. (He later paid Paul and Swede one hundred dollars apiece for the books they delivered to him.) He was invigorated. He had a wonderful, saleable book in his hand, and it would not be long before he would turn it into cash; and the near future held the promise of even better books. Plus, he had gotten them from the one place books supposedly could not be gotten from. It was not exactly the Mount Everest of book thefts, but it was some kind of peak.

If Gold recognized the change in Dupree's demeanor, it did not make a dent in his own mood. He offered him another proposition, sliding across the table a typewritten list he had copied from *Book Prices Current*, then pushed back his chair so he could make his exit. Rising, Gold dropped a few coins down near Dupree and told him he was welcome at the Aberdeen anytime with any of these books in hand. Then he turned and walked out, leaving the Southerner with only the cash.

Back at the NYPL, Elliot was distraught. He knew if any fault was to be assigned, it belonged to him. He never should have left the man alone with the books—even for a moment. But Metcalf was more concerned with the entirety of the crime. Elliot had filled him in on what he thought was stolen, and how the crime had taken place, and Metcalf was thinking it all through. A number of things had to have gone wrong for the books to get outside, and all of them had. There was enough blame to go around.

Metcalf thought long and hard about what the library's reaction should be. He decided against calling the police. (His thinking on the matter was similar to the rare book dealer in a 1936 Carolyn Wells novel: "The police are all right on a murder case, or most other crimes, but a rare book, especially this particular one, is a matter outside their technical knowledge.")[72] The cops might be able to help at some point, but probably not in the short term. Besides, he had his own policeman on staff. If he wanted to call someone in, that would be his decision. Metcalf picked up the phone and placed a call to Connecticut, home of the New York Public Library's second special investigator.

CHAPTER 4

Scholarship and Investigation

G WILLIAM BERGQUIST WAS NOT YET A RARE BOOK LEGEND WHEN Keyes Metcalf called him immediately after the theft. But he certainly had the backstory of a legend.

At age fourteen, Bergquist had run away from his Groton, Connecticut, home, unhappy with the woman his father had recently married. Over the course of the next two decades, he made his way in life, finding work where he could. That meant working in a rail yard, a lumberyard, a stable, and a foundry; among the jobs he had was cowhand, cook, stable boy, and horse trainer. If there was a low-level, menial job to be done, he did it. When World War I came around, the thirty-three-year-old joined the army and was sent to France.[1] Mustered with the 108th Engineers, Bergquist arrived in Europe in early 1918 and was in the war zone by June—as soon as his company was issued its Enfield rifles and gas masks.[2] Despite being engineers, Bergquist's regiment was often under fire. They cut fences, patrolled battle zones, repaired trenches, and, when called upon, took a hand in fighting. They also built a whole lot of bridges and roads, mostly on or around the front lines, and suffered through directed artillery barrages as well as machine gun and sniper fire.

After the war, he moved back to Stamford, Connecticut, where he married and took various sales jobs to support his growing family. All of these disparate experiences eventually coalesced in the man to form an unusual combination of attitude: realistic about the basest instincts of human nature but still optimistic about man's ability for rehabilitation. (Again and again over the course of Bergquist's life, he gave book thieves second chances, and time and again he would be proven wrong. But he never stopped believing in the power of rehabilitation.)

Bergquist was not in Stamford long before he wanted a change. A librarian there, noticing his interest in books, encouraged him to strike out in yet another profession. Bergquist loved the idea and made the trip to New York and its public library on Fifth Avenue. Keyes Metcalf, by then chief of the reference department, was sitting at his desk there when he was approached by a man in his early forties who, though an inch or two shorter, outweighed him by a hundred pounds. "My name is Bergquist," the man said. "I want to become a librarian."[3]

Taken aback, Metcalf stammered for an answer, eventually coming up with: "Where did you go to school?"

"I had a year in high school at Groton, Connecticut, where my father was a groundskeeper at the Academy," Bergquist said. Then he mentioned some of his work experiences. Metcalf did not know what else to do but keep the man talking and, in that way, discovered that along with the wide variety of early jobs, after returning from war, he had managed a grocery store in Chicago, been a traveling salesman, and, at present, ran a cooperative store in Stamford. It was an impressively varied resume, but one that did not immediately strike Metcalf as qualifying him for library work.

Still, it seemed to Metcalf that Bergquist had been everywhere and done everything. He was obviously smart and clearly willing to do whatever it took to succeed. These were great traits to have in a librarian. So he excused himself and spoke with his boss, Edwin Anderson. He told Anderson the tale of Bergquist and, in that way, convinced Anderson to meet the man himself. Anderson did, and got the same treatment. He ended his brief meeting with Bergquist convinced he was almost certainly qualified for the library school affiliated with the NYPL.

"I think we should give Mr. Bergquist our library school examinations," Anderson told Metcalf.[4]

At about the same time as the completion of its building on Fifth Avenue, the NYPL opened its own library school. In 1911, there were not even a dozen such schools in the United States and certainly no consensus on their need. Apprenticeship, or the like, had been the main route to librarianship in the past, and the profession was only recently coming to the conclusion of the need for formal training.[5] Andrew Carnegie, who had already funded library schools at Western Reserve University in Cleveland and the Carnegie Library in Pittsburgh, agreed to give $15,000 a year toward the NYPL effort.

The most eminent library school director around, the Pratt Institute's Mary Wright Plummer, agreed to become the director. For many people, it was natural that New York would have such a school, and that the NYPL would host it. A *Library Journal* article from 1922, written by library school director Ernest J. Reece, explained the need to situate a school at the Fifth Avenue location. The "thought was to utilize a combination of advantages which is not to be equaled anywhere in the United States." The library:

> is concerned on the one hand with scholarship and investigation as provided for in the economics, technology, oriental, art, American history, rare book, and other divisions of the Reference Department: and that it typifies on the other hand the many varied activities which are more commonly identified with the free public library, such as branch work, extension methods, club work and general community service. Outside the New York Public Library, but in and about New York City, there are examples of libraries associated with schools, colleges, welfare institutions, educational and research foundations, banks, insurance companies, man- ufacturing plants, export houses, and with societies devoted to engi- neering, law, medicine, botany, history, geography, numismatics, and the literature of specific languages, and examples of county libraries. New York is also the home of a number of important private libraries; it is the book-publishing center of the United States; it leads in lectures, music and the drama; and it is the city in which the greatest variety of civic and community activities is observable. The Library School of the New York Public Library has sought to take full advantage of these opportunities, feeling that it is in a strategic position and that the maintenance of a strong school for librarians in connection with the New York Public Library is in its way as significant as the locating of a medical school in New York, or the conducting of a school of mines in Colorado or Michigan.[6]

The examination Bergquist was offered was the same one that Metcalf had taken upon entering library school. The school was of the mind that college graduation should not be the major criterion for admission— there were good candidates for librarianship who had not gone to uni- versity.[7] But applicants did have to have a wide range of knowledge. Rather than qualifying by resume, a potential student had to take a five- part examination consisting of general history, general literature, general information, and a reading knowledge of French and German. Bergquist, who had had very little formal training and almost no preparation, passed all five. Almost immediately, he began working in the stacks of the NYPL, studying librarianship on the side, and commuting from Connecticut.

He worked very successfully at the NYPL for the next few years, eventually becoming a full-time librarian. Shortly thereafter, in 1926, the navy came calling. The veteran was offered the director's job at the

United States Naval Station in San Diego, California, and it was an opportunity he could not pass up. He moved his family out West and spent three years there, getting yet more experience in a new area. Then, in early 1929, he received a letter from New York. In it, Metcalf explained that Edwin White Gaillard had died and that the NYPL wanted him to take his position. The plump, genial, white-haired Bergquist turned his sights back East.

Gaillard, who died in October 1928, had invented the job of special investigator. Thanks to his writing, speaking, and dedication to the job he was, for a librarian, also fairly well known. But though Galliard was popular, successful, and instrumental in bringing the scourge of library theft to light, he was destined to play Wally Pipp to Bergquist's Lou Gehrig.[8]

Book thieves are not known for their courage—most often they steal from libraries because the places are under-protected and the crimes against them under-punished. So it would be an exaggeration to call Harry Gold brave. But he was certainly a cool customer: less than two days after the theft he commissioned, Gold presented himself at the desk of Keyes Metcalf.[9] The dealer told Metcalf that he heard the NYPL had recently lost a copy of *Moby-Dick*. Gold said that, as it happened, he had his own copy of the book. It was a first edition sold to him by the NYPL years earlier and sophisticated with parts of a second edition. Since he was offering it for sale at his shop, he did not want Metcalf to think he had anything to do with the recent theft.

But Metcalf had already thought it, as had Bergquist. On the very day Gold waltzed in to talk to Metcalf—the first workday following the theft—the chief of reference and the special investigator had gotten together to talk about the situation and who might be responsible for it. Gathered in Bergquist's second-floor office, the men by consensus placed Gold near the top of a short list.[10] It was not that they had any illusions about the honesty of other New York City book dealers—they knew that, if given the opportunity, the NYPL's rare collection would be pilfered by any number of men at shops within a cab ride of the library. They just did not think very many of them would be brazen enough to attempt a caper like the one two days earlier. It did not make sense, on almost any level, to steal a book that was nearly impossible to resell. It particularly did not make sense to make such a ruckus in the effort. Gold, known to be both crooked and a bit reckless, seemed like one of the few who might commission the act. His attempt to throw them off his trail, before the crime had been largely publicized, sealed the deal.

"The individual who purloined it is known," Edgar Allan Poe's Auguste Dupin noted of the eponymous missive in his detective story

"The Purloined Letter." "It is known, also, that it still remains in his possession.... It is clearly inferred from the nature of the document, and from
the non-appearance of certain results which would at once arise from its
passing out of the robber's possession; that is to say, from his employing
it as he must design in the end to employ it."[11] Like that document, the
nature of the thing stolen was the NYPL's greatest asset. It would have
been difficult enough to sell any similar Poe book in the city without
causing a stir. But given the attention surrounding the theft, Metcalf and
Bergquist felt they had a fighting chance to get this one back. The
Hawthorne and Melville books were rare and important, and the library
certainly wanted them back, but a New York sale of one or the other of
those would not attract much attention.[12] The *Al Aaraaf* was the key.
Once it was up for sale, no matter how shrewd the thief was, word was
destined to get around. No one was going to pay what it was worth
without several people finding out about it. This became the central
focus of their plan to get it back.

"Plan," of course, was a generous term. Mostly what the men had was
an idea—and the hope for its success rested on a series of probable courses
of action coupled with the trust they had in allies who they could convince
to work on their behalf. Any of a hundred things could derail it, including
the not-remote possibility that the books had already been smuggled out of
the city, bound for Europe or the West. But like a man searching for his lost
key under the street lamp because that is where the light is, the men focused
on New York at least partially because that is where their allies were.

Simply making a general announcement to New York booksellers
was neither possible nor wise. There was, of course, a bookseller grape-
vine, but it was not particularly effective or fast working. (This was adequately demonstrated a few years later when a forger, over the course of
a year, went from store to store to store selling fake autographed books
and letters to dealers. A well-working and fast-acting network would
have put a stop to this in a matter of weeks.)[13] And given that there was
little at stake for the book dealers, even getting the word out was not
likely to be overly helpful—and might have been counterproductive, as
Gaillard had found out many years earlier. Their main problem was figuring out who, among the bookseller crowd, could be counted on as an
ally—and then recruiting that person to help.

Bergquist trusted just about everyone, of course. He had spent his
first couple of years as special investigator making friends in the book
business—milling about Fourth Avenue shops, eating lunch with
Midtown dealers, making his presence known in the community, and in
general winning over bookmen with his "gentle, cultivated voice and

kindly blue eyes."[14] Viewed from the book trade, it might even have seemed that he was trying to repair the somewhat unfavorable reputation the special investigator position had gotten thanks to Gaillard. But Bergquist was not making any conscious effort to do this at all—he was simply being himself. Metcalf, on the other hand, had a more discriminating idea about whom they could trust. In the immediate aftermath of the theft, he placed calls to Charles Lauriat in Boston and Rosenbach and William Campbell in Philadelphia.[15] These were the booksellers most likely to see *Al Aaraaf* if it made its way outside of New York, and he felt he could count on them to call if they heard anything. Inside New York was a bit trickier. There were a number of men who might see it, but the issue was which of them he could trust. After some discussion, Metcalf picked up the phone and called one of the "senior men in the book trade concerning whom we had no doubts," Arthur Swann.[16]

Swann was a very important bookseller in New York, particularly when it came to American first editions, and he was the one man they were sure would know if a rare Poe came on the market. A turn-of-the-century English émigré, Swann had worked at the Anderson Auction House until 1913, when he had established a rare book department at the American Art Association (AAA).[17] He was remarkably successful there. During his time at AAA, business in the book department rose from $36,000 in 1913 to $1 million in 1927.[18] In fact, it was Swann's work with nineteenth-century American books there that made him both an authority on the items stolen from the NYPL and at least partially to blame for their abduction. It was he who helped invigorate the field, starting in 1924 when the AAA auctioned, with great fanfare, the collection of the late Stephen Wakeman. (Swann did not actually do the auctioning. That task was "conducted by Mr. Bernet and Mr. Parke.")[19] The *New York Times* recounted this sale many years later, saying that more "than any of its predecessors, more, indeed, than any other single factor, it served to stimulate the interest of an apathetic public in the rich possibilities" of nineteenth century American literature.[20]

In 1928, Swann retired from AAA—largely due to a conflict with the new director, Cortlandt Bishop, and his friend Mitchell Kennerley—and became a private rare book dealer. This allowed him, at least for a short while, to take full advantage of the trend he had helped create. He founded a bookstore focusing on American and English firsts at 598 Madison Avenue, between 58th and 57th Streets—the place to be for high-end book dealers. It was to this area, specifically 57th and Madison, that AAA had made a similar move in the late 1920s, following the northward trend of rare book and fine art commerce.[21]

What Bergquist and Metcalf knew was that if someone was going to buy the Poe in New York City, the transaction would probably go through this area, and Swann would almost certainly be party to it. The best thing—maybe even the only thing—they could do was wait for it to pop up. Gold had backed the theft for a reason, and it was not for the joy of ownership. He needed to get the books sold. And Metcalf and Bergquist simply had to count on Arthur Swann to get wind of something. It did not take long.

Abe Shiffrin was the owner of the Academy Book Shop on 59th Street. Formerly an employee of the Madison Book Store (a contemporary there of the Argosy's Lou Cohen), Shiffrin was successful, well known, and in the market for American firsts. But for Shiffrin, bookselling was not the passion it had once been; it was merely a way to make a living. His heart was in writing. This, of course, was not exactly a mark of distinction in the book business. A good number of dealers, or people associated with bookselling, wrote novels or plays—most involving some aspect of the trade. The thing that separated Shiffrin from the rest was that he was pretty good at it: in February 1931, Shiffrin's book of poetry was mentioned in the *New York Times*. A novel he was working on, called *Mr. Pirate: A Romance*, would be published a few years later and reviewed favorably by the *Times*. The newspaper said the story was "told with rare deftness and clothed with a reticent beauty."[22] Fifteen years later, one of his plays, *Angel in the Pawnshop*, enjoyed a brief run on Broadway. The play told the story of a young woman who, after discovering she was married to a thief and murderer, found refuge in a crusty but good-hearted shop owner.[23] (It did not do as well with critics. *Time* described the play as a "sentimental fantasy in which everything that doesn't seem banal seems borrowed, and in which he displays a kind of genius for crushing the life of words."[24] Another reviewer called it a "staggering dose of whimsy.")[25]

But in 1931, most of this writing success was in his future—he was still very much in the market for quality items of the sort Gold had just come into. For that reason Shiffrin, like a great many Midtown dealers struggling to survive, routinely scouted various shops on Book Row looking for bargains. "One of the pleasantest and almost unvarying routines in the rare-book world," wrote Americana dealer Charles Everitt, "is that by which you go into a store, ask the bookseller if he has anything new, to which he usually replies not, sit down, and begin passing the time of day. Meanwhile, however, your eyes are wandering around the shelves."[26] For Shiffrin, late March seemed as good a time as any for this exercise. There was not a whole lot going on in Midtown and the temperature, rising suddenly to the low fifties, turned what had been snow flurries into a light rain. So he left his father-in-law in charge of the store, walked out onto the wet pavement, and made his way to a Fifth Avenue sidewalk rich with umbrellas and bargain shoppers. At the slick edge of the bustling street he eventually managed to hail one of Manhattan's six thousand cabs and point it in the direction of Harry Gold's crowded little store.

Like many dealers, Shiffrin got into the business because he loved books. And although the profession may have cured him of his more mawkish sentiments, he was still a sucker for the romance of the book-shop. He confided, in prose, the experience of a patron upon first entering a bookshop, how the "odor of old paper and ink and glue and cloth and leather and dust would strike him very pleasantly, or very unpleasantly, depending on how much of a true lover of secondhand books he happened to be. But, if through his veins coursed only a drop of the pale, honorable blood of the bibliomaniac, his fingers would be reaching for the nearest volume even before he had advanced the distance of twelve inches from the doorway."[27] That is about how far he made it into Gold's shop before he was noticed.

Harry Gold was as much a student of booksellers as of books. He was a social animal by nature, so insinuating himself into the lives of his con-temporaries for the sake of business was as easy as breathing. When he was not hosting after-hours gatherings in his shop, he spent a great deal of his downtime in Greenwich Village bars or local pool halls talking books with various other Book Row dealers and collectors.[28] So, from his stool-elevated vantage point, he recognized Abe Shiffrin with ease and climbed down to welcome him. Shiffrin was just the sort of man he was looking for, and he was not going to let him get away. Gold had had the Poe in reserve for nearly two months, unable to find a discreet buyer, and he was getting anxious to unload it. This Midtown dealer was a fine opportunity.

Shiffrin, on the other hand, preferred to be left alone, unnoticed, appearing uninterested. He just wanted to browse privately without a dealer breathing down his neck. Quiet time with the books was really the only way to find good stuff in a jam-packed store. He knew that was a relative impossibility in Gold's shop—the dealer was legendary for his attentiveness—but he thought he could at least browse awhile before having to talk to Gold.

But Gold would have none of that. He walked up to Shiffrin and shook his hand. Pulling him close, he asked him directly if he "could use something good."[29] Ordinarily Shiffrin would have declined and then left the store. Every bookseller in Manhattan who had been in the business for any amount of time knew Gold's reputation. Not only was his role as a fence legendary, but he was also known to traffic heavily in banned erotica—a practice so dangerous that only the most desperate or well connected partook in it.[30] But he knew the Aberdeen had been getting some good items lately, so he bit his tongue and played along. "What do you mean, something good?" Shiffrin said.

Gold told him about the Poe, and Shiffrin was visibly surprised. That *was* something good, and it was nearly the last thing he figured Gold would ever have. Shiffrin had handled some high-quality material, to be sure, but he had never seen an *Al Aaraaf*. And he did not have any idea how this Book Row dealer got it. Of course, Shiffrin knew as much as anybody that Poe's works were legendary for turning up in the oddest places. Reluctant to be left out of the latest discovery jackpot, Shiffrin asked Gold how much he wanted for the thing.

When Gold quoted him $2,000, it quickly put a stop to any ideas he had of purchase. Shiffrin knew that *Al Aaraaf* was valuable, but in a depressed market he did not know how quickly he could move it—and $2,000 did not leave a lot of room for Shiffrin to make a profit. He said he was not interested.[31]

But Gold persisted. Outright purchase was only one option. Dealers often represented books for other dealers, acting as a sort of intermediary between parties. This usually meant going between the original book-seller and the ultimate patron, but it also happened between one book-seller and another. This was particularly true in the New York market, where a low-end dealer like Gold might feel uncomfortable approaching a high-end Midtown dealer. Having Shiffrin do his selling for him was a savvy move on Gold's part. It would be far less suspicious for Shiffrin to possess *Al Aaraaf* than Gold. If Gold knew nothing else, it was the power of a good fence.

Shiffrin still had not seen the book—Gold told him it was at an off-site location—but he agreed to represent it to a dealer named Harry Stone. He told Gold he could probably only get $1,000 for it, though. Stone was one of the more famous, and longest-lasting, bookmen in town, known not only for his dealings in rare first editions but also prints and lithographs. Whatever he sold, business was good enough that he not only worked but also lived in Midtown—his store and home were only a few blocks apart.[32] As it happened, he too had once owned a store on Book Row, but success had driven him forty blocks north to 58th Street, away from the crowded, bric-a-brac tumult of Fourth Avenue and into the placid arms of an area where galleries "were bathed in peace and good taste."[33] Ambition, and a Fifth Avenue cab, drove Abe Shiffrin the same distance that rainy March morning.

Stone was not surprised to see Shiffrin. While they were not exactly friends, their businesses overlapped enough that they were certainly acquaintances; it was not at all strange for Shiffrin to bring him a high-value item like the Poe. It was common knowledge that Stone had sold a good many Poe first editions—even during the Depression, Stone's "want list" included the very best of American firsts.[34] It was also known that, while he was not outright dishonest—or "at least not very often," according to fellow bookman David Randall—he was willing to fudge the facts a bit when needed. For instance, he once sold a copy of Sarah Helen Whitman's *Poe and His Critics* to J. K. Lilly, describing it as a "presentation copy from Mrs. Clemm to Annie E. Johnson to whom Poe was engaged at the time of his death."[35] When Lilly pointed out that this was simply not true, Stone knocked $500 off the price and announced he had gotten his Annies confused. By that point, Lilly had discovered that it could not have been inscribed by Mrs. Clemm at all, and suggested Stone have a "private cremation" for the book. After another Poe-related mis-description a short time later, Lilly stopped doing business with Stone altogether.

So Shiffrin knew exactly what he was doing, particularly if he had any doubts about the book's provenance; he figured Stone, of all dealers, would not be timid about paying the right price. He quoted him $2,000—a 100 percent profit if he could pull it off. Stone figured the little book was worth twice that much, but he was not in the habit of letting on to potential sellers the value of the items they were selling. And he knew the power of bargaining in the depressed market. So he told Shiffrin that $2,000 was a great deal of money for the Poe, especially one that had unconvincing provenance. In any event, he had to see the thing before he would buy it. But if he liked it, he said, he might be willing to pay $1,500.

Sold.

Shiffrin left Stone's store heading south to pick up the book from Gold. This one sale was looking like it was going to consume his whole day, what with two trips down and back car-packed Fifth Avenue. But if he was successful, his profit would be more than worth the trouble. As Shiffrin suspected, once he got to Book Row the little dealer gave the book up with the promise of $1,000. The only delay was the time it took him to get it. Gold suggested that Shiffrin walk around for a few minutes and then come back. That allowed Gold time to get it from his vault without letting Shiffrin know he kept the book on premises. Shiffrin walked out into the drizzle on Fourth Avenue, his sightline dominated by the block-long edifice of Wanamaker's. He turned to the books on a neighboring sidewalk stand and absentmindedly started to rifle through them. It was how he planned on spending most of this day anyway, but with the prospect of a big payoff like the Poe, these nickel-priced books held no interest. After fifteen minutes, Gold stepped out of his store and called Shiffrin back in. He showed him the book briefly, and then, without ceremony, wrapped it up like a parcel, glad to be rid of it. Gold did not have any money in his pocket yet, but the fact that the Poe was leaving his store tucked into Shiffrin's satchel represented a crucial step toward that end.

Back up Fifth Avenue, with the book put away against the weather, Shiffrin, in turn, went right into Stone's store, handed the Poe over, and got a receipt in lieu of a check. As part of the bargain, Stone wanted to have the thing for at least an hour to look it over. Shiffrin was in no position to object to this common practice, so he left the store and walked back to his own place. He might just have made an easy $500 or he might not have made a dime. Whatever the case, he was tired and chilled, so he stopped by a diner and got something hot to eat.

Stone inspected the book carefully. He noticed some peculiar erasures, and it looked as if the *Al Aaraaf* had been bleached. And there was a blue oval on the reverse of the title page that marked it as property of Lenox Library. This worried him. He decided he was not going to lay out that kind of money for an item he was not absolutely sure about.[36] But he knew someone who might.

If Stone had been less circumspect about the book—if he had simply bought it outright and put it in his vault to wait for the right buyer to wander into his store, or simply listed the work for sale in a catalog, it might have been months before anyone at the NYPL heard about it. And in any other market, that would have been the perfectly natural thing to do. For obvious reasons, book dealers try not to become attached to books, but hanging on to a particularly unique piece is not unusual in the rare book trade. Book dealers tend to get into the business because they love books, so most would get a charge out of owning, at least for a short while, something like *Al Aaraaf*. (For dealers like A. S. W. Rosenbach and H. P. Kraus, the fact of having owned and sold particularly notable books was a badge of honor worn proudly on the memoir vestment.)[37] Even dealers who think of business first often like to sit on such a purchase and watch it mature. With an item like *Al Aaraaf*, there was no reason to think it wouldn't appreciate with age, so waiting to sell it would have certainly seemed to have its financial rewards. But with this particular Poe, no one seemed to want to have anything to do with it for very long. Stone suspected the book was pilfered—or, as he later put it, he found the Poe "would not be a good investment . . . due to the markings in the book." So he did what the two dealers before him had done: He immediately passed it up the food chain.[38] In his case, that meant a trip of about two blocks to the store of a man he had been both colleague and friend to for many years: Arthur Swann.

The end of work came early that day for people who had a choice in the matter, as the gray skies turned navy blue and the sidewalks were visible only by the light from storefronts and teardrop street lamps. With a falling temperature that might scare away whatever walk-in customers were not afraid of the dark, there were not many reasons for bookstore owners to stay open late when they could get a jump on traffic. Nevertheless, Swann was in his shop at 4:30 when Stone walked in with the look of a man who had something good to sell. Keyes Metcalf, who could not leave work regardless of the conditions outside, was in his office, too, when his phone started to ring a few minutes later. Swann, upon reviewing the copy offered to him by Stone, noticed immediately the small stamp on the reverse of the title page. He was not the first dealer to notice it, but he was the first for whom it was a deal breaker. He suspected this was the NYPL's copy as soon as Stone presented it, and the unscrubbed stamp sealed it.

It is impossible to know what Swann was thinking at that point, but he almost certainly did a quick cost-benefit analysis in his head. If he seized the book from Stone, or even pretended that he needed to hold it on approval for an hour, he would be doing the NYPL, and the people of New York, a tremendous favor. On the other hand, he might be doing himself a bit of harm. He had known Stone for many years, and confiscating the book might be putting his friend in a bind.[39] But there was also a larger issue. The relationship between antiquarian book dealers and librarians at that point was an especially complex one, and Swann had to consider this fact. Taking the book from Harry Stone and giving it back to its rightful owner was a course of action that might scare away future sellers in possession of items of dubious provenance. At the very least, it would not earn Swann the admiration of his fellow dealers, a group for whom libraries had become almost an enemy.

The relationship between booksellers and libraries had long been a contentious one, with the animosity pretty much traveling in one direction. Dealers naturally resented the very idea of libraries, an attitude expressed succinctly in 1931 by bookseller Norman Hall. "From Samuel Pepys to date, the buying of a book has been an adventure and a delight; the borrowing of a book a makeshift imposed by indigence real or assumed, laziness, or intellectual impotence. I have yet to read or hear a glowing account on having borrowed a book."[40] Still, this outlook had largely been confined to the general booksellers. High-end antiquarian dealers traditionally had little to fear in terms of competition from libraries. But then came the second decade of the twentieth century.

All of a sudden, book collectors of the Lenox and Astor sort started a trend—instead of selling off their collections, the great (and even less than great) collectors were giving them to institutions, their remuneration taken in the form of tax write-offs or the inscription of their name in stone. J. Pierpont Morgan was a good example. By the time Morgan died in March 1913, he had accumulated one of the great private libraries in collecting history. This library was willed to his son with the fond wish that it eventually be made available "for the instruction and pleasure of the American people." Any lingering chance that the collection might someday fall back onto the market was dispelled when the son created the Morgan Library, "as a memorial to my father and for the use of scholars."[41] The trend of books being gathered by rich men and eventually donated to libraries was in such full swing by 1923 that Rosenbach predicted, with some authority, that the "rarities that have been passing through the market have been bought mainly by book lovers and collectors, not speculators, and will largely go into great university and public libraries, never to appear again at public or private sale."[42]

What made this sort of thing particularly irksome to dealers like Rosenbach was that, in the normal course of a career, they expected to buy and sell the same copy of a book many times. It was an article of faith among antiquarian book dealers that upon the death—either physical or financial—of one of their clients, the books would all come back onto the market, to be bought and sold again. It was a self-replenishing business. For many high-end dealers, selling a book to a collector often felt more like renting it out. Early twentieth-century book dealer and Walt Whitman expert Alfred Goldsmith bought and sold the same first-edition copy of *Leaves of Grass* six times.[43] At the Kern sale, Rosenbach, Wells, James Drake, Barnet Beyer, and Charles Sessler were all attempting to buy back books they had sold the songwriter in previous years. In 1928, Rosenbach bought at auction what was considered the most valuable manuscript in the world, *Alice's Adventures Under Ground*. He sold it to Eldridge Johnson, founder of the Victor Talking Machine Company, for a profit of some $20,000. When Johnson's library was sold eighteen years later, in an audience made up, according to a reporter from the *New Yorker*, of people appearing "far too slight to support the weight of [their] thick-rimmed tortoise-shell glasses," Rosenbach bought the manuscript again.[44]

But by the 1930s, this sort of thing was becoming increasingly difficult. Or, at least, that was the popular wisdom—something the biggest voices in antiquarian bookselling complained about. Charles Everitt regularly derided libraries. David Randall noted that the rare book business had been transformed by libraries that had gone "completely berserk in their sudden frantic attempts to achieve 'status,' or something, by appallingly ignorant mass purchasing of rare books."[45] Randall's colleague, and the top English bookman of his generation, John Carter, noted in 1960 that the "real enemies of the book collector are the institutional libraries, which swallow inexorably more and more rare books and manuscripts, more and more whole collections, every year."[46] And the complaining that began in the 1920s never really ceased: In a 1974 *New York Magazine* article, William Targ, a former rare book collector and dealer who started in the 1930s, noted that people wanting to get into book collecting had better hurry: "The great rarities will soon be out of circulation because of institutional buying."[47]

What made this all so ridiculous was that every generation of bookmen that complained about the "problem" was very much complicit in it. Places like Harvard, Yale, NYPL, and the Library of Congress were absolutely essential to the survival of most antiquarian booksellers. Regardless of what they said in newsletters or back rooms, dealers relied on libraries for their livelihood. Rosenbach routinely bought collections on the behalf of libraries, and even donated some of his own books to the NYPL.[48] Charles Everitt allowed that libraries "are by far the biggest buyers of rare Americana"—a fact that kept him in the black.[49] In the first fifty years of the Brick Row Book Shop (1915–65), virtually every rare book sale was to a library.[50] Madeleine Stern, the famous New York bookseller-turned-historian, had libraries to thank for her entire career: She sold her very first book to the NYPL. Her second went to Harvard. She sold so many books to these institutions, other dealers referred to her and her partner as "library dealers."[51] Everyone depended on libraries. And even as dealers complained about the gaping maw of these institutions, they kept shoveling books in.

Swann, like most dealers, straddled this line. He wanted to maintain a good relationship with the NYPL, but he did not want to cut off future prospects. So whether out of friendship, professional courtesy, economic self-interest, or the least bit of spite, Swann handed the *Al Aaraaf* back to Stone and told him he was sure it was stolen—right before he picked up the phone to call Metcalf. While Swann talked to the librarian (who begged him to hang on to both the book and the dealer who tried to sell it to him), Harry Stone left the store. He did not want to get caught holding the bag, so *Al Aaraaf* was about to make a hurried trip south on Fifth Avenue. Bergquist and Metcalf, who left the library as soon as they heard from Swann, passed the stolen book going the other way.

There was no quick way to get from 42nd Street to 58th Street at any time around 5:00, so the two men from the NYPL just walked the distance on darkened New York streets, like Abe Shiffrin before them, not knowing whether they were going to end the day very happy or very sad. When they arrived finally at Swann's place and he told them what he had done, they hurried through the puddles and crowds to Stone's store. When they got there, Stone told the men he'd given the book back to Shiffrin. When they went *there*, the fatigued and frustrated men were informed he had sent it, with one of his employees, back down Fifth Avenue to Gold. And, upon later arriving at the Book Row shop, they found the store closed tight and dark, not a soul stirring inside as they peered through the front windows. There was nothing for their efforts but to go back to the library, angry and frustrated at how close they had come.

The next morning, they were at Gold's store shortly after it opened. They walked in the door and reintroduced themselves to the man who had paid them a visit a couple of months earlier. But they did not have a chance to say much else.

"You want to know about that book, don't you?" Gold said. Bergquist admitted as much.

"A very peculiar thing," Gold said. "I had no sooner opened the store this morning when the fellow who left that book with me on consignment came in. I said to him, see here, there is something phony about that book." Gold then described the man as a fellow by the name of "Smith" who "comes from Canada. He pronounces his A's with a broad 'ah.'"[52]

But Bergquist knew the truth: the book was in a safe just a few feet from where the three men were standing. And there was absolutely nothing they could do about it.

It is worth noting, in the midst of a story about booksellers who handle clearly stolen property without a modicum of reluctance, that one famous Poe collector appears near spotless. J. K. Lilly, whose Poe collection now resides at Indiana University, started collecting Americana in 1925. He acquired his *Tamerlane* in 1929 and, shortly after, was visited by some Pinkerton detectives; they thought the book might have been one stolen from a New York farmhouse. Lilly immediately telegraphed Charles Goodspeed, the man who had sold him the Poe. "Please advise name of Nashua man from whom you procured the book and other pertinent data.... Feel we should render every assistance in tracing theft."[53] By the time that the NYPL's copy of *Al Aaraaf* was out in the open a couple of years later, it was the only truly rare Poe title Lilly did not have. When a Maryland dealer approached him with an offer to fill that gap, Lilly wrote to James Drake, a New York dealer whose judgment he relied upon. "As you know, I have waited for some time to turn up a copy of this book [*Al Aaraaf*] but I have been a little disturbed by receiving any offers to sell me the item on account of the recent disappearance of the title from the New York Public Library. Was the Library's copy ever recovered? Were there any distinguishing marks?"[54] This demonstrates not only that word was out on the Poe, but that some people were emphatically not in the market for stolen goods. (Lilly eventually passed on the offer, and in 1934 got an imperfect, rebound copy of *Al Aaraaf* from Goodspeed for $3,000.)

Bergquist was chagrined. None of this was his fault, of course, but it was difficult for him not to think it so. He had been on the job two years—exactly the time Gaillard had said it took *him* to get up to speed. But whereas Gaillard had had many problems creating the job of special investigator, he had been essentially inventing the position from scratch and so no one expected much. For Bergquist, it was different. He was meant to hit the ground running—in the footsteps of a legend. He had been hired for his competence, his doggedness, and the fact that

G. William Bergquist in an NYPL staff photograph. He was described in many ways by many people, most of whom noted his gentle nature and his reassuring attitude. *New York Public Library visual materials, Manuscripts and Archives Division, The New York Public Library, Astor, Lenox and Tilden Foundations.*

he met nicely Gaillard's requirements for the job. But what he had not been hired for was his personal philosophy; he was expected to act like Gaillard. The first special investigator had not only been successful, but also very well liked by many in the administration, including the library's director, Edwin Anderson. In fact, the first thing Anderson had done upon greeting Bergquist was to hand him a report Gaillard had finished just months before his death, to be pored over before he began the job.[55]

This report, a synopsis of Gaillard's thoughts on book crime gleaned from his fifteen years' experience, ran contrary to many of Bergquist's own ideas.[56] For one thing, Gaillard suggested that 10 percent of the men he arrested for book theft and mutilation were mentally ill. This was understandable, given that just about that percentage wound up in state mental institutions. But it was not an outlook Bergquist shared. Also, Gaillard was inclined to treat those he thought guilty of a crime sternly— even roughly—and he took particular pride in seeing them punished by the legal system. Again, Bergquist felt differently.[57] His first loyalty was always to repairing the damage, and seeing that it did not happen again. He would much rather see a book returned than its thief go to jail or a mental institution. Though both men ultimately had the same goal, it was clear right from the beginning they had different outlooks on the best way to accomplish it. Worst of all, Bergquist had inherited the job in the midst of the most dire book theft climate in American history. While his techniques might have worked wonders in a gentler era, in the late 1920s there seemed to be all-out warfare against libraries. It was not clear how well his approach would work. So far, Bergquist's success at tracking down book thieves had been humble at best. In particular, he was spending a lot of time trying to unravel a mystery involving a man known only as "Hilderwald" or "Hilderbrand," a man from Boston who had been spending a lot of time stealing books and selling them to book dealers in New York. But the man was a shadow, and nothing Bergquist did seemed to get him an inch closer to the thief.

Of course, none of that would have mattered much had it not been for the Poe theft, which changed everything. Suddenly, Bergquist went from his wide-ranging and general duties to focusing on a book he had never touched, never even laid eyes on.[58] He was expected to do something. And though nothing like this had happened during the Gaillard years—the *Saturday Evening Post* noted "only a chump would try it, and only a chump ever did"—it was clear to everyone that Bergquist was approaching the Poe theft differently than the first special investigator would have.[59] If he failed, it meant more than just the loss of a book.

That made the morning trip to Harry Gold's store all the more frustrating. They had come very close to getting the Poe book back. But close was all. And now Bergquist and Metcalf had tipped their hand to the man who controlled the fate of the book. Bergquist had two things going for him, however. The first was his patience. He knew their calculations had been right: Gold had to sell the Poe work in a way that exposed him to detection. Bergquist knew that sooner or later it had to resurface. And the longer they waited, the more desperate Gold would be, even if a delay made Bergquist uncomfortable. The second was Bergquist's demeanor. He had a way of making friends with dealers that scared the crooked ones and reassured the honest. In a strange way, he was able to get information from them with a sort of soft sell without their even knowing it. He let everyone know that he was going to be around, and the best thing to do was to help him do his job. He knew, and he let everyone else know, that he would eventually get the Poe back.[60]

In the meantime, he started making some changes at the library. He put out a new list of regulations that, while not markedly different from the old list, added a couple of important points about usage. One new restriction put immediately into effect was a registration card. Patrons wishing to use the RBR had to apply for a card and be admitted specially for study. This system was designed to give "improved facilities to serious investigators and better protection to the Library's property."[61] Another rule was basically just a reminder to staff, along with patrons: "Specially rare and valuable books can only be obtained by permission of the librarian in charge and under such conditions and restrictions as he may prescribe."[62] Bergquist's new rules probably would not have prevented the Poe theft—"Lloyd Hoffman" would simply had to have applied for a card—but they were at least another line of defense. More important, they were an outward reaction, a sign to anyone paying attention that he was doing something.

Not that "doing something" was a trait lacking in Bergquist. He always seemed to be busy, aiming his curiosity at one dark corner or another. And with his attention focused on the recovery of *Al Aaraaf*, a happy resolution to the whole episode seemed to have an air of inevitability about it, as if the wealth of his desire to make it so was reason enough for it to happen. This was an outlook that might have been worn down by an accumulation of disappointing progress, but before even one frustrating month could intervene, he received a call from Boston.

CHAPTER 5

The Boston Scene

NEW YORK–AREA LIBRARIES WERE NOT THE ONLY ONES with a long pedigree of theft. In fact, the Massachusetts towns ringing Boston had been book thief prey nearly as long as there had been libraries. Starting in the middle of the nineteenth century—and continuing to very late in the twentieth—the small-town library in the Bay State was a book thief staple. This was a fact at first important and, eventually, essential to the health of the Romm Gang and its confederate dealers. Massachusetts was like a field of cash crops, available for harvest year-round, gray skies or blue.

It was a fact that had not escaped the notice of nineteenth-century Boston bookseller William B. Clarke (no relation to Harold). He had gotten to know a number of thieves, many as they attempted to sell their stolen wares to him. One of the most notorious was William H. Brown, described by Brookline librarian Mary Bean as a "quiet, well-disposed person, who knew how to choose good books"—a trait that was not surprising, given how much practice he had gotten in Massachusetts libraries throughout the latter half of the 1870s.[1] Like most such thieves, Brown found a technique that worked and stuck with it. His was to go to local libraries and register for a library card either for himself, using some form of the alias William H. Sheridan, or an invented female relative. Then he would check out five or six books, depending upon what was available, and simply never return them. For instance, at the Brookline Public Library in the fall of 1878 he registered on his mother's behalf. He told the library staff that she was too infirm to get there herself. Then he took out six books he knew he could easily sell to Boston dealers—among them W. E. H. Lecky's *History of European Morals* and Benson Lossing's *Pictorial Field Book of the Revolution*—and never came back.

In Milford, he registered one Saturday afternoon for himself and his "wife," Mary Sheridan. Giving a false street address, he took out two books, Samuel Drake's *The History and Antiquities of Boston* and John Russell Bartlett's *Dictionary of Americanisms*. Knowing there would probably be a different librarian the following Monday evening, he returned, reregistered as "William and Ellen Kelley" of Upton Street, and took out two volumes of Lossing.[2]

It was William Clarke who finally caught Brown selling some of these library books in Boston, and saw him prosecuted. And though few of the books were ever returned—Brookline got back only one—word began to circulate among local libraries that Brown had been stealing from them. As it did, some libraries promised to make an effort to aid in the prosecution, lining up to press charges against Brown after he was released from jail. In February 1879, the Brookline librarian said she was waiting her turn to "take him in hand, so that after having served a round of sentences for his various offences in Brockton, Stoughton, Stoneham, Melrose, Somerville and other places, he may discover that stealing library books is unprofitable."[3]

It was a nice idea, but one that rarely worked out in practice. Librarians forgot their promises, or prosecutors lost interest, or other things just got in the way. In any event, Brown was out of jail and back on the prowl by mid-1879.

It was shortly after the thief's release from prison that bookseller William Clarke tried to convey to American librarians—first at the American Library Association conference in Boston and then in the pages of *Library Journal*—the danger posed by the likes of Brown, and the lack of seriousness with which thieves were generally treated. In Clarke's experience, the book thieves he had seen were "not confined to any one class in the community, but include school boys, clerks, students, teachers, soldiers, physicians, lawyers, clergyman, etc. . . . in only one of these has there been a reasonable possibility that the crime was committed in consequence of want or suffering. Yet notwithstanding the fact that the offenders have been proven guilty in every instance, I can recall but two where sentence has been enforced."[4]

For libraries and booksellers alike, thieves were a scourge, and there were only a couple of ways to ensure their demise. One was by "systematic and well-directed efforts on [librarians'] part, to make conviction and enforcement of the severest penalties an absolute certainty in case of detection." Clarke insisted that "Library Directors shall mutually agree to make every possible effort to secure the conviction of all offenders, always remembering that any person who will deliberately mutilate a book by stealing the illustrations, cutting out pages, etc. or who will take a volume from a library and carefully remove all traces of ownership for the purpose of selling, is utterly inexcusable, and has no claim for mercy." In an effort to prevent such thefts in the first place, "every book in a library shall be stamped on the title page, and also on a given page in each volume, such page to be decided upon by this Association, all libraries adopting the same page, in addition to their own special one already selected." This was so booksellers could know which page was marked or, if that page was missing, know why.

It seemed like sound advice, and it was well received by many librarians. The Brown affair, at least, had shown that librarians were willing to involve law enforcement and that law enforcement, when it took the thefts seriously, put thieves in jail. The problem was getting local authorities to see things in the same light. And, in fact, Clarke had no sooner given his talk in Boston than Samuel Green, librarian at the nearby Worcester Public Library, was confronted with just this issue.

In July 1879, a young man named Arthur Knight was caught stealing from Worcester Public. After catching the young man in the act, and doing a bit of subsequent investigation into the matter, Green discovered that Knight made a habit of stealing from local libraries. The board of directors of the library, spurred on by the librarian, decided to swear out a criminal complaint against the boy, despite his family's local prominence. Knight was convicted by a judge and fined forty-five dollars. He was not jailed, however, on the theory that the fine then would have had to have been paid by his relatives instead of the boy himself. Knight was allowed to go free under the supervision of a relative with a view to earning the money himself. "In this way," the judge said, "a direct lesson is enforced, the community protected, and a young man, is perhaps, prevented from more serious crimes."[5] The attitude that library theft was not counted among "serious crimes" was one that, over the course of subsequent history, afflicted many members of the American judiciary.

Unfortunately for Green, he did not have much of a chance to stew about the lack of punishment in the Knight case. Almost as soon as the judgment was handed down, rumors began circulating of another thief traveling from library to library. His technique, in fact, was strangely reminiscent of William Brown's, the man who most librarians assumed was still in jail for his earlier library thefts. Green began preparations for the appearance of this new thief.

The librarian at the Bigelow Free Library in the town of Clinton, Massachusetts—not quite fifteen miles from Worcester—got the news, too. The nearby Weston library had recently been victimized by "a

well-dressed, light complexioned young man, of short stature" who
went into the library and took out a borrower's card using a false
name—something like "William Sheridan"—and one purported to be
in the name of his wife.[6] Then the man searched the library's stacks for
a certain few books, checked them out using his new card, and never
returned. A librarian paying close attention, with a memory that
stretched back two years, would recognize the M.O., if not the actual
names being used. But if anyone did, word did not circulate widely that
this new book thief appeared remarkably similar to an old book thief.
Still, word of a stack prowler did get around.

One Wednesday that autumn, this Bigelow librarian, cognizant of this
thief, went away for an hour-long lunch. Before leaving, he left specific
instructions with his staff to be on the lookout for a man fitting the
description given by the Weston librarian and attempting to borrow
books in his wife's name. As if on cue, the thief arrived shortly after the
librarian left and, inventing false names, including one for himself and
one for his mother, took several books from the shelves. History does not
record the librarian's reaction when told by his employees upon his
return that the man had substituted "mother" for "wife" and in that way
fooled the library staff. In any event, the thief left town and promptly sold
some of Bigelow's books to a dealer in Worcester. The next day, that
dealer brought one of those books, Lossing's *Pictorial Field Book of the
Revolution*, to a local bindery; he did not like the cover, and he wanted a
new one. The binder immediately recognized the book as stolen and,
upon lifting a flyleaf that had been pasted down, confirmed the fact by
finding the library bookplate. The binder sent the book, via messenger,
to Samuel Green at the Worcester Library, thinking he would know what
to do. After all, he had recently—and very publicly—dealt with another
book thief. Green did know what to do. He sent a letter to the Bigelow
librarian notifying him of the discovery and then took the book to the
local police.

That was sufficient excitement for Green, but, as it happened, things
were just getting started. Shortly after Green contacted the local police
and told them the story of the Bigelow book, William Brown showed up
at Green's own Worcester library, looking to shop. It made perfect sense:
Brown was in town anyway to sell books, and he had never been to this
library before. Not knowing that Green was on to him, let alone that the
librarian had recently contacted the police, the thief went about the
business of attempting to take out a borrower's card at Worcester. He
asked one librarian about a couple of books and whether the library had
them. Green, in his nearby office, overheard this conversation and

recognized the request. He got up from his desk, walked over to Brown, and explained to him that they did not give cards to anyone who had not been living in town for at least six months. But, Green said, if Brown would like to sign a form that said he agreed to obey the rules, they might be able to work something out.

The thief agreed to the terms and came behind the circulation desk for that purpose. On a sheet of paper, he signed his name William H. Sheridan. Green, thinking this was evidence enough of guilt, told the man he was placing him under arrest. Then he and his library assistant, standing on either side of "Sheridan," walked him to the marshal's office.

The marshal searched the man and discovered that he had borrower's cards from Milford, Walpole, Franklin, Medfield, Marlborough, Northborough, Sherborn, and Foxborough. While the name W. H. Sheridan (or Mrs. W. H. Sheridan) was used most often, other cards used the names Mary Sheridan, Wm. H. Sullivan, Michael Sullivan, or Wm. H. Brown. Along with the cards, they found on him a notebook with a list of the libraries from which he had stolen and what he had taken. The notebook also had a list of what each book had sold for. Two volumes of Samuel Drake's *The History and Antiquities of Boston*, for instance, sold for $5.20.

In his defense, Brown stated that he was impelled by an irresistible passion to steal books. It was an excuse that was old then and was used with regularity by Brown's book thief heirs forever after. Then, as now, it did little to explain why the man—who was a regular with Boston book dealers—had the apparent passion to also *sell* the books. While he was being held, word that he had been captured was sent out to the various libraries he was thought to have stolen from—and to bookseller William Clarke, who replied to Green with a telegram that advised him to "put Sheridan, alias Brown, through as a common thief. Has served two sentences already." Within a week, Brown was brought before a judge in Clinton and sentenced to a year in jail.

The day after the sentencing, Green received a longer note from Clarke:

> I see that you have caught my old friend Brown. I hope that my telegram reached you in season to have him put through for something more than petty larceny. He is the young man whom I arrested for stealing from the Public Libraries of Brookline, Stoneham, Melrose, Medford, Somerville, Brockton, etc. From Brockton he was sentenced to six months in jail. Immediately upon being released commenced stealing again, from Plymouth, I believe, and Concord. Was again sentenced from the latter place for six months. Was again released a few weeks since and

almost immediately found to have taken books from the Weston Library. Waltham officers now have a warrant out against him. The names which he used to use were Wm. Brown, Wm. H Brown, Mrs. Wm Brown, Mrs. and Miss Mary Brown, and Mrs. and Miss Mary L. Brown. Books generally taken were Drake's *Boston, European Morals, Mycenae,* Lossing's *Field Books*, etc. etc.[7]

In January 1880, Brown was still in jail, but Samuel Green hoped that, when Worcester was done with him, he could get several of the other victim libraries to also seek prosecution. It is "the duty of such libraries as can identify him as the person who stole books from them to proceed against him one after another before the expiration of his term of imprisonment, and thus make the period of his confinement long enough to convince him that it is foolish to try to get a living by purloining" library books.

It was a nice idea but one that rarely worked out in practice.

Two generations later, the local situation remained largely the same. The names were different and the books were different—fifty years had a way of maturing the value of items Brown would not have stopped for—but little else was. The small-town Massachusetts libraries that had been victims before were victims again. And the man leading the charge was every bit as ruthless and without conscience as had been his predecessors.

Harold Borden Clarke was a piece of work. He hailed from Annapolis Royal, near Halifax, Nova Scotia, a town that was, according to him, both the birthplace of Canada and home of the country's first bookshelf. (This, he noted, predated the first American bookshelf by some forty-four years.)[8] Endlessly ambitious, he moved from one job to the other and one location to the next in search of success—or, at least, to escape the reach of failure. He thought he had found his place early on in the burgeoning radio business. In 1923, at age twenty-one, he started working at a small company called Radio Engineering, Canada's second radio station.[9] Within a couple of years, he was its president. (He was also, at roughly the same time, a tour guide at Niagara Falls. Fond of stories in which he himself factored heavily, he once told of taking Sir Arthur Conan Doyle on a tour of the falls and hearing the author remark that it would have been a better place for Sherlock Holmes to die than the Alps.)[10] But by age twenty-six, it had all come apart—Clarke was out of the radio business and on the run from a Nova Scotia larceny charge. He later blamed historical forces beyond his control for most of his woes, but he was in trouble—and a two-time failure in business—well before October 1929. In fact, by that time, he had been in the United States making a hash of things for years.[11]

At twenty-nine, Clarke cut a strange figure. He was of average height, stocky, and almost completely bald, with a face that was quick to color when he was excited or, much more commonly, irritated. His large nose seemed to come right down from his forehead with no dip between his eyes. In overhead light, this gave him a shadowy, almost sinister look— one that was entirely appropriate both to his personality and his trade. When talking, he liked to insinuate himself into his target's personal space to force an idea of intimacy he shared with no one in real life. Prickly, quick with an insult, and perfectly comfortable assuming whatever role would get him the greatest short-term gain, he spent much of his adult life pretending to be a scholar and medical doctor. And when he was not putting on airs as an educated blue blood, he was presenting himself as a living example of a Horatio Alger story—a man from humblest Canada who had pulled himself up by his bootstraps. He did not mind using others in his pursuit of money, and there was nothing—large or small—he would not lie about. In a society where introductions and personal references were important, he was constantly inventing associations with famous or prominent men. When his lies were found out, he would patch them with still more lies.

He was a flashy dresser and liked to wear a soft hat with tilted brim. It was all part of a package meant to distract. Like most confidence men, he had a great deal of vitriol for people with regular jobs, whether laborers, policemen, shopkeepers, or lawyers, and he routinely insulted them all. But no one earned his scorn more than librarians, a group he found to be both ignorant and stingy. He blamed them for the rash of book thefts he was himself responsible for and claimed, only slightly in humor, that they spent their time "heavily engaged with American Library Association conventions, index card problems," and plumbing issues and in "excited perusal of American Library Association Bulletins offering '5000 Suggested Label Border Designs.'"[12] In many ways, his contempt for librarians was as much a qualification for bookselling as any other he possessed.

Clarke had come to Boston on the run from Nova Scotia in 1927 and was living there in a Mills Hotel ("designed to appeal to poor men seeking steady employment")[13] when he got into the book theft business. In much the same way Samuel Dupree found Harry Gold, Clarke found William "Babyface" Mahoney, the king of Boston book theft. Blessed with a forgettable face, Clarke quickly discovered he was a natural at the crime. Not only did he have many of the attributes important to a book thief, but there was this appealing fact: it was a profession at which failure was difficult.

Clarke was a quick learner, and he picked up easily all the little tricks Mahoney taught him. Mahoney was, by all accounts, a virtuoso book thief. On one occasion, he stuffed fourteen books into his pants and coat just before closing time at small library in a town north of Boston. He then helped "the young and lovely Librarian close at 9 p.m., escort[ed] her leisurely to her nearby home," and, according to Clarke, there performed the "traditional farewells on the darkened verandah." He still made the 9:45 train to Boston. Much as a bookseller might, Clarke apprenticed at Mahoney's elbow. From that perspective, the Canadian got to know not only the theft part, but also the whole industry arrayed around book theft—the "leading receivers, fences, thieves and their agents, binderies, shops and storage plants, working up to the top directors and big money boys."[14]

As a criminal, his technique was straight from Book Theft 101. Unlike less skilled scouts, who relied chiefly on stealth and quickness, Clarke trafficked in bluster. He would go to a library and represent himself as a doctor doing research; he would feign a particular interest in old books and manuscripts. His routine was so polished, and his bookish nature so properly affected, that librarians often gave him special access to books that they would not give to regular patrons. Using a heavy coat—a prop that made him fond of winter—and a confident smile, Clarke would sign in with a false name and simply pocket whatever books he could get away with. If he could, he would also steal, or destroy, the card catalog entry. That made it even more difficult for a library to prove a book was stolen, and nearly impossible to prosecute.

Though Clarke's crimes were technically related to those of Samuel Dupree and the bookstore thieves Gold had patrolling Midtown Manhattan, he did not enjoy the comparison. To him, not all book theft was equal. His brand of library theft was unique. It required more skill than daring, and more knowledge of books than simply what another man circled in a dealer catalog. Bookstore theft was the smash-and-grab of the industry; library theft—particularly his sort—was more deliberate and nuanced, befitting the nature of a scholar. It was also, ultimately, a lot more lucrative. For most of the 1920s, libraries simply had more good material ripe for the stealing.

But even in the field of library theft, Clarke considered himself something special. Early on he was one of Mahoney's best book scouts, and it did not take long for him to discover that fact. By 1929 he knew that library work was basically entry level, and he was already leveraging his talents into a higher position in the theft ring supplying Book Row. He was becoming Mahoney's right-hand man. Having run a business, however poorly, Clarke had the organizational skills to supervise other thieves—and he did not mind doing all the small jobs management required. Perhaps more important, he had the technical skills and patience to scrub books. By 1929, he was the Romm Gang's utility infielder, doing whatever was necessary to loot the Boston area and get the books back to New York. And the more time he put in, the more he began to usurp the role of Mahoney—though, in truth, it was a voluntary relinquishment on Babyface's part. By that point, book theft was not as easy as it had once been—and most of the really good material that was not already sitting on the shelves of collectors was languishing in Manhattan warehouses. In either case, libraries were becoming picked over and Mahoney was trying to parlay his professional knowledge into something a little more stable, if less lucrative. But Clarke was happy with book theft. It was the only thing he was really good at, and he planned on using it to the very end.

In April 1929, the Boston Public Library (BPL) discovered missing from its "treasure room" a very rare book.[15] In the immediate aftermath of the January 1929 Kern sale, men who had once loved books for their own sake suddenly saw dollar signs sitting on their shelves. One of these men was Perry Walton, a local collector who wanted to sell his copy of Benjamin Waterhouse's *Oregon: or, a short history of a long journey from the Atlantic Ocean to the regions of the Pacific by land* (1837) with the Anderson Auction House in New York. But before that, he wanted to know how his book stacked up against the BPL's copy. When the rare book librarian at the BPL went to find its copy to do the comparison, what he found instead was another pamphlet sewn into the binding meant to house *Oregon*. At that point, no one quite knew what to make of the theft, other than that the thief was very skilled and had somehow gained intimate access to the collection. For that reason it was assumed to be an inside job. (This mirrors the thinking of the 1994 discovery of thefts from Columbia University's Rare Book and Manuscript Library. Also discovered when an employee sought a particular book for means of comparison, the crime was thought to be an inside job given the comprehensive and repeated access the thief had to the most secure treasures of the library. But that crime, like the BPL theft, was not the work of an insider.)[16]

Since there was very little that could be done about the disappearance of *Oregon*, BPL director Charles Belden did pretty much the only thing he could do: he got word out. He spoke with several local book dealers to ask them to keep an eye out for the work, in case someone brought it to them for sale. As with most such thefts of high-profile books, publicity was the most important weapon in his arsenal.

In early February 1930, this community involvement paid off. The Americana buyer at Charles Goodspeed's shop was offered a copy of *Oregon* in its original paper covers. But something in the seller's manner aroused his suspicion, and so he looked more closely at the book than he ordinarily might. Under this added scrutiny, the book showed faint remains of an embossed library stamp.[17] Goodspeed's, both in its capacity as owner and purchaser of books, had been a frequent target of thieves. Many years after this *Oregon* episode, Charles's son, George Goodspeed, noted that a "book thief is a great nuisance. Not only does he steal your property, but unless you are alert, he can make you a fence unaware, and thus steal your good name."[18] It was a fact he was in a position to know firsthand.

Young Goodspeed had been working at his father's shop only a short while when he had his first run-in with a thief who had made the shop an unknowing fence. The man, representing himself as Edmund Brown, offered George in 1927 a number of books of poetry signed by their respective authors. George bought them and had them included in the next catalog, only to find out they were stolen when the actual Edmund Brown presented himself at the shop to say as much. Goodspeed's returned the books, which they still had in stock, and bought back those they had sold. The man who stole the books was thought to be one of Brown's ex-employees, but a local judge refused to issue a warrant on such flimsy evidence.

Whether it was the memory of this recent incident or simply the sketchy nature of the man who had offered the *Oregon*, the sale of the book was turned down that February day in 1930, and the man who offered it, Harold Clarke, was told something he already knew: it was stolen. Unfortunately, it was only after he left the shop with the book in hand that Goodspeed's contacted BPL. Upon receiving the call, Charles Belden felt the same mix of frustration and anger that Keyes Metcalf felt a year later hearing from Arthur Swann. But instead of trying to chase the man down, Belden reacted by immediately creating and sending out close to sixty circulars to rare book dealers in New York, Boston, Philadelphia, Hartford, and Albany. In his missive, he stressed that if "the pamphlet be offered to you will you be good enough to try to secure possession of it 'for examination by a customer' for long enough to allow us to identify it."[19]

By the time Belden was writing the circular, Clarke was in New York offering *Oregon* and several other stolen books to various other antiquarian dealers. Taking over the reins from Babyface Mahoney meant frequent trips to NewYork to organize payment, coordinate with the Romm Gang, and make inroads with other dealers. Certain books, like *Oregon*, were retail sales of the sort that needed to be handled by Midtown dealers, so on this trip Clarke stayed away from Book Row. He went, instead, to a number of stores he had never visited before. He presented himself with a card attesting to the fact that he was Harold Clarke, managing editor of *The Malden Times*—a newspaper that no longer existed. He said he could also be reached at 2005 McGill College Avenue, Montreal, Canada. (This address, too, was a fabrication. Montreal Police once went to 2005 McGill and discovered that although the place existed, no one living there knew Clarke. But the they had gotten mail for him: one missive they had in hand was from the Boston Museum of Fine Arts.)[20] Among the other pieces Clarke offered the New York dealers were Thomas Nuttall's *Journal of Travels into the Arkansas Territory* (1821), H. J. Kelly's *A History of the Settlement of Oregon* (1868), and a couple of "rare Georgia titles." Each of these had evidence of erased or destroyed marks—the Kelly book looked to one dealer to have been torn from its cover and had a spot on its title page bleached—and all were offered very cheaply.[21]

One of the places he visited was Oscar Wegelin Rare Books and Prints, a store located in the shadow of the NYPL. By that point, Wegelin was one of the "old men of Americana," a famous bibliographer and author of *Early American Plays, 1714–1830, Early American Fiction, 1774–1830*, and two volumes of *Early American Poetry, 1650–1820*.[22] He happened to be having a conversation with another Americana dealer, Adolph Stager, whose Cadmus Book Shop was then on 34th Street but was just about to make a move farther north into Midtown. Stager, and his son, Samuel, while well north of Fourth Avenue, were said "to have the Book Row spirit."[23] Part of that was in evidence with a particular eccentricity of the elder Stager: He wore his coat and hat in his store at all times. He was on disability insurance and, as part of the deal, was not allowed to work. So he always maintained the illusion that he was in the shop just visiting his son, even when working a full day.

Whatever his feelings on insurance fraud, he did not stoop to buying books from Harold Clarke. Both Stager and Wegelin suspected the books offered them were stolen, and demurred, Wegelin later writing that he had "reached the point where I will buy no rare book from a stranger."[24] Clarke, in order to spur a sale, told the men if they did not buy the books, he would make a trip to Albany and sell them to the Scopes bookstore. This was a name dropped with very specific purpose. John Scopes was, according to Charles Everitt, "one of the dozen greatest living Americana dealers in all the world."[25] This was high praise indeed, considering Everitt was almost certainly at the top of that list. (And not much further down was Adolph Stager. He had learned the book trade from his own father, Solomon Stager, and had been partners at the Cadmus with Charles Everitt for eighteen years.) Clarke was a zero next to these men—even if he knew the right names to drop—and they had been in the business long enough to know it. So they did not respond to his threat, even after he gave them a chance to think about it: he returned to the store not long after to sweeten the deal with a first-edition *Moby-Dick*. Again, no sale.

The BPL's Belden later heard from numerous New York dealers by telephone and post that they had had contact with Clarke (a fact demonstrating the usefulness of publicity in book theft) but none had purchased the book. Belden called Scopes in Albany to tell him to be on the lookout. But Clarke, of course, was lying about Albany. Instead of going upstate he merely went back to Boston. Once there he approached another of the important local booksellers, Bartlett's, with a range of other items that did not include *Oregon*. The bookseller immediately recognized Clarke from all the attention he had generated in the past few days and, taking direction from Belden's circular, asked to keep some of the books Clarke offered on approval. Then he called the BPL.

In the grand tradition of library theft, a person with little prior experience in the subject was assigned to handle the matter for the BPL. This was L. Felix Ranlett, a man with a life story every bit as interesting as G. William Bergquist's. And what he lacked in experience dealing with book theft he more than made up for in smarts and overall competence.

The chief of acquisitions at the BPL, Ranlett was a Harvard graduate who, like Bergquist, had served in World War I. Unlike Bergquist, Ranlett had been in a forward position in northern France, "in the trenches," as he later wrote. He was constantly under the threat of fire and, aside from being shot at, had been shelled by both standard artillery and poison gas. His book on the subject, *Let's Go*, published in 1927, is still an important account of the war experience. He later authored several other books, including *Master Mariner of Maine*, a biography of his grandfather, and the *Bangor Book of Honor*, thumbnail sketches of local men who died in World War II.[26] He was also an avid mountaineer, outdoorsman, book collector, and essayist and later director of the Bangor Public Library.

But he had been at the BPL for barely a year (coming from the Millicent Library in Fairhaven, Massachusetts) when he heard from Belden that there might be a lead on *Oregon*.[27] Once he got the information from the bookseller, he was able to be at the store when Clarke returned to Bartlett's to inquire after the books he had left. They had no proof of any books Clarke had stolen, and still less of books stolen from the library, so there was nothing Ranlett could do when the thief came back to the store. But they knew this was the man with *Oregon*, and the encounter allowed Ranlett to get a good long look at the thief. Lacking the artistic ability of Lenox librarian Victor Paltsits, he did not sketch Clarke. But he was able to explain to the employees at the BPL, in great detail, just what to look for if the man ever showed up again.

On February 27, 1930, Clarke did just that. As he had on dozens of prior occasions, he walked right back into the BPL in the company of Babyface Mahoney. Not only did he not know anyone was on to him, but he could not have stayed away anyway: the BPL was where they did most of their research. While the two were looking at *Book Prices Current*, one of the library assistants recognized Clarke from the description Ranlett had given the staff. Upon being told the thief was in the building, Ranlett came down and accosted Clarke—an act that made Mahoney hurry toward the exit—and let him know that it would be in his best interest to report himself to Belden and explain how it was he came to have stolen property in his possession.[28] Never one to be scared away by authority, Clarke agreed. He was nothing if not a smooth talker, and he knew that with a combination of indignation, bluster, and strategically dropped names, he could talk his way out of just about anything, not least his possession of *Oregon*. So he returned the next day to talk to the library director.[29] Unfortunately for Clarke, Belden was not in. And since he had to aim his voice at someone, he made his way to Ranlett's office, where he stayed for hours.

The one major problem with Clarke's career as a thief was his inability to keep his mouth shut. He talked incessantly. And not only could he not stay on topic, but once he got going he could not for long hide the slew of naturally occurring traits that made him so disagreeable. Nor did he have the sort of memory an expert liar needs. He started off by claiming he had gotten the *Oregon* pamphlet from a man in Worcester named Robinson who, hearing he was going to New York, asked Clarke to sell it for him. When he discovered, thanks to Belden's circular, that the book might be stolen, Clarke said he returned it to the man, with sufficient dudgeon, and thought nothing more of the matter. He told Ranlett he was certain that the copy of *Oregon* he handled was not the

BPL's anyway—he had overheard a conversation, between dealers he could not name, in which they had said the BPL's copy of the book had been sold months earlier to another dealer whose name he also could not remember. Over the course of his story, he also mentioned the names of several men he had worked with who could vouch for his honesty and integrity. Ranlett wrote these names down.

In the end, the librarian came away unimpressed. He concluded that the "fact that Mr. Clarke forgot so many important details, gave fictitious addresses before finally giving his correct address and is confused on many points of his story results in his story's being largely incredible."[30] It was the same thing a great many people decided independently over the course of the next couple of years.

Still, Ranlett acted as if Clarke was telling the truth and went about trying to track down the man from whom he claimed to have gotten the book. He did not have much to go on, except the name and city. So he sent a letter to the police chief in Worcester, Massachusetts, asking if he had heard of the man. He also sent letters to several other men whom Clarke had listed as character references. The men who wrote back all said basically the same thing: They knew who Clarke was, but they could not vouch for his character. One vice-president of a large company wrote it most succinctly: "I am not associated with him in business and I do not vouch for his financial stability."[31]

Worcester police reported back that there was no one in their town fitting the description given and no one who would give Clarke a reference. It was all just a waste of time anyway. "Robinson" did not exist. Clarke had gotten the book from Mahoney, a fact he denied right up until he admitted it, some sixteen months later.

Given the way people followed up on such things in that era, Clarke offered personal references with astonishing recklessness. One of the other names he gave Ranlett turned out not only to be a gross exaggeration, but it brought Clarke the sort of unwanted attention from police that serial thieves generally like to avoid. It was a strange mistake for the Canadian to make, and was the result simply of his having said so much that he had finally moved from the unbelievable—a milieu in which he was comfortable working—to the patently ridiculous.

The chief of the Identification Division of the Boston Police Department was as surprised as anyone to find that Clarke had listed him as a reference. When contacted by Ranlett, he reacted the way some other men Clarke mentioned reacted: he said he had never heard of Clarke. And though the chief had met a great many men in his career, both personally and professionally, he was right. He had never met Clarke. Ranlett's inquiry, however, piqued his interest enough that he did a little research on the subject. What he discovered was that someone else in his department had had some contact with Clarke in the recent past.

Six months before Harold Clarke spoke with Ranlett, he filed a complaint with the police. He said he was being harassed, through the mail and in person, by two men from Hartford, Connecticut. In fact, it was Clarke who had done the harassing. The men, a Hartford sheriff and an attorney, had once been involved in a legal dispute on behalf of Clarke. They had enforced an order to collect some money owed Clarke by another man. Unfortunately, the Canadian felt the two men had collected more money than they told him—and pocketed the difference. He prosecuted this grief by means of a letter-writing campaign against the pair, alluding to and threatening the commission of various acts. The Hartford sheriff, for his part, returned the threats, noting that he was about to have Clarke "arrested for violation of the Mann Act," a reference to the law most typically enforced against men who had sex with underage girls.

In the matter of the men from Hartford, the detective assigned to meet Clarke that October 1929 day was Warren Liese. The detective heard Clarke's story and said he would look into the matter but, upon researching it, discovered nothing from Hartford that led him to believe it anything other than an overreaction on Clarke's part. But his interaction with Clarke did not sit well. He found him objectionable and unreliable, and worthy of a closer look. The Canadian struck the detective as the sort of man who might have had other interpersonal problems in his past—problems of the sort that might have come to police attention. What he discovered in his research was an interesting item sent from Halifax, Nova Scotia. As of October 12, 1927, Harold Borden Clarke was a wanted man. He had been charged with the "theft of rugs and cushions and canoe accessories"—amounting to $500—and had skipped his province. The circular sent to the Boston Police Department had included a fair description of Clarke, including that he "is a good talker and may be endeavoring to sell advertising. May be found around Radio concerns."

Detective Liese told his superiors about this warrant, and the Boston chief inspector sent a telegram to Halifax asking if Clarke was still wanted. If so, the Canadians needed to "have request for his arrest come through British Consul."[32] The Halifax chief of police sent a terse note of demurrer back, suggesting it was not worth the effort, and Clarke was not arrested. In the meantime, the case of the Hartford harassment never amounted to anything at all, except bringing Clarke to the attention of the Boston Police Department and, in particular, Detective Liese.

Clarke did not mind lies about himself as long as he was the one telling them. But he objected to the truth about himself, particularly if it came from others. He especially did not like book dealers acting under the impression he was a thief. In the aftermath of the *Oregon* affair in the spring of 1930, his name recognition was getting in the way of business. So during one of his increasingly frequent stays in New York, on the letterhead of the Hotel Pennsylvania, a large place ("2,200 rooms, 2,200 baths") conveniently located across from Penn Station, Clarke wrote a long letter to Belden to let him know he was aggrieved. According to Clarke, the BPL had done nothing to "correct the situation which you created when you so rashly sent out a general letter" indicating he was selling property stolen from the library.[33] That Belden had done no such thing—his letter did not indicate it was Clarke selling the material—was of no moment. Facts rarely got in Clarke's way, particularly when he was venting. He wanted Belden to know that most men in his position would sue the BPL for $100,000. In order to avoid that, or something very much like it, Clarke told Belden that he needed to send a second letter out in order to correct the record. Once the librarian did this, Clarke would be more than willing to help the BPL "and about twenty other libraries of the East." They were being taken for a good deal of their books and he knew "exactly where stolen books are going—exactly who is buying them—and can prove it." He alluded to a number of New York book dealers, "all of a certain type and location," but gave no names.

Clarke said he knew all this because he had almost completed his investigation of the "book situation," resulting in a publication meant to document the theft ring pilfering the Northeast. He told Belden he meant to publish it as a series of articles "in a national weekly medium." (Clarke had first mentioned this supposed exposé to Ranlett and would subsequently tell of its existence to everyone who would pay attention, but that is as close as it ever came to finding an audience.) He knew all book dealers were crooked—for a book dealer to be honest was "a physical and mental impossibility"—and he aimed to bring the racket down. He just needed Belden to help clear his name, and then he would give the librarian all the information he had about stolen books.

Belden, like Ranlett before him, was unimpressed. Three days after the BPL received the letter, Joseph Lyons, the library's attorney, sent a reply to Clarke at the Pennsylvania. He first noted, as a legal matter, that Belden had never mentioned Clarke's name in the circular. He also said that Belden would not retract any part of the letter because everything in it was factual. Lyons mentioned "facts" several times in the letter as an indication to Clarke that, in the BPL's opinion, any sort of defamation suit would be groundless. In truth, they need not have worried. Clarke was a man prone to spouting off threats at the drop of a hat, but he never followed through. He did, however, upon finding his threats ineffective, ratchet them up a bit. In this case, the response came two days later. Another long letter—again on Hotel Pennsylvania stationery—allowed Clarke to exhort some more. This one came complete with exclamation points and many underlined words. It was vintage Clarke—a screed full of malice and dropped names.

Ranlett found these two letters especially interesting, having spoken at length with Clarke three months prior. He particularly found it strange that Clarke was suddenly reporting he knew "exactly where the stolen books are going and can prove it" given his lack of recall during their meeting. "The conspicuous thing about his interview," Ranlett recalled of his meeting with Clarke, "was that he forgot nearly every name that would have tended to prove his statement, and that his story contradicted itself in many points, and also that several of his references did not prove, upon investigations, to be as good as he would have liked."[34]

It is entirely possible that if Clarke had simply forgotten all of what he perceived as slights against him and, as Babyface Mahoney did, merely blended back into obscurity, everything would have worked out well for him. But something in his personality would not permit it. He needed to continually poke and pick, reminding people of his existence and almost challenging them to come after him. It was as if his need to be thought well of—or thought of at all—was worth risking all the negative attention he brought to himself. Until the spring of 1930, Clarke had managed to operate below the radar of even those few people who were trying to put a stop to book thieves. But through his own insistence, he shoved himself onto the short list of people considered the enemies of libraries. Pretty soon, he moved himself right to the top of it.

On April 5, 1930, William Bergquist wrote a letter to Charles Belden. He had taken note of the recent dustup involving books stolen from the BPL and offered for sale in New York. Bergquist knew this not because he had been informed by the Boston library, but because he had heard from some of the local dealers he commiserated with. In his letter, he mentioned "an investigation that we have been making of the activities of certain 'book scouts' who have been offering for sale books obviously stolen from public and subscription libraries."[35]

The special investigator had barely been on the job a year by that point but was already knee-deep in local book thefts. As far as he knew, the thefts had not touched the NYPL. But he had been assisting other librarians around town in trying to get a handle on the problem. He also routinely made it clear to both bookstore owners and librarians alike that he was willing to aid them with their problems, too. In this respect, he was building upon Edwin White Gaillard's willingness to help. Within a few years, Bergquist was working on as many cases for other libraries as he was for the NYPL.[36]

When Bergquist wrote Charles Belden, he was on the cusp of arresting a man who had recently stolen books from the City College of New York. But the only thing he knew of the Boston connection was that a couple of men from the city seemed to come down to New York quite often, loaded with good books to sell at cheap prices. One of these men was known only to him as "Hilderwald" or "Hilderbrand," a shadowy figure that no one could seem to put a finger on. He was known to be both a thief and director of other thieves. The other was a man named William Mahoney. The special investigator, like most everyone else, had never given a thought to a man named Harold Borden Clarke.

Bergquist asked Belden what he knew about Mahoney, and some more particulars about the Boston scene, before offering his help. "To the best of our knowledge, we have not suffered from the depredations of any of these book thieves but our facilities are always at the service of any institution who may have so suffered and we like to take steps to prevent any possible raids on our collection. We would be grateful for any information that you may have in regard to these matters and stand ready to assist you in any way if you have suffered any losses." Belden took Bergquist up on his offer, inviting him to Boston.

Two months later, Bergquist made the trip. He went with the ostensible aim of helping the BPL with its Clarke issue, though his ulterior motive was to find out about Hilderwald and whatever else he could about the Boston scene. He thought there might be some connection between this latest thief and the ones he had been tracking in New York. After meeting with Belden, Bergquist and Ranlett had a long discussion about the matter, and all three came to the same basic conclusion: there was a consistent effort by certain men to rob local libraries and sell the books in New York. They were not certain exactly how much Clarke had to do with it, but Bergquist wanted to talk to the man anyway. He requested that Ranlett and Belden, if they ever had contact with Clarke again, have him get hold of the special investigator the next time he was in New York. If Clarke was serious about stopping book crime, as he claimed, Bergquist would very much like to talk to him.

As for Clarke's offer to help the library avoid being targeted by the theft ring—his special ways of detecting thieves and keeping books safe—in exchange for certain considerations, Bergquist thought it a lie. Even without meeting the man, he told Ranlett, it was nothing but a shakedown. This, as it happened, was a popular opinion with folks who knew human nature. And it was about to be shared by Harvard's Alfred Potter.

The Widener Library at Harvard University first discovered it had a problem right around the time Clarke was becoming the focus of conversations across the Charles River. In the early summer of 1930, professors from Harvard's English department noticed that books they wanted to reserve—often first-edition American—were disappearing. A survey of the collection found that roughly $10,000 worth of the books was missing, though this figure was actually extremely low. (Harvard had absolutely no idea how many books were leaving its shelves never to return and, like a great many libraries, did not seem to want to know. Alfred Potter constantly underestimated how much had been stolen from his library.) Harvard was a particularly rich target and had been pilfered by a range of people, both professional and amateur, over the course of many decades. One of the men regularly stealing from the library at the time, in fact, had no affiliation with Mahoney, Clarke, or Romm. He was just an enterprising thief with good access. Joel C. Williams, a graduate of Boston University, the *Harvard Crimson* noted, also had a master's degree from Harvard. Because of this latter credential, he had the run of the library and noticed it as a target of opportunity. When he was later caught trying to sell a couple of Harvard books—complete with identifying stamps—to local book dealers, police discovered some two thousand Widener books at his home.[37] (The Cambridge charges against him were later dropped because a grand jury in another town charged him with ten counts of larceny for book theft—and that was apparently thought remedy enough.)[38]

Many, many books were leaving Harvard's shelves. In his annual report, Potter put it this way: "We discovered that certain sections of our collections had suffered systematic depredation; the books missing were those which would especially appeal to collectors."[39] Once they realized the astounding scope of the thefts, the matter was brought before Harvard's Library Council. Like most victim libraries forced by events to act, it decided "stringent measures should be taken to safeguard the security of the books in the Library, and access to and egress from the stacks should be subject to more rigid control."[40] On June 16, 1930, the faculty agreed "in hearty sympathy with the efforts of the Council to that end."

One of the things the library did was curtail the use of the stacks by regular library patrons. More important, the library closed off a back exit and put a manned turnstile at the front, noting that though the new regulations "involve a certain amount of inconvenience to both faculty and students, they have been equally endured by almost all members of both bodies." (Sort of. The barriers caused some consternation with the students, who, unlike the faculty, had not been consulted. Predictably, the relatively humorless guards at the exits became the target of a *Harvard Lampoon* editor. He was run off while attempting to make a sketch of the new turnstiles and told "You can't do that in here.")[41]

The other important thing the library did was to go through the collection and move certain valuable books to a more secure location in the "Treasure Room." This meant several thousand books moved per year for the next few years, a number that represented three-quarters of the additions to the rare book collection. These were the same basic security measures the NYPL had adopted nearly two decades earlier, and they were just as effective, if late. At the very least, the posting of guards at a library's front door let thieves know the library was suddenly taking these sorts of crimes seriously.

Clarke took immediate notice. When he realized that the open-air market that had been Widener Library was becoming less hospitable, he decided to become part of the solution. He sent a letter to Alfred Potter that was of the same basic tone of most of his interactions with the BPL: self-righteous and vague. He noted that, as a secondhand book dealer, he had seen many stolen Harvard books cross his path. His claim of having "seen some $25,000 walk out the Widener open stacks" one year may have been an exaggeration, but by mentioning a few books that even Potter did not yet know were missing—books that Clarke, of course, had caused to be stolen—he got the librarian's attention.[42] Then, "with incredible brass," Clarke got to the heart of the matter: He offered his services to the school.[43] He said that if Widener employed him he could guarantee that their books would be safe since he had a particular marking technique that could not be defeated.

It was a shakedown identical to the one Clarke had proposed at the BPL, and Potter did not fall for it, either. Instead, he hired men from the Pinkerton Detective Agency to tail Clarke.[44] (If it seems unusual that neither Harvard nor the NYPL felt compelled to contact the police, it is not. Both institutions almost certainly felt that their chances of catching the thieves would be improved if they had the work done privately. To this day, for other reasons altogether, libraries still often eschew involving the police in these matters.)[45] The Pinkertons got on the issue quickly, contacting area libraries to find out what they knew about Clarke, Mahoney, and Hilderwald. George Kallman, assistant superintendant of the Boston office of the agency, got hold of Bergquist, too. He thought the special investigator might be able to help.

In the meantime, the wholesale looting at Harvard came to a stop. The new security measures and the eyes on Clarke, coupled with the fact that there were plenty of easier places to steal from, did the trick. In his annual report the next year, the library director noted that experience had "amply justified the slight inconvenience inflicted upon the users of the Library. While definite and final totals are not yet available, it would appear that the book losses in the Library have decreased by 85 percent from last year's totals. The psychological effect upon the users of the Library has also been a favorable one.... Heavy penalties were inflicted upon transgressors of the library rules and those who frequent the building have to come realize very clearly that the use of the Library is a privilege and not a right."[46]

And while plugging the holes at Widener and the BPL simply put pressure on other libraries, it also marked a turning point for the theft ring in the Boston area. Word began to spread of a traveling thief. And, to the extent possible, other local libraries started to implement security measures—and keep an eye out for the likes of Clarke.

CHAPTER 6

Someone Qualified
as a Bookman

B Y THE TIME *AL AARAAF* WAS SPIRITED OUT OF THE NYPL, Harold Borden Clarke was pretty much running the Boston scene. The elusive Hilderwald was still around, but he was not really the cooperative type, preferring to come and go as he pleased and sell to those he knew; in particular, he shipped most of the material he stole to Ohio. Meanwhile, Mahoney's dedication was foundering. He was increasingly afraid of getting caught as his exploits became better known, and he was taking less and less of a role in the book business. The Canadian, on the other hand, was still consumed by the trade. It was the one unqualified success in a lifetime of failure, and he was not anxious to give it up. In fact, even as the general climate of book theft became less hospitable, Clarke was continually working to rehabilitate it, taking on more jobs and traveling constantly. He was both actively running a team of scouts and doing his own stealing. As soon as he could get books in, he would clean them and get them out the door.

He was, at the same time, working less and less for the Book Row gang. He had been trying to establish his own business, and he sought to get away from the Romm folks. This was simple economics. Almost as soon as he started stealing for them, he knew they did not have the appetite for the amount of books he could provide. By the time they were filling up warehouses, he was selling to whatever other dealers he could find. This obviously meant other dealers in New York, like Wegelin and Stager. But Clarke was not picky in his dealings; he would sell to anyone. That still occasionally included Boston dealers, though by 1931 he had reasons to avoid the city. There was a much greater risk of getting caught selling in Boston than stealing in Boston, as his one run-in with the BPL had shown him. But also, the antiquarian book scene there just did not compare to that of New York, or most cities in Europe. Charles Goodspeed explained this to a young dealer who longed to have a shop as nice as those in New York. "I told him that, in my opinion, he could not make it pay. Heavy local taxes, interest on the investment, depreciation, and other overhead charges would be too heavy a burden. There has never been a volume trade of rare books in Boston sufficient to make profitable such a stock which, in value, might amount to half a million or more dollars."[1]

So the Boston area was a net exporter of books. Aside from the other major American cities, Clarke had customers in London, Paris, Berlin, Budapest, Rio de Janeiro, and Buenos Aires.[2] If there was a market for stolen books, Clarke had his hands in it. But it did not end there; like the Romm gang, he was accumulating books. Even as he tried to keep the Boston gig alive, he knew it could not last forever, so he intended to become a legitimate dealer himself. He liked the lifestyle it provided, and the level of respect it accorded some of the top bookmen. Part of this plan meant accumulating stock, part meant accumulating wealth, and part meant accumulating a good name. (As an example of the latter, he sent some of his stolen rare books back to Dalhousie University in his home province of Nova Scotia. The books came with a note telling the school that, if they already had the books, they should pass them along to the Halifax Library.)[3] His cache consisted of hundreds of books stored around Boston in train station lockers, hotel rooms, and a large freight shed.[4]

Despite the attention his theft ring was attracting—thirty-four libraries were said to have complained to Boston police about the gang of thieves—no one could put a finger on Clarke.[5] He and his scouts were routinely hitting repositories on the outskirts of Boston and deeper west in Massachusetts, coming and going with the regularity of the train schedule. The book theft ring plaguing the Northeast was no longer the secret it had been even just a few years earlier, but still no one could stop him. This was despite the fact that many of Clarke's excursions to libraries were repeat trips. Like a hyena picking over already-picked-over bones, he was cleaning libraries of items thought unimportant on earlier trips.

For instance, he visited the Lancaster (Massachusetts) Library four times between mid-March and mid-April 1931—the height of his notoriety—managing to get about a hundred books. Along with some typical first editions and some lesser works by popular authors (Henry David

Thoreau's *A Yankee in Canada* and Oliver Wendell Holmes's *Poems*), these Lancaster books included Jonathan Carter's *Travels Through North America* (1776), Lucretia Parker's *Piratical Barbarities* (1825), Ellis Huske's *The Present State of North America* (1755), Laurence Sterne's *A Sentimental Journey Through France and England* (1780), and George Ogden's *Letters from the West* (1823). They also included several of the sorts of unique items Clarke could not describe to scouts in a list but knew on sight, like Convers Francis's *Sketch of Watertown* (1830), a copy of a Daniel Webster speech, and a letter from the Middlesex Union Association.[6] Not all of these were on the open shelves. In fact, part of the reason this material still existed was because it was housed in locked cabinets or in restricted-access areas. Clarke was able to obtain some of this fine material by insinuating himself into areas ordinarily closed to the public. And though he usually waited for a librarian's blessing to do so, he sometimes went even if not given permission; one afternoon in late March he was caught in one of these off-limits spaces, but the librarian merely asked him to leave.

At nearby Lowell, he stole a similar type and number of books. One of these was *The Conchologist's First Book* (1840), attributed to Edgar Allan Poe but written by Thomas Wyatt. This turned out to be one of Poe's most controversial books—not because it was macabre or shocking, but because it was thought he plagiarized it from an earlier version of Wyatt's work. He had not—it had been published with the author's permission. (What is most interesting to note is that Wyatt thought Poe's name attached to the book would improve the chances of sales.[7] This was less than a decade after Poe could barely get his work into print.)

As in Lancaster, and everywhere else he went, Clarke made no attempt to hide from the librarians at Lowell. He used the library as a regular researcher would, calling for as many as forty books at a time and interacting with six different librarians during his two-day stay in the town. Two of the books he used were reference works, *American First Editions* and *Americana*—works that aided him in his effort to squeeze the last bits of good material out of the collection.

He was constantly on the move, and not just for the sake of theft. From South Boston to Roslindale to Revere, every month or so that spring he changed residences like a man who knew he was being pursued. All the while, right up through early summer, with the authorities alerted to his presence, he and his scouts stole from libraries in towns all around the city, including Andover, Billerica, Concord, Lancaster, Lawrence, Lowell, Milton, Nahant, Natick, Salem, and Wakefield. Not that they were exclusive to Massachusetts. They stole from Rhode Island institutions, too, including the very nice collection at the Redwood

Library.[8] It was a blitz of theft that had the feel of a last big score before retirement, though Clarke, of course, had no immediate plan to quit.

By late spring 1931, the situation had become intolerable. Enough libraries had been hit a sufficient amount of times that local police could no longer ignore the problem. In Boston, detective Warren Liese began investigating the matter, consulting with librarians and policemen in towns all around the region. The most important thing he discovered was that this Boston problem might have a New York solution—a man who specialized in just this sort of thing. So Detective Liese got in contact with Bergquist. Though there was little evidence that the Boston thief also prowled New York, and less that Clarke had stolen anything from the NYPL, he hoped that William Bergquist would be willing to help.[9]

Bergquist was not surprised by the call. He had long suspected that Fourth Avenue booksellers were doing big business in Massachusetts books—sometimes they had not even bothered to scrub the library stamps. The special investigator had talked informally to many Bostonians about the matter, though very little had come of it. There were a lot of rumors, conjecture, and scuttlebutt within the book trade, but not a whole lot of real evidence. Or, at least, not a whole lot of people willing to come forward and offer it on the record. But shortly after he talked with the Boston Police, Bergquist started making his bookstore rounds with renewed interest in a particular angle: he focused on books of a certain type that libraries claimed were disappearing from their shelves.

By looking closely at copies of certain Americana books, he made an interesting discovery at the Fourth Avenue store of Irving Alpert. The store was in possession of a copy of *Moby-Dick* that, upon close inspection, still had the marking of the Lancaster Library. This tipped him off to the fact that there might be other such books in the store, and after a little searching, he found more than a dozen with similar, half-obliterated markings.[10] These included Charles Dickens's *American Notes*, Stephen Crane's *In the Valley*, William Dean Howells's *Rise of Silas Lapham*, Henry Wadsworth Longfellow's *Voices of the Night*, and William Cowper's *Poems*.

Bergquist took note of some of the book titles, returned to his office at the NYPL, and placed a phone call to Virginia Keyes, the Lancaster librarian. She checked the shelves and discovered that the books Bergquist had found in New York were missing from their places in her library. Then she checked internal records and talked to her staff. It turned out that Clarke, using his real name, was the one who had checked the books out; and several people remembered having actually helped the man. With that information, Keyes petitioned Chief Peter Sonia of the

Lancaster Police Department to swear out a warrant for Clarke's arrest.[11] Since no one was entirely sure Clarke *was* using his real name, it was sworn out for "John Doe."

What Bergquist knew was that most dealers were in a pinch when approached by Clarke or men like him. Even if the dealer was leery of buying books he suspected were stolen, he knew his competitors might not be so honest. Worse, book criminals often implied that dealers who did not buy their wares might find themselves the target of future heists. Clarke had been willing to shake down major institutions like Harvard and the Boston Public—he certainly was not above doing the same to store owners. What Bergquist did throughout his career was to flip this equation, trying to keep booksellers on his side. He did this by establishing and maintaining relationships and instilling confidence in the bookseller in his ability to catch the thieves. When it worked, it paid big dividends.

In the matter of Clarke, this got Bergquist two things. The first was Alpert's willingness to cooperate in the prosecution of the thief. The second, and most immediate, was information. As a customer, Alpert knew how to get in contact with men from the gang. And though Alpert's information did not immediately lead Bergquist to Clarke, it did lead him to Babyface Mahoney. And that was just as good. Mahoney had been spending a lot of time in New York. He was losing his stomach for the theft business, and much of his dissatisfaction had to do with Clarke. His former friend had been steadily encroaching on his territory for years. With the book theft business, that was fine. Mahoney was looking to get out anyway, and having Clarke usurp his role was not that bad. But despite the fact that the Canadian lothario was recently married, he had made significant inroads, too, with Mahoney's girl.[12] And that clinched it.

For Bergquist, this was the opportunity he needed. He could sense Mahoney wanted to change. (Though, in truth, Bergquist sensed that in everyone.) So he got hold of the book thief and set up a meeting. And while Mahoney might indeed have been looking to get out of the business, Bergquist still had to do a good job of convincing him that going straight was the best way—particularly when jobs were notably scarce. Still, however much effort it took him to turn Mahoney, the special investigator did not make a big deal of it in retrospect, boiling his conversation down to its 1930s pulp novel essence: "You're all washed up. Why not come over to our side?"[13]

To seal the deal, Bergquist invited Mahoney to an extraordinary dinner with a group of legendary bookmen. His aim was to get the thief talking and, in that way, find out about the Boston area thefts as well as obtain any information he might have about the New York connection. In particular, he wanted to know anything at all about Harry Gold and the likelihood that he was still in possession of *Al Aaraaf.* The alcohol-soaked event included, along with Bergquist and Metcalf, Arthur Swann, A. S. W. Rosenbach, and Byrne Hackett, founder of the Brick Row Book Shop and the social group for booksellers known as the Old Book Table. (Aside from their overall stature in the rare book business, all three of the dealers had close ties to the NYPL; both Rosenbach and Hackett had even donated rare books to the collection in the months before and after the theft.) It was quite a gathering.

For Rosenbach, it might have been an uncomfortable event, considering the subject matter. The author of a number of short stories involving the lengths to which men go to get books, he had written in *The Evasive Pamphlet* of a book dealer, almost certainly based on himself, who consigned a thief to "go the limit" to steal an early copy of Poe's *The Murders in the Rue Morgue*—and then paid the thief $3,000 for the successful effort.[14] Given that some of the details dovetailed nicely with the actual theft with which Bergquist was concerned, any other man might have been red-faced about the coincidence. (Edwin White Gaillard, had he been alive, might not have thought it a coincidence at all. He had noted back in 1920 that Rosenbach had "a rather disquieting familiarity with some of the phases of [book theft's] more difficult technique and method. Indeed, in certain circumstances it is not impossible that [Rosenbach's] evident acquaintance with the professional devices of the biblioklept for acquiring property may lead an inquiry in his own direction.")[15] But Rosenbach was rarely inclined to feel embarrassment about anything, least of all a story he had written nearly two decades earlier. The only things that colored his face at that point were copious amounts of whiskey and the attention of young women.

For him, even at the beginning of the Depression (and the middle of Prohibition), drinking was a daily occurrence: He was "riding the crest of his wave," one of his biographers noted, and "the wave had a high alcoholic content."[16] He was rich, respected, and had the impulse control of an adolescent, so the drinks-soaked night of book talk and ribald tales was typical. Not that it was exactly out of the ordinary for any of the dealers: fine dinners with colleagues and customers were par for the course.[17] But for Mahoney, it was a unique experience. He was used to hanging out with the dregs, scurrying underfoot to sell stolen goods and drinking bathtub gin. Being feted by these already legendary bookmen was intoxicating, and it was where he wanted to be. Eventually, the talk turned, as it always does with bibliophiles, to books.[18] With the drinks, camaraderie, and, according to Bergquist, the inherently good nature of thieves, Mahoney was gotten.

He told them all about the theft ring and, more important, professed his willingness to change sides, giving up Clarke, Gold, and Romm in the process. And while this whiskey-pried information was mostly just confirmation of what the bookmen already suspected—or even if they knew a great deal more than they were letting on about—it did have one solid new fact: Mahoney knew all of the places Clarke liked to stay. Clarke had various hotel rooms in and around Boston, some of which he kept longer than others. These were mostly used as places to receive mail or, sometimes, spend a night. Boston police had found one of these places by tracing the address where he, at one point, had received some telegrams. But Clarke was long gone by the time they got there.

When Mahoney gave up several of the more reliable Boston locations, Bergquist contacted Detective Liese and told him the place Clarke would most likely be. (The special investigator also talked to Alfred Potter and Felix Ranlett.) But when police went to that location, they found it, too, abandoned. What they did discover, however, were several letters and telegrams waiting for Clarke. With these, they found the address in nearby Revere to which he was having some of his more important mail forwarded. They finally knew where to find him.

The day after Bergquist spoke with the police, he left for Boston. If he could not be there when they caught Clarke, he wanted to be there just afterward. He thought Clarke the key to unraveling a lot of book theft—including the whereabouts of Hilderwald—and he thought he may even have some information on the *Al Aaraaf*. At the very least, Bergquist knew he could help Clarke turn his life around. After all, he had already put Babyface Mahoney on the right track.

In the early evening of June 8, 1931, the rain blew in gusts off Broad Sound, cooling a balmy late-spring Boston. But Winnie Clarke felt no relief. The windows in her room at the Hotel Pleasanton, just northwest of the city, were shut tight against the night, so the heat of the day was—very much like Winnie herself—trapped inside.

At twenty-four years old, she knew the score. She knew the man she had married was no saint. He came on too strong to be a nice guy, and was too smooth a talker to be fully trustworthy. And even when he was being polite, he seemed to be boiling beneath the surface. But he dressed flashily, spoke clearly, and seemed to have a lot of extra cash at a time when very few others had anything at all. Since she loved to be fawned over and pampered, she had been attracted to him right from the start. But what had been exciting in a boyfriend turned out to be awful in a husband. Less than a year into her marriage, she understood the truth: she was an ancillary concern, maybe even an imposition. The only thing that mattered to her husband that night was that wind and water were bad for books; if that meant she had to be hot, then she would just have to be hot.

Winnie tried to be understanding. In the midst of the Depression, this was her husband's livelihood, so a little discomfort in aid of financial success was necessary. And if she needed reminding, the stack of dollar bills in a neat heap on his desk was enough to do the trick. What was difficult for her to accept was how little luxury that money ever bought. She was languishing in a hot, cheap hotel stinking with a rancid mix of bleach, scorched iron, and book dust. Their meal that day had been a pint of milk and three rolls between the two. Books were stacked on every flat surface and, hunched in the middle of them, was a man who barely breathed a word. When he was not scrubbing them of library marks and making notes on papers he kept, he was organizing a steady rabble of dirty and desperate men—all of it with a level of enthusiasm he had only briefly shown for her. Worse yet, the whole thing was feeling less and less like a temporary situation: the only thing that changed anymore was the name of the hotel.

Unfortunately for Winnie, things were about to get worse.

The sound of footsteps on the boards outside would have been hard enough to hear, what with the weather lashing the windows. But the stacks of books, dampening every stray decibel, made it impossible. That meant neither she nor her husband heard anything until there was a sudden pounding at the door, so violent it shook the hinges. Then the door flew open and two men stood framed in the failing light. Her first assumption, having never seen either of them before, was that they were enemies of her husband's book racket, here to make good on the threats he sometimes talked about. But those threats were mostly illusion—at best, exaggeration—meant to keep her interested and close by. What her husband knew as soon as he got a good look at the men in the doorway was that they were no threat at all. The taller one—the man in charge, the one wearing a boater hat and long coat—was Detective Sergeant Warren Liese. It had been twenty months, but even in the dim light Clarke recognized him.

Systematic library theft is a quiet, solitary crime, requiring the patience of a watchmaker. Long hours spent in travel and hidden in dusty book stacks—punctuated by the uniquely tedious work of scrubbing library books of their marks—tends to force a man to live inside his head. So placidity is an expectation. But even by this standard the man who still referred to himself as "Doctor" Harold Borden Clarke was unruffled. He rose from his desk, faced the policemen from the middle of the room (later said to resemble a "bookbinder's workshop"), and started to speak.[19] He knew this was the sort of thing that, in his business, might happen sooner or later. And though this was information he had not shared with his wife, he was at least personally prepared for it. Of course, he was the sort of man prepared for just about anything. Rarely caught at a loss for words, he was confident he could talk his way out of any trouble he'd promised his way into. He started to explain to Detective Liese why he was in a hotel room scrubbing library books—while also acting very much as if most of what he had to say would be wasted on the policeman.

Still, it did not much matter what he said. Clarke had been in the process of removing identifying stamps from the books he had just stolen from the Lowell Library, and it did not take long for police to discover this evidence. After sufficient time was given for Clarke to fill the dead air with words, he was placed under arrest. And though it was not an ideal night to be hauling books, the police set about removing what they estimated to be $7,000 worth of American first editions stolen from libraries in Lowell, Lancaster, Billerica, and other towns west of Boston.[20]

Even as Winnie, who was asked to come to the police station with her husband, trembled from all the excitement, Clarke remained aloof. He had dealt with the authorities before and so assumed he had little to lose. Nothing in his experience had demonstrated anything other than that library theft was no big deal. On top of that, he had an ace in the hole. He knew himself to be the loose thread that, when pulled, could unravel the blanket of book thieves—an "interlocking directorate" he would call it—covering the three major cities of the American Northeast. And that had to be worth something.

Of the hundreds of purloined books, including dozens of first editions, found in the Hotel Pleasanton that night, most had been stolen within the past couple of days. So if there had been a lessening in local book thefts thanks to all the attention Clarke had received that spring, it was difficult to perceive. Among the books found in his possession in that hotel room were ones by James Fenimore Cooper, James Russell Lowell, Mark Twain, Emily Dickinson, John Whittier, Oliver Wendell Holmes, Henry David Thoreau, and Booth Tarkington. And while the little library of firsts also included books by Poe, Hawthorne, and Melville, none of them had been stolen from the NYPL.

It seemed to be exactly the sort of predicament a man could not talk his way out of. But that did not stop Clarke from giving it a good try. Even after losing interest with talking to the authorities, he said he would be willing to make a statement to a bookman, or some other person with the ability to understand his talents. Why he thought qualified bookmen would stream to his cell for pearls of wisdom is unclear. The only ones really interested in what he had to say were law enforcement and victims. What he got was the attention of cops—most of whom he thought were corrupt—and librarians, whom he felt "don't know a First Edition of Robinson Crusoe from a last edition of the Telephone Directory."[21]

By the next morning, he was receiving visits to his cell by librarians from Lancaster, Lowell, Boston Public, Harvard College, and various "other centers interested in Dr. Clarke's activities." And even if a bit put out by the people with whom he was forced to interact, he was enamored of all the attention. He loved to be listened to, particularly by librarians, and like a kid in a confessional, he was not afraid to shock. So he told many librarians about books they did not even know were missing. In one case, he told a local library about a book that was theirs that police assumed belonged to Harvard. He convinced them by pointing to the place on page twenty where their mark had been wiped out.[22] And while libraries knew they had been robbed, the scope of the crimes was almost always a surprise. (When the head of the Lowell Library, Frederick Chase, was told that many of the books found in Clarke's possession were thought to come from his library, he found the idea preposterous and ridiculed the suggestion that the thief could have stolen some thirty books from them. Checking their records, they could confirm only one missing book. Still, Chase agreed to view the loot seized in Revere to see if anything belonged to Lowell. Upon returning from that trip, the librarian somewhat sheepishly admitted to identifying twenty-eight Lowell books stolen, and not yet sold, by Clarke.)[23]

But in telling his tales, Clarke still denied committing any of the thefts. Despite his intimate knowledge of their places on the library shelves, he claimed the books in his collection had been bought from book scouts, in his capacity as a book dealer. He also said he could not be expected to know a stolen book from a regular one. This was a consistent excuse used by men caught with loads of library books, and it was never less believable than when used by Clarke.

But if that excuse seemed preposterous to the authorities, it was nothing compared to his next statement. Asked to explain why the books in his possession bore clear library stamps, he said he was investigating the activity of a ring of book thieves for the purpose of exposing their racket; it was essentially a more evolved version of the story he had mentioned in his communications with the BPL. In his hotel room, he claimed, was the manuscript for a book titled *Startling Revelations of the Wholesale Looting of Priceless Literature from Maine to California*, which he said had been accepted for publication by a New York firm. He had been prowling around the trade to get an accurate and comprehensive look at the theft industry—for the sake of exposing it—and what he found out had been memorialized in this manuscript. The books in the room, along with four times as many in a nearby storage shed, had all been, according to Clarke, saved as evidence to be presented to Governor Joseph Ely in hopes of taking down the racket.[24]

Clarke also noted that he had procured the books in the hotel room not only for research but also to get illustrations for his book on the subject. When it was noticed that he did not possess a camera, he claimed that he was planning on acquiring one. The move to the Hotel Pleasanton in Revere, from a hotel more local to Boston, was also said to have been done in this effort: his room in Revere had four windows that allowed better light to work on his manuscript and, eventually, take better photographs.[25] As further proof of his book-thief-hunting credentials, he noted the fact that, sometime earlier, he had offered Harvard's Widener Library his theft-prevention service. He still did not know why the offer had been declined.

"Doctor" Harold Borden Clarke always assumed that one day he would make headlines. But he certainly never thought the news media would treat him as harshly as it did. The front page of the *Boston Daily Globe* the day after his arrest declared, "Allege Wholesale Book Loot by Ruse" in a two-page story complete with a picture of the strange-looking man. It was not that Boston newspapers (or Bostonians in general) were particularly interested in library security or book theft, but rather that readers loved crime and adventure stories. The two biggest pieces of news on the day Clarke was arrested were "A 45 Minute Battle For Life Dangling From Tail of Airplane 2000 Feet in Air" (complete with dramatic picture) and a gigantic headline stating that the daughter of a wealthy coffee merchant had gone missing: "Search Cape Tip for Ill Rich Girl."[26] The next day, along with Clarke's story (center column, above the fold) was news that the rich girl's coat had been found "in the water on the shore of Provincetown Harbor" and the large headline "Hathaway Jury Box Filled; Woman Among 12 Locked Up." (This was regarding the rather sensational story of Elliot Hathaway, accused of killing a twenty-year-old student nurse.) Bostonians loved to read about crime, and their newspapers gave them what they wanted.

The newspapers accused Clarke of sneak thievery and being in league with some very bad men. But maybe the unkindest cut of all was that almost no one believed he was a doctor. He told people he had a medical degree from the University of Chicago, but after talking to him for any length of time, few reporters believed it. On June 13, he was described in *Publishers Weekly* as "Dr. Clarke, thus self-styled on the strength of a diploma from a Chicago school of chiropractice" and by the *New York Times* with the word *doctor* in quotation marks. Within a couple of weeks, the newspapers dropped the title altogether. (As a further slight, one Boston paper referred to him as "the New York youth.") Pretending to be a doctor was a ruse, of course, but for Clarke it was more than that. The idea dovetailed nicely with his personality, and it pained him that people were skeptical.

But if his educational credentials were not all that he represented them to be, he could take comfort that his book theft bona fides were nonpareil. And it was not long before news of that fact got out. Within a few weeks, it was clear to the press that this was not the twenty-nine-year-old's first brush with trouble. A brief (mostly inaccurate) version of the *Oregon* affair came out. As did the fact that Clarke had frequently changed addresses, jobs, and names. Of the latter, Gordon Forrest and Rodney Livingston were the best known, but there certainly were others.[27] For a professional criminal, Clarke had always been exceedingly careless. Of course, this was not exactly rare in his field. Years of experience had taught him that very few people were paying attention to libraries and their collections. And after a while, library thieves simply stopped being careful.

But the sloppiness caught up with him in Revere. In his room were tickets for lockers full of books in New York railroad terminals and various places in and around Boston. One of the best pieces of evidence police found was a notebook: Its pages indicated the names and addresses of book dealers with whom he was in the habit of doing business. He had listings for customers in cities across the United States and around the world. Particular note was made of five New York, two Philadelphia, and two Boston bookshops. There were also letters. Book scouts robbing libraries far from home had no way of communicating with their book dealers, usually, except for the mail. They often received orders from dealers by post and, if on long trips, sent packages of stolen books back in return. For Clarke, most of these letters concerned things like special orders or complaints about books he had sent—whether they were in bad shape, were bad editions, or had not been properly scrubbed: one of the letters in Clarke's room chastised him for failing to adequately remove a particular library mark. All of these missives left a substantial paper trail when one or the other recipient failed to destroy them—as Clarke, in this case, had failed to do.

As police went through these letters, they implicated a number of fairly well-known booksellers. Though this was not much of a surprise to Bergquist, police were often astonished at how many otherwise honest dealers were offering to buy stolen material.[28] Most of the letters were from dealers outside Boston, of course, since Clarke did not need the mail to communicate with nearby dealers. But some of the material linked a number of local dealers to the thief. (One area bookseller, when later pressed on the matter, admitted to having recently bought thirty-five books from Clarke.)

To add to the mounting evidence against him, three more packages of books—two in the form of full suitcases—arrived at Clarke's hotel room while he was in custody. One had been sent via post by Clarke himself in the days before his arrest. Some of the books were from the Phillips Academy in Andover, the Peabody Institute in Salem, the Nahant Public Library, and the Lawrence Public Library.[29] Landlords at two of the other drops Clarke had in Boston reported that there were packages waiting for him there, too, sent by scouts who did not know he had moved. Almost as soon as he needed it, Clarke's major bargaining chip—his knowledge of the book theft ring—was becoming less exclusive. Evidence was piling up telling authorities basically everything he could tell them. Nothing was going quite the way he assumed it would, right down to the support of his friends.

For some reason, he had expected aid—both emotional and financial—from the people he knew in the Boston book theft business. But those people stayed away from him like he was poison. He also thought that certain librarians—from places like Watertown, New Bedford, Salem, and the Widener Library—would attest to his helpfulness and honestly. He thought his shakedowns of these places, masquerading as aid, were going to work in his favor. It was a futile hope that stayed with him for months. As for his wife, he had a right to expect some support initially, but he did not very long labor under the misapprehension that he would get it. Winnie Clarke was brought to the Boston station with him on the night of his arrest. After being questioned, she was released and returned to Revere. She then came to the jail the next morning for a curt visit. She had sent for money from her family, and once it arrived, she went back to New York.[30]

Clarke was arrested on Monday evening; word arrived in Lancaster shortly thereafter. On Tuesday, Chief Peter Sonia of the Lancaster Police, on the strength of the earlier warrant, accompanied Virginia Keyes of the Lancaster Library to Boston to collect him. After his big day talking to other librarians, Clarke was released into the custody of Sonia. Along with Keyes, the two men headed west that afternoon toward a jail in Worcester, Massachusetts. They were accompanied by a curious hanger-on. Bergquist had arrived in Boston earlier that day but had not had a chance to meet with Clarke, so he followed the librarian, police chief, and prisoner. He just could not wait to talk to Clarke. Clarke, for his part, could also not wait to talk to Bergquist. That is, he literally could not wait—on the way back to Lancaster, he regaled Keyes with stories of books and libraries and people he worked with and the amount of money he could (and did) earn on sales and pretty much everything under the sun. As usual, he simply would not shut up.

Clarke spent the night in jail and was arraigned on larceny charges on Wednesday morning in the Clinton District Court. He was accused of stealing six books from the Lancaster Library on or about April 10. Library records indicated Clarke had been there several times in the spring, just before thirty-four books had gone missing—only some of which had been found by Bergquist in New York. Keyes and another librarian, Lena Martin, offered testimony as to the amount and value of the stolen goods.

On the day he was arraigned, Clarke was, according to one reporter, "somewhat disheveled when he entered the dock, but he had all the poise and the ability to talk that is said to have gained him the confidence of librarians."[31] He told Judge George O'Toole that he was not prepared for a hearing that day, that he was without counsel and had no money. He was under the impression that some friends had hired Boston's John Feeney to represent him, but the lawyer had not yet made it to town. The hearing was postponed until Saturday and Judge O'Toole ordered Clarke held on $5,000 bond. (O'Toole later made *Time* magazine in a brief story noting that in Clinton, "Mark O'Toole [was], arrested by Policeman Martin O'Toole, on complaint of John O'Toole. He was booked at headquarters by Desk Officer Edward O'Toole, fined $10 for drunkenness by Judge George O'Toole.")[32]

Unable to make bail, Clarke was held in the Worcester jail.[33] The developing situation did not agree with him one bit. The lavish attention paid to him by local librarians and police was one thing, but sitting alone in a cell wore him down. And the more time he spent alone, the more he got to thinking about Winnie. When he did not hear from her for the next few days, he told whatever newspaper reporters came by to let her know he was doing well. The *New York Herald* conveyed the message this way: "He wants his wife to know that his jail is comfortable and that he is mentally serene and tranquil. He seems to be enjoying the adventure of a life behind bars with the intellectual relish of an author looking for 'local color.'"[34]

But Clarke's demeanor around newspapermen was just bluster. He was going batty in the jail cell, and it was taking a toll on his health. After enough time alone, he decided that the reason no one was coming to visit him—and, of more immediate concern, represent him—was because they were afraid of Romm. It dawned on him that word of his arrest might have gotten around, and to keep him from testifying, the leaders of the theft ring had intimidated his friends into abandoning him. If that was the case, he thought, they were also likely to have him killed. To hear him tell it, he got for his earlier efforts to "help" local libraries "a neat little .32 drilled in my hat one dark night."[35] His paranoia might well have been justified—people who threatened profitable criminal enterprises in the 1930s often came to a violent end—if members of the Romm Gang cared that much about him. But to the extent that anyone from New York knew of his arrest at all, they were not sweating his testimony.

On Wednesday, after his first hearing, Bergquist stopped by the jail to see him. One of the things Bergquist told Clarke was that he was most interested in arresting the book dealers in New York—the "big money men" Clarke liked to mention. If Clarke could help with that, and return to New York to testify, Bergquist would see what he could do about getting the charges reduced. He would also see that the Canadian got a lot of police protection in the meantime. With no other allies to turn to, Clarke gave in to the special investigator. Feeling he had nothing to lose, he was as effusive with Bergquist as he had been with everyone else, even admitting his part in the book theft ring. And it did not end there. He liked to write nearly as much as talk, and with so much time on his hands, he jotted down a long statement for Bergquist of the sort he could carry with him to New York. This letter implicated a number of men, including Romm, Harris, Gold, Mahoney, and a man he called Jack Brocher.[36]

Bergquist still was not sure what the local Massachusetts prosecutor was going to do, so he could not promise Clarke anything, but after he left the Canadian he met with the prosecutor to find out. He wanted to see how soon he could get Clarke back to New York. After he talked with the prosecutor—and was disappointed to find out the man was not going to release Clarke until after he had been sentenced—Bergquist spent another night in Worcester and then, with a lot of new and precise information about the Book Row theft ring, went back to New York. Once there he met almost immediately with, and "placed all the facts before," Manhattan Assistant District Attorney Morris Panger.[37]

Even though Bergquist had not been able to get Clarke out of jail, he at least got him the protection he thought he needed. The authorities in Worcester agreed to escort Clarke at all times when he was outside his cell. For his first court appearance on Wednesday, the only people in the audience had been the two Lancaster librarians testifying against him, and Bergquist. For his next appearance on Saturday, it was the librarians plus a couple of police officers. If anyone planned on killing him, or even intimidating him into keeping his mouth shut, they were not making their intentions obvious.

One of the few consolations Clarke had while sitting in the Worcester jail awaiting his Saturday hearing was a list of books Virginia Keyes of the Lancaster Library thought he had stolen. She gave it to him on Wednesday, after his first court appearance, for him to peruse. She had noticed he talked a lot about how much he wanted to help libraries, so she'd decided to call his bluff. He got a kick out of the list, telling authorities that they had severely overestimated the amount the listed books could get. They had figured the items to be worth more than $1,000—he let them know they were worth $114.50. And whether they believed him or not, Clarke was certainly in a position to know.

By Saturday, it was clear to him that he was not going to get any material support from anyone in Boston. At the hearing to determine if there was cause to bring his case before a grand jury, Clarke asked Judge Allan Buttrick if he could represent himself.[38] Buttrick allowed this, noting he would afford Clarke as much latitude as possible—a kindness everyone in the courtroom came to regret.

As an opening statement, Clarke told the judge he was particularly forlorn because he had "been forsaken by those he supposed to be friends." This was a strange claim from a man who, if his own confession was to be believed, had written a book whose purpose was to betray those very same people; a book—just to bring the paranoia full circle—he suspected had been destroyed by the Boston Police Department "acting on orders from New York."[39] In any event, he also noted that he was not guilty of the crimes for which he was in jail.

Keyes testified against him, telling the court that books found by Bergquist in New York matched books Clarke was known to have either looked at or actually checked out of the Lancaster Library. Also, she said, he admitted to her over the previous days that he had been to the library numerous times. Keyes also mentioned that she had seen him on at least two occasions, wearing a large coat and looking at the card catalog. There was something about his manner that had drawn her attention. This was not a rare assessment of Clarke. "He did seem to act peculiarly," was the impression later offered by one of the Lowell librarians.[40]

Clarke's defense strategy in the preliminary hearing—aside from a politesse that bordered on creepy—was not to deny he had been in any of the libraries whose books he was found in possession of. It was to suggest that he had been accompanied by another man, and that it was this other man who was the ringleader of the book scouts. In his cross-examination of Keyes, Clarke tried to get her to admit that he was usually in the company of this man while in the library. Later, in explaining why he had been in the Lancaster Library at all, he said that he had been traveling on business and stopped in a Worcester hotel. There, he said, he had met a man named John Potter, a "book racketeer." The two decided they had go to the local library and attempt to buy duplicate copies of some of their rare books. But once there, Clarke said, he realized that the library would never sell him the books. So while he waited, Potter stole some books and then sold them to Clarke. In addition to Potter, Clarke noted, there was a man named Babyface Mahoney who ran all the thieves in Boston. It was Mahoney, he said, who had first gotten him into the business by having him sell an $800 book stolen from the BPL. (Just for good measure, Clarke also noted the possibility that children had gotten into the stacks and taken some of the missing books. But Keyes rebutted that, generally, "Children were not seeking out first editions.")[41] Clarke mentioned, again, that all of his efforts were on behalf of exposing this theft ring. Just in case Judge Buttrick had missed some of the testimony, Clarke pulled out a lengthier written version of his remarks—similar to what he had written for Bergquist—and presented it to the court.

Thanks largely to Judge Buttrick's willingness to give Clarke latitude, the hearing took two hours. Newspaper coverage of the proceedings suggested that his effort took so much time primarily because of an overly long cross-examination and Clarke's tendency to talk "in rambling fashion."[42] But despite all the talk, Judge Buttrick found Clarke's astounding tale to be outside the realm of believability; at the very least, he found the man to be a good candidate for a grand jury look-see. Since the next session was not until August, he decided Clarke would remain in custody until then.

Clarke's time in jail waiting for the grand jury certainly took its toll on the man, but at least by August he had found proper counsel. Boston attorney Robert J. Curran made the trip to Worcester to meet with his client. And while this did not spare Clarke from the grand jury, which found enough evidence to go forward with a trial, it did bolster his spirits. On August 11, after he had been indicted, Clarke pleaded not guilty. Curran asked the court to allow his client to go to the Worcester State Hospital for thirty days to undergo mental examinations. This was to see if he was sane enough to go to trial—a fairly standard issue in the case of book thieves, who were often thought to be suffering from "bibliomania." To bolster the idea that he was mentally ill, Clarke's father sent a letter to prosecutor Edwin Norman claiming that, some years earlier, his son had "received an injury that affected his head."[43] As it was in most other cases of the kind, this was just a ruse. Clarke had been charged with stealing and then selling books, not hoarding them, as someone suffering "bibliomania" presumably would. The idea that an injury could bring on such a disease was another layer of absurdity altogether. Despite this, the judge granted the motion and sent Clarke to the "hospital" for testing.

Built in the mid-nineteenth century at the top of a small hill—its gothic towers and sharp angles stood out against the horizon like something straight from spooky central casting—it had at one point been called the Worcester Lunatic Asylum.[44] In 1931, it still had chains hanging from interior walls and halls echoing with the screams of inmates. Clarke spent the rest of August and some of September there.

He was, of course, perfectly sane. Still, he continued to labor under illusions of the sort that suggested there was actually something wrong with him mentally. For instance, one of the things Clarke told his attorney was that he could expect letters of support from, among other places, the BPL. Clarke had told Curran that he had aided the library in its prevention of thefts by a roving gang of thieves. Curran wrote the library to ask if they might furnish him with copies of the letters of commendation they had sent Clarke for his efforts on their behalf.[45]

Felix Ranlett responded immediately, informing the attorney that Clarke "never gave this library any information that was of the least value to it, nor did he ever receive from us any letters of recommendation." Ranlett then explained his relationship with Clarke, their "very long conversation," and the fact that Clarke spoke "in such general terms as to be entirely valueless as a warning, and even though it had been supplied with authentic details would hardly have been of any service to the library for it is a matter of common knowledge."[46]

After being released from the asylum, Clarke was still unable to make bail, so he spent another three months in the local jail awaiting trial. Finally, on November 10, his trial for the theft of some fifty books began, in a courtroom crowded with book lovers.[47] Also in the courtroom were many of the books Clarke had stolen, several librarians who had been victims, and at least one New York book dealer to whom Clarke had sold stolen books. All testified to his guilt in a trial presided over by Judge Daniel O'Connell. (A decade and a half later, Judge O'Connell was one of the American jurists assigned to the trial held in Nuremberg of fourteen members of the SS charged with war crimes.)

The case was prosecuted by Arthur Houghton, and his major piece of evidence at trial was the group of Lancaster books that Bergquist had found in New York. Clarke had never denied bringing the books to the store, but in his defense, he said he *gifted*, instead of sold, the box of books to the dealer right before he headed back to Boston. Of course, his story changed depending upon when, and to whom, it was told. One version, consistent with his much-mentioned role as a book crime fighter, was that the Lancaster books were a box of "discarded defectives" given to a "suspected fence with labels, stamps still attached to see if he would take it."[48] Why a man would go to the trouble of bringing a box of books, particularly those described as defective, to New York just so he could give them away was not explained—and did not make any sense on any level. Finally, the New York book dealer took the stand and cleared up any lingering confusion. Irving Alpert noted that Clarke had come to his store at least ten times in the prior eighteen months looking to sell books "at most any price." When Alpert told him he did not think he could sell the latest passel of items Clarke brought in—the quality of items was worsening—the Canadian did indeed leave them there without taking any money. He simply asked the dealer to sell them for him on consignment.

With testimony like that, an hour into the trial Clarke's attorney sensed disaster. He promptly withdrew his plea of not guilty and substituted one of guilty—to five counts of larceny. Two days later, Clarke was sentenced to a year in prison, six months of which he had already served. In the meantime, a number of other libraries showed interest in getting their hands on the thief. Charles Belden wanted him still for the *Oregon* theft, and requests for transfers of "jurisdiction of Clarke were expected to come from a score of towns throughout New England."[49]

It was a nice idea, but one that did not work out in practice.

CHAPTER 7

The People of the State of New York and Their Dignity

WILLIAM BERGQUIST RETURNED TO NEW YORK WITH SOME helpful details about the Book Row theft ring. Clarke's report on his years of collaboration with members of the Romm Gang was specific, comprehensive, and quite detailed. Unfortunately, it was not enough. The fact that Romm, Harris, Gold, and several other booksellers were dealing in stolen books was not exactly news. The problem was getting enough evidence to make something out of it. And while Assistant DA Panger was impressed by what Clarke knew, had written down, and was willing to testify to, he needed more than just the say-so of a soon-to-be-convicted thief. For one thing, he needed Clarke himself, not just his written testimony. And as the summer of 1931 wore on, it became increasingly clear he was not going to get him. The Canadian was in a Massachusetts jail awaiting the grand jury, and the more time he spent behind bars, the less he felt the New York DA could do for him. If the Worcester prosecutor was not going to show any leniency, then Clarke was not going to testify.

That did not mean Panger was going to ignore the issue. But what Bergquist had brought him was only a start. He needed specific evidence, the exact sort of thing Bergquist had found in Manhattan that linked Clarke to Lancaster. Panger had been working as a prosecutor for a turbulent decade—an age when punishment was matched imperfectly with guilt. He had been part of the internal investigation into corruption in Manhattan courts, had worked on cases involving police graft and organized crime, and had lasted in the office through the election of three different district attorneys. He knew what he needed for a successful prosecution—and he knew he did not yet have it.[1] What he needed was evidence of a crime having been committed in New York. It was a tragedy, and certainly a crime, that the Book Row gang was stealing books from other states. And that evidence could be used in a receipt of stolen goods charge. But in addition to what Clarke knew, Panger wanted to have evidence of thefts that were both local and recent. He needed stolen books sitting on shelves. In a strange way, Clarke knew too much of the wrong thing. He knew big-picture stuff—names and places, normal routines, and techniques. But the DA wanted hard evidence on a few specific items—*Al Aaraaf*, for instance—and Clarke did not have it. Even in the pre-*Miranda*, prosecution-friendly 1930s, knowing these guys were crooked in the abstract and being able to absolutely prove it were two different things.

Worse yet, New York papers had announced the arrest of Clarke and noted his ties to local booksellers. So the Book Row gang was aware of the possibility of scrutiny and acted accordingly, getting rid of much that might link them to Clarke. By August, Bergquist and Panger knew that the best thing to do was to gather more evidence, and maybe wait for a calm to settle back onto Book Row. Besides, with two major thieves out of commission, the special investigator could be happy with what he had already accomplished.

Still, the publicity had been good and it was worth every effort to capitalize on it. Although it did not exactly galvanize public support, it did light a fire under people in the library community, some of whom had powerful connections. For the first time, it brought home the nature and scope of the theft ring to people inclined to care about such things. It also instilled in Bergquist the idea that he could not afford to go after the book dealers piecemeal—he wanted to go after the three men all at once. He knew that if he focused on just one, the others would be warned, a situation that might force the remaining dealers to hide or even purge their stolen items. Bergquist set about collecting more evidence.

Part of his plan was simply a long debrief of William Mahoney; he had access to one of the most prolific thieves in American history—he might as well take advantage of it. Besides, Bergquist had always been serious about turning the thief to the library side of things, so spending time with Mahoney was a natural part of that. The question was whether, after the high of his initial conversion, Mahoney would make good on his promise. Many thieves had made similar promises to Bergquist, and most had lasted only as long as it took for them to be sprung from jail. But Mahoney seemed different. In the weeks and months after they had met, Mahoney at least acted like he was going to follow through. He was happy to have a straight job working in libraries, and he was more than willing to talk to Bergquist about the men he knew in the theft racket. When the special investigator asked about Jack Brocher, one of the men Clarke had mentioned, Mahoney told him everything he knew.

Brocher was another of the Romm suppliers, and he mostly worked out of Connecticut. Using Mahoney's connections, Bergquist discovered that Brocher was going to be in New Haven on a certain day to steal some books from the Brick Row Book Shop—a sister store to the one in New York.[2] Bergquist knew that the more thieves he had on his side of things, the better chance he had of getting evidence. He wanted to lay a trap for Brocher and, if possible, turn him the way he was turning Mahoney. The special investigator worked out a quick plan to capture the thief; he alerted the store and local authorities to Brocher's pending visit and counted on them to do the rest. In the event, he came very close to being disappointed. Even though the store owners expected the thief and assigned two men to watch him during his entire visit, Brocher still managed to make it out of the Brick Row with a book that was twelve inches wide, nineteen inches long, and three inches thick. He was caught only later that day when, as he left another store, police stopped him on suspicion of theft. They searched his car and found the Brick Row book under the carpet.

Brocher, like Clarke and Mahoney before him, gave up all the information he had on the Romm Gang. What made Brocher's information crucial was not only that it was more current—he had worked with Book Row more recently than either Clarke or Mahoney—it was more specific. Brocher was still in the business and, in many ways, filling in the spaces left by his two predecessors. While most of what he knew had to do with New England, at least one of the major thefts Brocher knew about was from Columbia University. Mahoney, as it turned out, knew about that one, too.

Prolific author and longtime Columbia professor Brander Matthews had, over the course of his long life, accumulated an interesting and diverse stock of valuable books. Not long before his death in 1929, he had given a small portion of these books to the NYPL. He had been particularly generous with Columbia, however, donating, upon his death, a good deal of his most personal and valuable books to the university. These included his own copies of books he had written and those of other authors that had been dedicated or inscribed to him. Matthews was an important author at the time, and a well-known figure in the New York literary world, so this collection was, by any standard, quite impressive. It was certainly very valuable.

For example, among the items in this small library was a copy of *The Man That Corrupted Hadleyburg*, which Mark Twain had inscribed "To Brander Matthews with the belated compliments but ever present affection of the Author." Another was a copy of *Tess of the D'Urbervilles* in which the author wrote a simple inscription—"to Brander Matthews: From Thomas Hardy." James Whitcomb Riley wrote a dedication in his *Afterwhiles*, as did Owen Wister in *Neighbors Henceforth* and Theodore Roosevelt in *Historic Towns* ("Brander Matthews Esq. with warm regards from his friend the author. January '91.") Even Harry Houdini wrote "To my good friend Prof. Brander Matthews, Regards, Houdini," in one of his books. (Matthews was a big student of magicians and sleight-of-hand.)[3] These books, along with nearly six hundred others, sat on Columbia's shelves, ready to be picked.

With little effort, Romm had secured a list of books donated by Matthews and, knowing how valuable they would be, sent Mahoney and a couple of others up to the Morningside Heights campus. Much the same way they had done the work at Harvard a couple of years earlier— and in many places since—the scouts stole numerous of the requested Matthews books and delivered them to him.

These thefts from Columbia, of course, were no more an exception at Manhattan's Ivy League campus than the thefts from Harvard had been: both were porous collections. This was demonstrated adequately enough again in November 1932. As part of the Sir Walter Scott centenary, Columbia put on an exhibit of Scott treasures, including several manuscripts. A quarter of the exhibits, including the written manuscripts of *Waverly*, *Ivanhoe*, and *Guy Mannering*, were on loan from the Morgan Library—similar to the way items had been loaned to the NYPL for its manuscript exhibit.[4] In a daylight theft from a highly trafficked and patrolled exhibition space, someone stole two hundred pages of *Guy Mannering* despite the fact that two guards were present in the room. The thief apparently used a dummy key to unlock the display case and smuggled the pages out under his coat. A month later, a no-questions-asked reward of $500 was offered for return of the manuscript; six months after that, *Guy Mannering* was returned. It was noted that "some of the mystery that attended the departure of the manuscript seems to have marked its return." No one attached to either Columbia or the Morgan admitted how much, if any, money was exchanged for return of the manuscript. But for an item with a quoted value of tens of thousands of dollars, there was some speculation that it ran higher than the stated reward.

Mahoney, for his part, still remembered many of the books he had stolen from Columbia on Romm's behalf and where they had come to rest on the dealer's shelves. This was of particular importance since Bergquist could not simply go into the store and browse around looking for stolen items. He wanted to be able to describe to others what to look for on the shelf so that they could go right to it.

Finally, after months of waiting, and weeks of meticulous planning—consisting of both store visits and extensive interviews with thieves—they had what they thought was enough. Bergquist, along with his assistant Arthur Heinle and Keyes Metcalf from the NYPL, Frank Erb from Columbia, and several police officers and representatives from the DA's office, was all set. The idea was to approach all three dealers simultaneously. With knowledge of where specific books were housed, the men would enter the respective stores at the same time, gather some quick evidence about thefts, and then have the dealers arrested. As a plan, it was ambitious and had a lot of moving parts. But it was also what Bergquist thought was in the best interest of the books.

At the appointed time that November afternoon, the group moved en masse from the library down to Book Row. Metcalf and Erb went to Romm's store, where they quickly found many pieces of evidence implicating Romm in thefts from several libraries. Erb, knowing where Columbia's secret marks were, easily confirmed that at least thirteen books stolen from his library were sitting on the store's shelves. Arthur Heinle did similar work at Ben Harris's place—Columbia books were plentiful there, too.

But Harry Gold's luck held out. By the time Bergquist got to his store, it was cleansed of stolen books. Gold had been tipped off. Metcalf assumed that this was just one of those eventualities that could not be planned for (and always seemed to break Harry Gold's way). The weather was unseasonably warm for late November—setting heat records in some parts of New York, even—so the men were not afforded the protection of large coats, scarves, and upturned collars. Instead, they approached Book Row in the sort of attire worn inside a library. It was in that way, according to Metcalf, that a disgruntled former employee of the NYPL chanced to see the two men walking down Fourth Avenue in the company of a crowd of other men, all looking like they meant business. The former employee deduced that they were there for only one reason, and went immediately to warn Gold.

Metcalf's version of things might be the truth. But it is at least possible that Gold was alerted thanks to something less capricious than luck. The dealer trafficked flagrantly in both stolen goods and pornography, and while the former had rarely gotten anyone in trouble, the latter was responsible for the routine closing of stores and the doling out of prison sentences. Gold made a great deal of money in the book business, much of it from trafficking in illicit goods. It was logical that, in a time of rampant police corruption in New York, Gold had well-paid informants in the local precinct.[5]

In any event, Gold was warned by someone and the special investigator was frustrated again. The Poe book remained at large.

The dealer with the longest fall hit the ground first. On November 25, 1931, Charles Romm was indicted on eight counts of grand larceny and criminal receipt of books in what the district attorney described as "a conspiracy in which many rare books in the last five years have been stolen from Harvard, Columbia and Dartmouth Universities and from public libraries."[6] Along with Frank Erb, Potter of Harvard and Catherine DeVine of the Newark Public Library also found books from their collections in Romm's store.[7] They all testified against him at the grand jury hearing.

Romm was charged, specifically, with grand larceny in the second degree "of goods, chattels and personal property of a certain corporation called President and Fellows of Harvard College."[8] The DA brought similar indictments on behalf of Columbia University and Dartmouth College. Some of these books were listed in particular, including a copy of *Fragment of a Sentimental Philosopher*, a work ascribed to New York author Washington Irving.

Two weeks later, five more indictments were handed down against Romm's associate and neighbor, Ben Harris. Harris was charged with purchasing and receiving books stolen from Columbia University. These included *Bibliography of Sir William Schwenk Gilbert*, *Mining in the Pacific States* by John Hittell, *Letter from a Merchant Who Has Left Off Trade*, *Dess Spiegels der Seefart von Navigation* from 1589, and *Norte de la navegación hallado por el quadrante de reducción*, published in Seville in 1692.[9] (Harris eventually admitted to receiving some sixty more Columbia books.)

Aside from the physical evidence linking the men to the thefts of books at Columbia, Harvard, Dartmouth, Princeton, and other small university and public libraries throughout the Northeast, they faced the potential testimony of Clarke, Mahoney, and Jack Brocher. The prosecution also lined up to testify at the trial Erb, Erhard Weyhe (owner of a bookstore and gallery on Lexington Avenue in Midtown), Potter, Heinle, and Bergquist. Facing a Murderer's Row of bookmen, on December 11, 1931, Romm pleaded guilty to one count of larceny to cover the thefts from Harvard, Columbia, and Newark Public.

In the meantime, the crimes of the Book Row dealers garnered only tepid coverage by newspapers in the major cities of the East; certainly nothing more than any of a dozen other sensational stories that made the papers every day. Only Clarke ever made the front page, and that was in Boston. In New York, the Romm and Harris indictments generally got Associated Press accounts, and they were buried in the local section. Unlike other thefts, these prompted no editorial comment or corollary stories. Only a few book-related magazines mentioned the issue, and *Publishers Weekly* was the only one with a significant readership that provided any substantial coverage. Still, *PW* managed to sum up the feeling of those concerned in its December 26, 1931, issue:

> The book wealth of the country is made available to scholarship on a very free and liberal basis. The approach to the stacks of books is not difficult, and to curtail this freedom means a hindrance to the work of scholars and their successful use of the vast accumulations of scholarly literature. If scholars should be deprived of this opportunity to consult such books freely, because of the criminal activities of a man like Romm, the loss to creative work would be tremendous. This is no light matter, and public opinion ought to register itself upon the court in order that the seriousness of what has been done be fully realized.[10]

The next week, most people with an opinion on the matter were pleasantly surprised. Romm was sentenced to a term of up to three years in the penitentiary. When he asked for leniency, based on his age and nature of his crimes, Judge Max Levine said that he had already received leniency in being allowed to plea. "Word must go out from this court to book purchasers and sellers," the judge said, "that a conspiracy such as uncovered in this case cannot continue. The libraries of New York must be protected from book thieves."[11]

Worse yet for Romm, the penitentiary in question was Sing Sing, a prison that in the 1930s was notorious for its violent criminals and medieval accommodations. In the six months before Romm was arrested in New York, three inmates had been stabbed to death.[12] This was aside from the inmates who lived through their injuries, and the more mundane brutalities of everyday prison life. Even potential guards were scared of the place. In 1931, two years into the Depression, half of the men on civil service lists eligible to work at Sing Sing turned the job down when it was offered.[13] (Sing Sing had had this reputation for many years. One of the dealers whom Edwin White Gaillard caught selling stolen books two decades earlier, upon hearing that if he was convicted he would go to that prison, said, "You'll never send me to Sing Sing. I won't go and no one can make me go." He then promptly escaped to Philadelphia and hanged himself.)[14]

Thirty-six-year-old Ben Harris, facing the same basic charges, also agreed to plead guilty to a single count of larceny. But that was before Romm had been sentenced, when Harris thought there was at least the possibility that he could get off with relatively minor punishment. After the Romm judgment, Harris knew what was coming. If Judge Levine had shown no leniency to an older man, he was not likely to do so with a man in his thirties. Harris was rightfully terrified, and the sentiment focused his thinking: he began devising ways to avoid the same fate as Romm. The solution he finally came up with was, in terms of ways to avoid prison time, pretty good.

Everyone involved knew how Bergquist felt about recovering the NYPL books, particularly *Al Aaraaf*. Harris reasoned that if he could help the special investigator do just that, he might be spared prison. The day before he was due to be sentenced, he went, along with his brother Ed, to Harry Gold's store. The young dealer had, thus far, been spared almost any consequence for his involvement in the theft ring despite the fact that, it could be argued, he was the one who had brought all the heat down on the group. The book theft business had been humming right along until Gold decided it was a good idea to steal from the Reserve Book Room. But whatever the origins of their problems, Harris knew that if he could get *Al Aaraaf* back, it would be very helpful in lessening—even precluding—his sentence. To that end, he begged Gold to give him the book so he could bargain with Bergquist.

He should have known the plan would be fruitless. Gold refused.[15] Whether the Poe book had achieved an iconic status for Gold—and he was not simply going to give it away—or whether he was not entirely upset to see Harris go to jail, or for a combination of these and other reasons, Gold pretended he no longer had *Al Aaraaf* in his possession. Eventually, to placate Harris—and avoid the risk that the Dane might roll over—Gold said he would try to get the book back from the people who *did* have it. But this was a hollow promise. Gold never planned on helping out one bit, and the next day Judge Levine, nothing if not consistent, gave Harris the same sentence he had given Romm.[16]

As predicted, Sing Sing did not agree with either Romm or Harris. The ringleader of the project, by then in his fifties, had a rough time in the notorious prison right from the start. After a little more than a year there, spent mostly in the sick ward, he became so ill with what was termed "cardia asthma" that he was allowed to go home. He lingered there, a broken man in a crowded tenement on East 12th Street, a few blocks away from his former shop, for a couple of years before dying of heart disease.[17]

Ben Harris was not so lucky. He was in perfect health.

It did not take long for Harris to realize that the worst place in America was as bad as he had thought. His cell was no bigger than a tall coffin, and for a bookish Danish immigrant, there were not a lot of natural allies in the prison population. He had not been inside a week before he was talking to his brother, Ed—the man who was tending his store—about how they might get the book back. Whatever it took, Harris had to get out of prison, and he knew Gold was the key. He also realized that the dealer was not working on his behalf. But in a strange way, this was good news. It meant that Gold was predictable. His first interest was to stay out of jail; his second, to make money. Harris knew that those two things, taken together, were the best way to get *Al Aaraaf* back. Instead of counting on Gold to *give* the Poe work back, Harris would simply buy it from him. Then he could give it to Bergquist in exchange for getting him out of prison.

Of course, it was not that simple. Harris knew he could not just offer to buy the book from Gold. There was no way the paranoid dealer would think it was anything other than a setup. Harris had to approach Gold through an intermediary—someone Gold trusted. So Harris sent his brother, Ed, to see a man named Oscar Chudnowsky.[18]

Chudnowsky was a fellow bookseller known to operate on the periphery of the business. Not only did he deal in erotica, but he was also a library thief and fence. It was in all of these capacities that both Harris and Gold had worked with him before, and it was because of this that Harris knew Chudnowsky would be the perfect man to approach Gold. He was believable, and Gold would not suspect him of working on Harris's behalf. In February, Ed Harris met Chudnowsky and told him he was taking over his brother's store. Then he told him he needed him to do a little business. He wanted Chudnowsky to find out how much Gold wanted for *Al Aaraaf*—if things worked out, there would be a nice commission in it for the go-between. The only moderately difficult part of the whole thing, Harris told him, was that it all had to be kept anonymous. That was no problem, Chudnowsky assured him. Discretion was his specialty.

Knowing there might be a way to make a serious profit, Chudnowsky approached Gold as soon as he got a chance. He discovered, after a little dickering, that the dealer would sell it for $425. It was a significant discount, to be sure, but Gold realized that the book was so hot he would be lucky to get anything, and he was happy to just be rid of it. Chudnowsky took the information to Harris, telling him Gold wanted $500. While that was a lot money, it was not as much as Harris thought. He said he would try to raise it and get back to Chudnowsky.

Despite the relatively humble price of the book, by the middle of the summer it was clear to the Harris brothers that raising the needed $500 was an impossibility. Without a steady stream of stolen property, it was difficult to turn a profit in the secondhand book business. At the same time, they realized they were going to need to involve Bergquist at some point anyway, so they decided it might as well be in an effort to get the money, too. With that in mind, Ben Harris sent Ed on another errand, this one to the NYPL, with an entreaty to Metcalf and Bergquist.[19]

By this point, Gold was rightfully scared of the authorities. His major allies in the ring were in jail or out of business, and it was an open secret that he had the Poe work. He knew that if he tried to sell it, he stood a good chance of getting caught. In an attempt to erase any identifying marks on the copy, he had already torn the cover off and taken bleach to several pages. While this significantly lessened the retail value, Gold did not much care. Getting anything was better than nothing, and getting nothing was better than a trip to Sing Sing. Harris told as much to Bergquist, playing up the investigator's fears that Gold's next step was to destroy the book. Since this touched on Bergquist's two greatest motives—getting the item back and reforming the felon—he agreed. And they started working out just what to do.

By this point, Bergquist, always an optimist, had engineered two failed attempts at getting the *Al Aaraaf* back. He knew absolutely that he would only get one more shot at it before the book disappeared forever, so he was going to do it right. After talking to Harris about the matter, he contacted Assistant District Attorney Archibald Firestone. The library had been pleased with the serious way the authorities had handled the Harris and Romm cases, so they trusted the DA to do well by the *Al Aaraaf*. They approached Firestone with a plan that, thanks to Ben Harris, was pretty much in place. The only thing missing was $500.

Harris's plan went as follows: Chudnowsky would be "hired" by Ed Harris to buy the *Al Aaraaf* from Harry Gold. (Chudnowsky would remain ignorant of the fact that he was working for the police—there was really nothing good that could come from him knowing the truth.) Armed with $500, he would contact Gold and set up the buy. He had spoken to Gold about the book a half-dozen times since February, so

Gold would not be surprised when the man finally had the money. The whole time Chudnowsky had the money he would be watched by representatives from the library and the police. Then, once the transaction was completed, Chudnowsky would turn the book over to Harris and the police would arrest Gold. It was as simple as that.

On Friday, September 2, 1932, Bergquist met Detective Maurice Gaughran, Ed Harris, and a representative of the DA at the local Amalgamated Bank. Gaughran was one of the police department's forgery and financial crime experts, and he was used to dealing with stings involving a lot of money.[20] On the city's account, they drew out $500 and painstakingly wrote down the serial numbers of the bills. Once that was done, Harris took the money in a satchel and made his way to the Book Row area. It was there, in a pool hall on 12th Street, just west of Fourth Avenue, that he met up with Chudnowsky.

Bergquist and the police were not far behind. They followed Harris to the pool hall at a distance—and then they followed Chudnowsky once he had received the money. They also had other officers posted around Book Row. But the NYPL representative closest to the scene was Charles Shaw, a reference librarian and sometime helper of Bergquist. The special investigator was known throughout Book Row and could not take the chance of being seen anywhere near the place. They also knew that police officers, no matter how inconspicuous they seemed, could be detected. Shaw, on the other hand, was just a regular guy who was unlikely to be noticed, and so it made the most sense that he would closely tail Chudnowsky. Several police officers would then follow Shaw.

Once Chudnowsky got the bundle from Harris, Shaw followed him to Harry Gold's place. Officer Gaughran followed Shaw. Everyone knew that if Gold—who was always on edge—got even the slightest hint of a setup, the deal would never work. But none of them really trusted Chudnowsky, either. So they always had plenty of eyes watching.

Still, Shaw was nervous. He knew how important his role was, and he did not want to do anything that might put the Poe work in jeopardy. He followed Chudnowsky to the Fourth Avenue store and then, once the money carrier was in, he followed him inside. Hiding behind some shelves of books, Shaw listened in on the transaction for a few minutes before walking out the front door onto Fourth Avenue. He stood in front of the shop, riffling through the tables of books on the sidewalk, periodically trying to catch a glimpse of Chudnowsky through the window. Gold, who always noticed everything, noticed this—and it made him uneasy. Still, he had to get rid of the *Al Aaraaf*, and Chudnowsky might be his last chance to make money off it.

A couple of minutes after Gold noticed Shaw, Chudnowsky left the store. He did not go anywhere in particular; he simply loitered on a street corner nearby, not unlike Abe Shiffrin had eighteen months earlier, mixing with the early weekend crowds browsing the book tables.[21] Then he walked down the street a bit to a public telephone and made a call. Shaw was not quite sure what was going on. He did not think Chudnowsky had the book, but he could not be sure, so he tried to catch glances of the man on the sly. By this point, sweat began to soak Shaw's clothes—he was nervous, and an early September heat wave was not helping things. Chudnowsky, for his part, was only pretending to dawdle. He was actually working on the part of the caper that was most important to him: rearranging the $500 so that seventy-five dollars of it stayed in one of his inside pockets.

After about fifteen minutes, Chudnowsky went back into the store. He handed the $425 over to Gold and took the *Al Aaraaf.* They said their good-byes and Chudnowsky slipped the book under his arm as if it were any other paperback. Then he left the store and walked straight up Fourth Avenue to Ben Harris's bookstore. Ed Harris was waiting there, along with Bergquist and, very soon after, Shaw and Gaughran, who had followed Chudnowsky the whole way. No one was more shocked than Chudnowsky to find out he had been working on behalf of the NYPL.[22]

Gold, on the other hand, would not have been shocked by anything. He had suspected something was amiss fairly soon after Chudnowsky came into his store. The whole thing just did not feel right to him. Besides, for as long as he had had that Poe book, it had brought nothing but trouble and there was very little chance that Chudnowsky was the man to change his fortune. Just as soon as the door had closed behind the go-between, the little dealer went out and pulled his sidewalk stock in, locked his place up, and left. Gold was so paranoid about being had that he did not come back for four days.

Still, it did not matter how long he stayed away. After twenty months, the whole thing was not just going to blow over in a vacant weekend. Bergquist and Metcalf had worked a long time to get the book back, and now they were going to see Gold in the dock. On September 6, Gold finally returned to his shop, and Bergquist was there to meet him. The special investigator asked him about the *Al Aaraaf,* and the book dealer denied knowing anything about it. He even denied having the conversation about it—the one in which a Canadian named "Smith" was the culprit—some eighteen months earlier.[23]

Though the dealer had taken about as many precautions as a man could with the stolen book—including destroying parts of it to erase any indication of its true owners—he had not done enough. Once the book was back in Bergquist's hands, it was simply a matter of time before Gold was finished. And despite all his precautions, he had not erased every mark. Marion Root, a cataloguer at the library, had marked the book in a secret spot on page sixty-seven, and Gold quite simply could not have known about it.

Gold was indicted by the grand jury on September 8, 1932, and was almost certainly surprised by the fact. He was not surprised to be treated the same way Romm and Harris had been treated, but surprised that any of them were subject to the legal system. He had been stealing—or having others steal on his behalf—from hundreds of libraries for years and years, with very little consequence. But one relatively minor theft from the NYPL—a theft that had brought him three books and not a great deal of money—had proven to be an unmitigated disaster. Partly this was because of Bergquist, a man whose sole role was to work against the likes of Gold. But it also had a great deal to do with the standing of the NYPL in the city. It was an important institution, and the people affiliated with its maintenance brought a lot of power to bear. Among the members of the board of trustees in the years leading up to the theft were Elihu Root, J. P. Morgan, Payne Whitney, Cleveland Dodge, John Finley (an editor at the *New York Times*), Edward Sheldon (chairman of the United States Trust Company), and various other powerful and influential men in the areas of commerce, industry, philanthropy, law, and the Roman Catholic Church. On September 19, one of these men, Frank L. Polk, president of the board of trustees and a well-known lawyer, wrote a letter to District Attorney Thomas Crain:

> I am taking the liberty of writing you in connection with the arrest of Harry Gold, second hand book dealer, on the charge of having received a book stolen from the New York Public Library. Gold was arraigned on September 7th, pleaded not guilty, and was released on $1,500 bail. I understand he has been indicted by the Grand Jury and probably has already been arraigned. This case we consider of tremendous importance to all libraries as many valuable books have been lost through the operations of a ring of thieves. Your office has been most helpful and courteous and last year secured the convictions of a man named Romm and a man named Harris on similar charges.
>
> I know the gentleman in charge of this case will do all he can but I take the liberty of calling your attention to the case as we feel that all the libraries, and particularly our library, have a deep interest in securing a conviction as it will have a great moral effect on the men who have been active in this particularly criminal activity.[24]

District Attorney Crain was himself an accomplished man, having, among other things, presided over the murder trial of the owners of the Triangle Waist Company. But his prestige had been battered in the past couple of years. A longtime member of the Tammany organization, he was described by Samuel Seabury—the lawyer who headed the commission investigating New York's courts and police department in the early 1930s—as "an ineffectual but honest man surrounded by thieves."[25] He had taken hits from the press, too, for his recent inability to resolve the murder of gangster Arnold Rothstein—after publicly stating he would—or find missing New York State Supreme Court Justice Joseph Crater. But whatever Crain's failings, he was still the district attorney. Though his office had done an admirable job with the other two dealers—and had already taken the same initial steps with Gold—a reminder that powerful people were anxious for justice could not hurt. The man who had Tammany to thank for every position he had gotten for the past forty years was exactly the sort of man who understood that message. The DA's office was not going to let Gold off the hook.

But the dealer was not ready to capitulate. He was a born fighter, and he had the resources for a legal battle. More important, the consequence of giving in was brought home to him early in the process: he was scheduled to plea in front of the very same judge who sentenced Romm and Harris so harshly. Three weeks after he was arraigned, he pleaded not guilty in front of Judge Levine, and he meant it. A court date was set for October 6, 1932, in the Criminal Courts Building at 32 Franklin Street.

Gold was very familiar with the disposition of his book theft buddies, so he was not taking any chances with his freedom. He sought the representation of Robert Daru, an important and successful New York attorney—his office was on Madison Avenue, one block away from the NYPL—who spent his career burnishing his anti-crime resume. Among other roles, Daru served as special counsel to the Commercial Crime Commission, counsel to the Federal Grand Jury Association, chairman of the Committee for the Repression of Racketeering, and chairman of the Federal Bar Association's Committee on Crime. Daru met with Gold and handled the preliminary matters of the trial, but after this first hearing, he handed the case off to an associate in his law firm.

Gold was predictably upset about being indicted and told Judge Levine as much. He noted that of the six people who had testified before the grand jury, three of them (Harry Stone, Max Fabricant, and Ed Harris) were in the book business. "I might say that none too friendly relations exist generally speaking, among the persons in our trade. Particularly during the Depression the competition has been very keen and there is an attitude among the persons in the trade, which amounts to more than just non-cooperation."[26] Of Chudnowsky, he said the man "bears a very bad reputation in the trade as a publisher of lascivious and obscene books in violation of the Penal Law and is known as one who has been engaged in stealing books from public libraries."

In protesting his innocence, in fact, Gold said a great many things to the court, including this mouthful:

> I realize, of course, that in the view of some persons, the interest of the Public Library is subserved by the return of an indictment charging criminally receiving a Public Library book because the attendant publicity tends to diminish stealing from the Public Library, but I respectfully submit to the Court, that as a reputable businessman who has never been in any kind of trouble, a sounder view would dictate that the proceedings commenced in the Magistrate's Court should not have been terminated by summarily indicting me and I have been done a great injustice thereby, which even the dismissal of this indictment will not vitiate, as I have been seriously injured in my trade by the publicity which has been given this matter.[27]

Unlike his compatriots, Gold did not have any illusions of leniency—he knew he had to win the case outright. He put his faith instead in a highly paid attorney and his ability to sway a jury. And given the charges against him, he thought he had a pretty good shot. Unlike the other men, he was charged with a mere two counts—one for grand larceny and the other for receiving stolen property—both related to *Al Aaraaf.* The first count charged that Gold "did feloniously, and with force and arms, steal, take, and carry away, against the form of the statute in such case made and provided, and against the peace of the People of the state of New York and their dignity, one rare book." The second count was that Gold "feloniously did buy, receive, conceal, withhold and aid in concealing and withholding, the said defendant then and there well knowing the said goods, chattels and personal property to have been feloniously stolen." This may have seemed like boilerplate language to all involved, but the last part of this charge would soon become very important to the Gold defense.

After months of delay, the trial began in earnest in May 1933, in the general sessions presided over by Judge Joseph Corrigan. Corrigan, like Recorder Goff, was a no-nonsense judge, respected by just about everyone. At a time when Tammany Hall pretty much ran New York, Judge Corrigan was unafraid of stepping on the toes of the political organization's influential members and district leaders. Despite that reputation, he had been appointed to the general sessions after many years as a magistrate and was confirmed to the post by the state senate in a rare unanimous vote.[28] On his first day of work in April 1931, there was no ceremony or celebration; he simply got right to work, disposing of twelve cases left over by his predecessor.[29] This was not the sort of judge to rule that a library was a heartless corporation or that men who stole from one had simply made a mistake. Worse yet for Gold, one month before his trial was set to start, Judge Corrigan had opined, on the creation of a new parole board by the state legislature, that "leniency to criminals is a menace to society." Making most criminals eligible for parole after a year in prison was, according to the judge, a disaster. "In my opinion," he said, "this would be in effect a repeal of all our criminal law, and if this suggestion is adopted by the Legislature and carried into effect we might almost as well disband our police departments, close up our courts and submit to the dictatorship of the underworld."[30]

Judge Corrigan made that statement a mere two weeks after he had clashed with Sing Sing warden Lewis Dawes on the value of incarceration. The warden encouraged the use of preventative agencies and effective parole in lieu of jail time. Judge Corrigan vehemently disagreed, noting, "The only way to prevent crime is to show that it is unprofitable and prison is a direct consequence."[31] That his judge was more predisposed toward the value of prison sentences than even America's most famous jailer was a message to Gold that, though he had escaped Judge Max Levine's frying pan, he had landed in Judge Corrigan's fire.

Not that he had very much more luck with his prosecutor. The attorney working on behalf of the city was Irving Mendelson, a graduate of New York University Law School who had been on the job for just over three years. He was young, ambitious, talented, and not at all intimidated by the specter of interesting defendants. His most high-profile case so far had been the prosecution (and conviction) of a former Sing Sing rabbi who claimed to have both a PhD and a law degree, but who had been financially preying upon immigrants trying to gain entry into the United States.[32] But not only was Mendelson good, he was also grieving. The Gold case started on the eve of the first anniversary of the sudden death of his wife. And if that were not enough, only a few days into the Gold case, someone stole Mendelson's brand-new spring coat right out of his office while he was in court.[33] He was in no mood for leniency.

Nor was his effort going to want for enthusiasm because of the nature of the crime. Mendelson's witness list included pretty much everyone involved in the saga: Bergquist, Metcalf, Arthur Swann, Abe Shiffrin, Ben Harris, Arthur Heinle, Harry Stone, John Elliot, and Charles Shaw.

A person who had little knowledge of the actual case, NYPL rare book cataloguer Marion Root, was called to "testify to the identification of her secret mark in this book." The witness list even included Chudnowsky— DA Crain sent a very specific Western Union telegram to Liberty, New York, where Chudnowsky operated the Liberty Book Shop. It asked him to be at the General Sessions courtroom at promptly 9:45 a.m. on May 16. Its only subject was "Harry Gold on Trial."[34]

They were all there, eventually, over the long course of the trial in that barren brown courtroom, where "an occasional sunbeam radiated through the windows only to disappear hastily behind the clouds as if to avoid being a witness of the wrangling between facts and evasions."[35] The booksellers each told his part—Arthur Swann, never a shrinking violet, acted nervously and spoke in a voice hardly above a whisper as he explained how he had briefly come to possess *Al Aaraaf*. Harry Stone told the same story with somewhat more force. But even though his testimony was not exactly damning to the defense—he was a minor link to a minor link—Gold's attorney tried to impugn his credibility with an old conviction for possession of obscene books. It was the same treatment, more or less, that all of the prosecution's witnesses got.

Whether he was spooked by the spirited defense or simply calculating the odds, during the course of the trial Mendelson decided to drop the first count. Though it might have been possible to prove grand larceny against Gold, it was certainly the weaker of the two counts. The prosecutor knew the second count, for receipt of stolen goods, was a sure thing, so he decided to focus on that. With the number and quality of witnesses arrayed to testify against the dealer, the verdict seemed a fait accompli. It was clear to anyone paying attention that Gold was, at the very least, guilty of receipt of stolen property.

Despite Gold's seemingly clear guilt, the trial lasted more than a week.[36] So whatever the verdict might be, Gold got his money's worth from his counsel. But not more than his money's worth. Judge Corrigan charged the jury with its instructions and sent it away for a decision. Over the objections of the defense, which stated that the prosecution had not proved its case, on May 23, the jury found Gold guilty of the one count. Judge Corrigan sent Gold to wait in the Tombs for a couple of weeks before sentencing. Then, on June 7, one day shy of the two-year anniversary of Clarke's arrest outside of Boston, Judge Corrigan made his decision. The jury had encouraged him to show some leniency to the twenty-six-year-old, who stood a chance of spending twenty years in prison, and the judge did, to a certain extent. He sentenced Gold to between two and four years in Sing Sing.[37]

But there was a problem, and the defense recognized it during the trial. Both the prosecution and the trial judge acted under the reasoning, based on §1308 of the Penal Law, that any person who "buys or receives any of the property specified in the section, which includes a book belonging to or bearing any mark or indicia of ownership by a public or incorporated library, *without ascertaining by diligent inquiry* that the person selling or delivering the same has a legal right to do so, is guilty of a felony."[38] In his jury instructions, this is the language the judge used in charging the twelve men who heard the testimony against Gold.

The copy of *Al Aaraaf, Tamerlane and Minor Poems* stolen in 1931. Harry Gold ripped the cover off to disguise its ownership, but marks within the book gave it away. *New York Public Library visual materials, Manuscripts and Archives Division, The New York Public Library, Astor, Lenox and Tilden Foundations.*

The Gold defense knew this was wrong and appealed the sentence, claiming the judge used faulty statutory interpretation in directing the jury. Gold's argument was based on the "knowledge" that a buyer of stolen goods needed to have to be convicted. Under the trial court's reasoning, he should have, through "diligent inquiry," ascertained that the person selling him the book did not own it. And that is what was proven beyond a reasonable doubt. But Gold's argument was that he had been charged under the common law (that is, judge-made law) theory of the crime, and that required, for receipt of stolen property, "actual or constructive knowledge" that the property was stolen. That was a higher burden. And while it may have seemed like a technicality, it was a serious problem for the prosecution. Instead of proving what Gold knew, they had only proven what he *should have* known.

On November 17, 1933, a majority of the First Department, Appellate Division of the Supreme Court, agreed with Gold. The appeals court found that under the trial court's reasoning, "The burden of proving that the defendant did make reasonable inquiry that the person selling or delivering the stolen or misappropriated property to him had a legal right to do so was upon the defendant, and that, not having made such an inquiry, the presumption was that the property was bought or received knowing it to have been stolen or misappropriated. We think this put an undue burden upon the defendant, and constituted prejudicial error. Under an indictment charging defendant with the common-law receiving of stolen property, the burden was always upon the people to show that said property was received with knowledge on the part of the defendant of its contraband character."[39] Gold was therefore not convicted of the crime with which he was charged.

After a mere six months in prison, he was released. He left the dank and stale cellblocks of Sing Sing and moved to a house on the south side of Long Island—from which he could see, smell, and hear the Atlantic Ocean—and plotted his return to Book Row.

The people who had worked so hard for so long to put Gold in jail were scandalized to see that he was out and back in the book business. While a chastened DA began to prepare for another trial, the library began to do what it could to help reassemble the folks who had testified the first time around. And in January 1934, as prosecutorial interest seemed to be flagging, Frank Polk brought his influence to bear once again. He wrote this time to prosecutor Irving Mendelson.

> Mr. Shaw and Mr. Bergquist sent me a report of their interview with you in regard to the Gold case. I am sorry this matter is taking up so much

of your time as I know how rushed you are but we are so keen about getting a conviction in this case I am sure you will forgive me.

The impression has gone out I am afraid that Gold is more or less immune and I think it is tremendously important that the case should be pressed in spite of the unfortunate decision of the Appellate Division. The Library is at the mercy of a man of this character and he will be able to recruit men to do the stealing with considerably more ease if he can point out that a plea of guilty was followed by a suspended sentence.

If there is anything we can do to help you in this case please command us for as I said before we feel very strongly.[40]

Harry Gold was buoyed by the appellate decision and felt confident a second trial would prove fruitless. Still, he was not taking any chances. He hired another of Manhattan's top attorneys, Jay Leo Rothschild. A former law professor, prolific scholar, and author of a casebook on New York practice, Rothschild had a Madison Avenue office—like Robert Daru, one block away from the NYPL—and a list of high-profile cases.[41] He took an aggressive stance from the beginning, fighting even the idea that the grand jury could return an indictment. Taking a page from Gold's victory at the appellate level, he noted to the trial court that "there were not stamps or marks on the book, visible to any person who came in possession" of it, so it would be impossible to prove statutory receipt of stolen goods.[42] But despite his protests, on February 26, 1934, Gold was reindicted, this time using the language of §1308 of the Penal Code.

The trial was basically a repeat of a year earlier, with a couple of slight variations. The judge was Morris Koenig, a nineteen-year veteran of the court who, though not as stern as Judge Corrigan, certainly did not shy from giving long sentences. He had sent people to Sing Sing on relatively minor charges, and he was not afraid of doing it again. The witness list, too, was slightly different. Among the people called to testify were John Elliot, Marion Root, A. S. W. Rosenbach ("Can testify as to the value of the book"), Harry Stone, Abe Shiffrin, Ed Harris, Det. Gaughran ("Can testify to what took place when the book was returned and arrests made"), Max Fabricant, Keyes Metcalf, and William Bergquist.[43] But Ben Harris was not called to testify. It may have had something to do with a hand-scrawled note—sent to "Red Headed Bastard"—from "Friends of Harry Gold." It read: "You are marked lousy squealing yellow rat. We settle with you soon."[44]

Harris's absence did not matter a whit. In early November, just before the appeals court set Gold free, Samuel Raynor Dupree was arrested trying to sell stolen books at the Madison Book Store. However guilty the

Southerner felt about stealing from the NYPL in January 1931, it had not stayed with him long. He was still in the theft business—and in and out of jail on a regular basis. In this case, the man he was with when he tried to sell the books was supposed to have had a reliable fence at Madison. If that was true, Dupree picked the wrong person—the man at the store to whom he talked about selling stolen books had him immediately arrested. Unfortunately for Dupree, he was just out on parole after serving a year in the New York County Reformatory for another larceny. But as bad as this was for Dupree, it was much worse for Harry Gold: Leery of going back to jail, Dupree was looking to bargain. He had been stealing books fairly constantly and selling them to Book Row dealers for many years. Worse yet, he had particular information about the *Al Aaraaf* theft and he made it clear to the DA that he was more than willing to testify to the fact.[45]

With Dupree on their side, the second trial of Harry Gold went much like the first. The New York prosecutors had prepared their case to the last detail—after an embarrassing reversal at the appellate level, they were not taking any chances. On June 27, 1934, Gold was reconvicted for his crimes just as certainly as he had been convicted. Judge Koenig, discharging the jurors, noted, "I don't see how by any rational reasoning you could have reached any other verdict."[46] Nine days later, Judge Koenig sentenced Gold to between one and two years in prison, taking his prior time served into consideration. The only thing Gold had gotten out of his appeal was a slightly shorter sentence and the chance to drain his coffers a little more for the sake of his legal defense.

It had taken more than three years, but Bergquist finally saw Gold punished. More important for him, he also saw *Al Aaraaf* rightfully returned to the NYPL. Shortly after the sentencing, the Poe work was delivered to the Fifth Avenue building—bruised by rough handling, and the wear and tear of commerce, it was in worse shape than when it left. Still, it was back, this time forever. In October 1934, the library paid for some repairs and the Poe work was rebound in dark blue goatskin at the NYPL's bindery.[47] It resides to this day in that same handsome cover as part of the library's rare book collection.

The stolen copies of *The Scarlet Letter* and *Moby-Dick* were never recovered.

CHAPTER 8

That's the End of the Rare Book

WILLIAM "BABYFACE" MAHONEY WAS, IN MANY WAYS, THE one unequivocal example of William Bergquist's notion of the redeemable thief. In a strange way, he became what his onetime accomplice Harold Clarke always pretended to want to be: a library asset. Clarke's ham-handed attempts at giving up information about the theft ring seemed more like extortion than aid, and his personality made it so no one wanted to work with him. Mahoney was different. He was not only earnest about wanting to get out of book theft, he was a much more pleasant fellow. With the special investigator's help, Mahoney started working at the Newark Public Library. He eventually became that library's special investigator and retained the post successfully for many years. It was in that capacity that, in 1937, he helped recover some of the books he had initially helped steal.

In February 1937, a person buying from a secondhand bookstore in Newark called Mahoney when he noticed something that seemed out of the ordinary. Spending a mere $1.15, this man was able to get a heap of very valuable first editions. Mahoney, following up on the tip, went to the store and discovered a box of books, most of which had marks suggesting they were stolen from libraries. He called Bergquist and the two began investigating.

The 103 books they found at the store turned out to be the fruit of a string of thefts that had taken place five or six years earlier from the Newark Public Library; Harvard University; Brown University; the Berkshire Athenaeum; and the Pittsfield, Massachusetts, Public Library—that is, a representative sample of the places from which the Romm Gang had stolen. Most of these books were nineteenth-century American first editions. One was a book by Emily Dickinson, one was by John Drinkwater, and one had once been Oliver Wendell Holmes's copy of Harriet Beecher Stowe's *Little Foxes*. (Holmes had signed it across his bookplate.) Also from Holmes's library was a copy of William Duane's *Ligan*.[1] These books were being sold as nearly worthless in this Newark bookstore.

Eventually, the bookseller was exonerated of any implication in the thefts, despite the fact that in most of the books, there was some sort of ownership mark. Apparently the collection of stolen books had been passed down through so many hands that they were effectively laundered.[2] They almost certainly were once a part of the Romm Gang's loot—maybe even stolen by Mahoney himself—and, in the aftermath of the gang's prosecution, hurriedly jettisoned from the large backlog of material housed in one of the various storage units.

This, finally, was the fate of tens of thousands of books carefully culled from the stacks of northeastern libraries. Forgotten, and often not thought valuable by the people who discovered them, they were sold off in boxed lots at yard sales and local bookstores. They were bought up again, usually one at a time, and placed on shelves in houses, or at other booksellers, to be bought and sold, bought and sold, bought and sold. These books traveled the way rare books often do in commerce— misidentified, undervalued, and marked, eventually found by a collector or trained book scout who cannot believe his luck. Very few ever made it back to their original owner library. But these particular books found in Newark were an exception to the rule. To the extent possible, they were returned to the libraries from which they came. Seven of them, including a Thomas Paine work from 1792, ultimately made it back to the Widener Library.[3]

Mahoney, for his part, became an important addition to the Newark library staff and also a big help to Bergquist. The two became close associates, consulting each other on various crimes and prosecutions throughout the subsequent years. But Mahoney's greatest contribution to stopping book crime, after his help bringing down the Romm Gang, did not take much work at all. He simply recognized a face, and in that way helped Bergquist finally capture the one man who had eluded him the longest: the notorious Hilderwald.

Before *Al Aaraaf* was stolen or William Bergquist had even heard the name Harold Borden Clarke spoken out loud, he had been after a man known only as "Hilder" something. Hilderwald, Hilderman, Hilderbrand—or maybe none of those. The man was slippery and thought to be responsible for more disappeared books than the Boston Fire of 1872. No one could get a bead on him. It was in pursuit of this character that Bergquist had first gone to Boston—but that only led him to Clarke. By 1936, "Hilderwald" seemed like proof of the idea that no one would ever know the identity of the greatest book thief of all time, because he simply would never be caught. The man was so notorious that there had been a sketch of him circulating among northeastern librarians for several years, but it was of little help. As longtime Philadelphia bookseller George Allen quipped, it merely "showed that he had a head, eye-lashes, eyes and nose and mouth."[4] In truth, the sketch artist could not be blamed. Even a picture of the man showed him to be perfectly average looking. A smidge over five foot seven, he had a thin, angular face with not a single distinguishing feature—his nose, mouth, eyes, ears, and hairline all seemed to be in keeping with most other men. Even his cleft chin was prominent only in certain light.

And while this may have contributed to his remaining at large seven long years after Bergquist first took an interest, it did little to placate the special investigator. His search for the man was not obsessive enough to call Hilderwald his white whale, but by the middle of the 1930s, another maritime cliché seemed to apply: the one that got away. But a book thief, like most criminals, is susceptible to the iron rule of statistics—the more times he commits a crime, the more chances there are to catch him. And Hildwerwald had pushed his luck more than most. Even after his confederates and competition in the East Coast book theft business had bowed out, been rehabilitated, or put out of business, he was still humming along. And this only added to the legend.

Of course, the legend did not exactly match up with the man. By any analysis, Hilderwald's life was almost comically mundane. The most feared book thief in America was the son of a prosperous Ohio family who had turned out to be a failure at just about everything he tried, right up until he tried book theft. From acting to storekeeping to sobriety, Stanley Wemyss had washed out of them all. Finally, with little else left to do, he had turned to theft. And two years after the incarceration of Harry Gold, he was still riding the same basic book circuit he had blazed a decade earlier—making the same money and stealing from the same places. Wemyss was the standard itinerant book thief. He lived on the road, out of a small suitcase and whatever else he could fit in train station lockers. Usually that was not much besides a few papers and sometimes a typewriter. This meant his clothes often had a rumpled, slept-in look, though, in the mid-1930s, that did not give away much. There were plenty of men in rumpled suits. Besides, his intellect and the wad of cash he kept in his pocket usually was more than enough to counteract first impressions.

He referred to himself as a book salesman, and it was as good a description as any. He had once been a legitimate bookseller in Cincinnati, running the Continental Bookshop. And he certainly still sold the first-edition American books he stole from public libraries, often within a day or two of acquiring them. But most of his time was spent on the stealing part. Like Clarke and Mahoney, Wemyss was an independent contractor, selling to whoever would buy his books. But he, too, relied on certain fences—and preferred one in particular, a man he had known in the southern Ohio book trade named William Smith. The men had been working fairly closely for a half decade, and the typewritten wish list of five thousand books Wemyss kept in his briefcase was partly the result of their collaboration.

But the list was merely something Wemyss was adding to, not bound by. And it was his ability to make actual choices about books that made him far more dangerous to libraries than almost any other book scout. He knew what had value and what he could sell. If Wemyss spent enough time in the stacks, he could usually find something to take. And he was used to spending a lot of time in libraries. Wemyss's technique was not markedly different from Clarke's, or most other book thieves at the time. But his thievery was different enough that he was able to make a steady living at it for a long time. Partly this was because he was willing to travel great distances, stopping in remote public libraries along the way. Partly it was because he was selective in his thefts, taking items that were not necessarily considered rare by librarians. And partly he was just a very good thief. Despite his sometimes disheveled look, he was a natty dresser, wearing spats with his suits and carrying a cigarette holder and cane. And like a lot of the great thieves, he did not avoid librarians—he warmed up to them. By feigning a particular academic interest, he was able to roam the stacks with impunity, either concealing the few books he chose to take in his waistband or, if need be, tossing them out the window and into the bushes. He was so trusted that librarians would sometimes lock him in the stacks while they took their lunch breaks.

Wemyss set out from southwestern Ohio in mid-September 1936, heading northeast. He had been on the road a lot that year and this was to be his last major excursion before the winter. It was a bookend of sorts, finishing the year along the same stretch he had started it: the East Coast. One of the places he had been particularly successful during that trip nine months earlier was the Library of Congress.

He had approached the federal library with Americana on his mind. He knew what was selling—and, more important, what a certain person was buying—and so he focused on books relating to Indians and the Indian wars of the United States. Most of what he wanted were the sensational accounts of Indian interactions that had been printed in limited quantities with very little dedication to either the craft of writing or to bookmaking. They were ephemeral, not meant to last. So, naturally, most of them hadn't. That's why, in 1936, they were in particular demand. Among the dozens Wemyss stole from the Library of Congress were Capt. James Barr's *Correct and Authentic Narrative of the Indian War in Florida* (1836), Ann Coleson's *Narrative of Her Captivity* (1864), J. H. Dripps' *Three Years among the Indians in Dakota* (1894), H. E. B. McConkey's *Dakota War Whoop* (1865), and A. B. Meacham's *Narrative of the Massacre by the Savages of the Wife and Children of Thomas Baldwin* (1837). None of the items he stole were available anywhere in real numbers, but a couple of them were particularly rare. M. Hodges's *The Life and Times and Wonderful Achievement of the Adventurous and Renowned Captain Kirby* was terribly hard to find (and remains so today—only a half dozen or so libraries own it). The same was true of *An Account of a Visit Lately Made to the People Called Quakers in Philadelphia, by Papoonah, An Indian Chief, and Several other Indians, Chiefly of the Minisink Tribe.*[5]

Almost all of these books were less than one hundred pages long and softbound, and so were fairly easily secreted into a pocket, pant leg, or waistband. But some proved more difficult. For instance, Josiah Priest's *A True Narrative of the Capture of David Ogden* (1841) was bound together by the library with Priest's *The Low Dutch Prisoner* (1839). So Wemyss tore these from their binding—leaving the husk behind on the shelf—to make it easier to sneak them out.[6] (This was not a particularly rare move on the part of thieves who wanted something, and has the added bonus of making the shelf look still complete. In a more recent theft in Ohio, that of an old state code from the Rutherford B. Hayes Presidential Library, the young man checked out a bound book from the closed stacks, took it into the women's restroom, tore out the part he wanted, and turned the rest back in. The librarian received the book back and replaced it on the shelf as if it was complete.) Not that Wemyss kept only to Indian subjects. He also took targets of opportunity that he spotted on his way in and out of the library. One of these was *A Geographical History of Nova Scotia*, from 1749. Another was Joseph Robson's *Account of Six Years Residence in Hudson's-Bay*, from 1752.

Wemyss packed up twenty-three of these Library of Congress books and sent them to William Smith; the dealer paid $237 for them upon

Wemyss's return to Cincinnati that winter. Then Smith promptly set about selling them, describing and listing the books in his March catalogue for a total of $1,137. This was a good deal for both men and was like most of the transactions in a relationship between the two that started many years earlier. Wemyss stole books and sent them back to Smith. The dealer priced the books and paid the thief upon his return to Cincinnati. But the relationship was even closer still. Wemyss spent a great deal of time in Smith's store, learning his inventory, his needs, and the business of Americana from one of the country's masters. Wemyss, on the other hand, also brought to bear his own information, including the names of the libraries from which he had stolen books. This was an important point since Smith dealt books to these institutions, and wanted to avoid the uncomfortable situation of trying to sell a library's books back to it.[7]

In September, Wemyss was retreading this same ground, looking for much of the same material. His plan was to make a small loop of the Northeast, which would take him across parts of Ohio, Pennsylvania, and New York before arriving in Massachusetts, where he would turn back south and west. He planned to take in the cities of New York, Boston, Philadelphia (his October 6 ledger entry for Philly noted his targets as "U.P., Drexel, &c."), and, finally, Washington before heading back to Ohio. Certainly he planned on stopping by libraries he had never visited before, but this was mostly familiar ground. All of the major places he planned on stopping had been victims before—some as many as a dozen times—and he was merely shifting his focus within their collections.

He headed first northeast of Lima, Ohio, toward the most important city in the state and its fantastic stock of books. The Cleveland Public Library was a grand collection, housed in a handsome building just about ten years old, in the heart of a thriving community. Cleveland had been one of America's great early cities, home to a number of corporations (and barons of industry) and the then famous Millionaire's Row. By the time Wemyss rolled into town that September, the library had been around for more than sixty years and in that time had managed to accrue quite a collection of the sorts of items Wemyss could easily sell. Like a great many urban libraries in the 1930s, it was seeing a record number of patrons crowding its lobby, stacks, and reading rooms. This was good for Wemyss, too.

After he left Cleveland, he continued his travels east, intending to stop at a number of small-town libraries along the route. These had the hidden gems he was particularly adept at discovering, and he knew them to be almost completely unprotected. And even if the books were locked away or the stacks were closed, he could always charm a librarian into giving him access. It was a circuit he was familiar with from years of practice, and by late September he had already been fabulously successful—so much so that he started having second thoughts. After Cleveland, he traveled across southern New York, by train or hitching rides along Highway 17, taking in the just-turning foliage of the state's magnificent low mountains. He hit libraries along a route that included Olean, Hornell, Corning, Binghamton, Middletown, and several other small communities and delivered him, finally, to the eastern part of the state. It was on the cusp of New Jersey that things went wrong.

His original plan had been to keep on heading east, eventually winding up in Providence, before turning back south. But then he changed his mind. Rhode Island was in the exact opposite direction from Ohio. And Ohio was where he wanted to be. He had already sent several packages to Cincinnati, and he was tired of traveling. The weather was turning bad in New England, and it seemed there was little to be gained from staying on. By turning south and west, however, he could be in Cincinnati in early October and collect his money from Smith. On top of which, he could steal all the way along the road home. So he turned south. He first hit Port Jervis, New York, then Paterson, New Jersey, and, finally, Newark—a big city with an impressive collection.

Wemyss arrived at the Public Services Terminal there on Monday, September 21, and stored his few belongings—including the books he had taken but had not yet sent to Cincinnati or sold to other dealers—in a locker. Then he went to scout the Newark Public Library, an institution noted both for its collection and the philosophy of openness instilled in it by librarian John Cotton Dana. Unfortunately for Wemyss, the Newark library also had another particular trait: William Mahoney.

Mahoney was five years into his new life on the right side of the book theft trade and was as surprised as anyone to see one of his old Boston rivals. In fact, at first Mahoney did not recognize Wemyss. The two had never been close, and the intervening five years had not done either one of them any good. But Wemyss looked moderately familiar to Mahoney—and anyway, he pegged him as a book thief right off. It only took a few more minutes before one of America's two most infamous book thieves recognized the other in the stacks of the Newark Public Library.

The Newark special investigator followed the thief for a while. Mahoney had always been pretty nimble in rows of books, managing to simultaneously browse and watch at the same time. But in Newark, he was especially good. Years of roaming the same stacks had taught him the angles and avenues. He shadowed Wemyss with great concentration, not wanting to miss a single motion. It was quite a task, since the thief was not in any hurry. But after a cat-and-mouse game, Mahoney finally saw Wemyss slip three slim books into his pants and make for the door. The special investigator stopped him before he got there.[8]

Mahoney reintroduced himself to Wemyss, and he got the books back. Then he sat the Ohioan down in a locked room and made a couple of phone calls. One was to the Newark Police Department. The other was to G. William Bergquist. When Mahoney told him he had Hildwerwald in his possession, Bergquist crossed the river immediately. In the meantime, Wemyss sat alone in a jail cell, considering his options. None of them seemed particularly good. In fact, he was apparently so distressed by his predicament that he tried to commit suicide in the holding cell. One fruitless attempt—cutting his wrist with a piece of broken eyeglass—left him with a serious wound, but nothing that proved mortal.[9]

Then Bergquist showed up and started working his magic. He told Wemyss that his book-stealing days were over and that the best thing he could do was to cooperate in putting the book dealers he sold to in jail. It was the same basic thing he had told Mahoney in 1931. Wemyss was initially reluctant to help—not least because, whatever little bit of a career he had left would certainly disappear once he testified against his fences. But after more time with Bergquist, the decency the special investigator managed to find in all of these guys—or, at least, all of the ones under arrest—came to the fore. Wemyss said he would come clean and help investigators track down the books and crooked dealers. As a first step toward this end, he took the men to his locker at the train station. It was packed with items of the sort a traveling man would need. It also housed nine books he had recently stolen along with eighty-five coins from the Roman and Byzantine eras. Not that there was any doubt about the matter, but he owned up to stealing these. In exchange for his complete and continuing cooperation, Bergquist agreed to do his best to keep Wemyss out of jail.

The wheels of Newark justice moved quickly in the 1930s, particularly if they were greased by locals in good standing. Wemyss was arraigned, pleaded out, and was sentenced within one week. Standing before Judge Seymour Klein, Wemyss was not so much contrite as practical. "I can't steal anymore because every library in the country has my picture now," Wemyss said. Beyond that, he "had to revise my psychology of crime to include a hackneyed conclusion—crime does not pay. I will help to get all the books back." And, for good measure: "I've tried to commit suicide three times in one day in jail. I thought I heard voices of other criminals condemn me for what I have done." It was all a bit melodramatic, but, in his defense, he had once very much wanted to be an actor.

On the strength of his promises, as well as the testimony of Bergquist and Beatrice Winser, head of the Newark library, Wemyss was given a suspended sentence and paroled in the custody of Bergquist. The rationale for this leniency, aside from Wemyss's cooperation in getting the books back, was that it was the crooked book dealers, not the thieves themselves, who were truly to blame. Without a place to sell stolen books, thieves would not exist. This was an idea shared by many librarians who, like Bergquist, felt that putting a thief in jail for a short period of time was less important than putting a crooked dealer out of business forever.[10] With one particular dealer in mind, Wemyss was on his way again to Cincinnati. But this time he was accompanied by the book detective so that he could live up to his end of the bargain.

The Queen City had briefly been the cultural center of the frontier. Founded on the Ohio River as one of the first American cities west of the mountains, Cincinnati was an early nineteenth-century boomtown full of people, commerce, and government. Books followed close behind. The first stores selling them had come to the city in the early 1800s, and by the beginning of the 1820s, the book trade was firmly established.[11] By the 1830s, the city was a literary hotbed of what was then still considered the West. Because it was situated in the hinterlands and had only sporadic access to the East Coast, its bookstores came early to rely on items published in the Western Reserve and in other territories on the Ohio side of the Alleghenies. That meant that by the end of the nineteenth century—when rail, instead of water, started to dominate travel, and the southern Ohio city was no longer what it once had been—the city's bookstores were still dominated by Americana. It was a wave William Smith rode for a half century.

Smith was a native of Cincinnati and the owner of the Smith Book Company, one of the five most important dealers in Americana in the United States. One historian later noted that anyone "attempting to write a definitive history of bookselling in America without devoting one chapter to Mr. Smith would do well to reconsider the subject."[12] Smith had gotten his start young, after a few years spent working in various trades taught him exactly what he did not want to do for a living. With books he collected as an avid reader, he opened his first bookstore in 1898, selling all types of books, new and used, at the corner of Fourth and Main. He issued his first catalogue—of an eventual 456—three years later, in 1901, comprising miscellanea and Americana. These were in abundance in the area, and pretty much the only things he could afford to buy. He kept this book business going for fifteen years until the start of World War I, when, running out of money, he closed it.

At the end of the war in 1918, he retooled his store and opened again as the Smith Book Company—incorporated in 1919 with $10,000 of capital stock.[13] He was not going to make the same mistakes that had cost him his business the first time around. No matter what, he was going to stay in the black until he was ready to retire. And at the beginning of this new business, at least, it looked like he need not worry. The market had caught up with his stock, and his expertise. Trade in Americana was starting an upward climb that lasted a decade, and he was right in the middle of it. And though—out of habit, mostly—he always made regular trips to New York to buy books, bringing much of it back to Cincinnati was like bringing coals to Newcastle. The great mass of Americana was in his backyard, on the shelves and in the attic trunks of middle America. So he tapped that rich vein for all it was worth. This initially meant a lot of traveling and a great deal of advertising in newspapers, particularly in southern Ohio, northern Kentucky, and southeastern Indiana.[14]

Within a few successful years, Smith was casting an even wider net, reaching to southern Kentucky and northern Indiana. In Logansport, he asked for items about former resident Stanislaus Lasselle, as well as "other books pertaining to the Middle and Western states."[15] In nearby Valparaiso, he advertised for "John Branco's Life and Adventures," published in the town in 1908, as well as any "book and pamphlets on California, Oregon, Mormons, Indians, overland journeys, county histories, family histories and genealogies."[16] In Massillon, Ohio, he was looking for Keller's "A Trip Across the Plains," published in the city in 1815, as well as "any books on Indians, Early Pioneers, Overland Journeys, Explorations" and "any book published in Ohio previous to 1820."[17] Soon he was placing ads as far away as New Hampshire.

In Cincinnati, he headquartered the Smith Book Company on the ninth floor of the Union Central Building, the tallest in the city. This was no coincidence. Selling "rare and fine editions, art, extra illustrated copies" and early printed works, he wanted to be seen as more than a simple bookseller. And by the early 1920s, he was. Quite in addition to his bookish accomplishments, the Ohio bookseller was a Rosenbachian figure, known for his ribald jokes, preference for drink, and the lavish parties he liked to throw. When Bergquist first set eyes on him in the midst of the Depression, he was known throughout southern Ohio simply as Rare Bill—a man who knew how to throw a party. Rotund and dapper, he smoked cigars, dressed in linen suits, and generally acted in a way very much like gentlemen across the river in Kentucky were thought to act. He was also known for sharing his high living with a certain class of people, treating important members of the community to lavish dinners and, during Prohibition, strong drinks. But being rich—and willing to spread the money around—was only part of Smith's persona. He was also opinionated, outspoken, and extraordinarily ruthless in his business practices.[18] By bullying and steam-rolling, and then undercutting, his competition, he had mostly cornered the southern Ohio Americana market. It was a combination of power and prestige that earned him exactly the sort of loyalty he needed in the fall of 1936 as Stanley Wemyss, and the knowledge he possessed, rumbled down the tracks toward Cincinnati.

Once Bergquist knew Wemyss was going to testify, he got in touch with Chalmers Headley, director of the Cincinnati Public Library. He wanted to know more about the area, and about Smith. The librarian set the special investigator up with the Hamilton County prosecutor, Louis Schneider. Almost immediately after Bergquist and Wemyss arrived in town, they met secretly with a grand jury. Schneider was an old hand at prosecuting big fish—he had recently done the job against "Foxy Bob" Zwick, southern Ohio's underworld king—and he was happy to go after another notable name. In bookseller William C. Smith, he had little to fear in the way of gangland violence, even if he did have plenty to fear politically. But almost regardless of the consequences, he was going after the man.

It was on the ninth floor of the by then second-tallest building in Cincinnati, on October 8, 1936, that Smith was presented the three indict-ments against him for receiving stolen books. The charges stated that on January 25, he received twenty-three books stolen from the Library of Congress, on September 16, he received four stolen from the Cleveland Public Library, and three days later he received nineteen books stolen from the Olean, New York, public library.[19] He was arrested, his store searched, and thirty books, identified as stolen from libraries, were seized. Most of the books still had marks of ownership either clearly present or only partially destroyed. It was all very much like Wemyss said it would be.

If convicted on the charges of receiving stolen property, the book-seller faced up to seven years in prison. He was arraigned the next day and his bond set at $3,000. This was paid by prominent local inventor, toolmaker, store owner, and president of a Fort Smith, Kentucky, bank, Oliver P. Schriver. Smith's benefactor was also, as it happened, his father-in-law.

Given his importance to the case—and, almost certainly, his unpop-ularity with locals—Wemyss, too, was held, as a material witness, and his bond set also at $3,000.[20] No one paid it for him.

Smith, for his part, did not deny that he had bought a number of books from Wemyss over the course of several years—an impossible claim anyway, given all the evidence. He simply relied on this old bookseller chestnut: He did not know they were stolen. He had been in the business for forty years but, apparently, had yet to develop an eye for spotting material that was too good to be true—even when it came from a single itinerant man who could not manage to keep his own store in business. And even when it came with partially erased stamps from the Library of Congress or various other public libraries. Smith told everyone who would listen that, as an honest bookman, he could not be expected to know he was dealing with thieves. With regard to the books stolen from Cleveland and Olean, Smith noted that he had not actually paid Wemyss for them because he was not, in fact, interested in them. Upon receipt, he said, he merely set them aside to return to the man.

This lie contained at least a partial truth: he had not paid Wemyss a dime for those books. But that was simply because Wemyss had not yet returned from his trip to collect his money. In any case, this allowed Smith to continue to insist that he never wanted the books Wemyss sent him that September. But what no one ever asked Smith was *why* he was not interested in the books. They were perfectly good pieces of Americana and would have been nice additions to his stock. If he suspected them of being stolen, why hadn't he turned Wemyss in—or, at the very least, contacted the librarians in the towns whose stamps the books bore? This question was never answered. (Though prosecutor Edward Strasser, who took over the case from Schneider, did suggest that Smith put the books aside only after he found out that Wemyss had been arrested in Newark—a far more plausible explanation than any given by Smith.)[21]

The trial date was set for November 17. In an unusual move for a man facing seven years in prison, Smith waived his right to a jury trial. The politically connected book dealer wanted his guilt or innocence decided, instead, by the judge presiding in the case, Alfred Mack. Judge Mack was, like Smith, a Cincinnati native, though he had traveled far afield before returning to the Queen City. A graduate of Harvard, he had been a student in the 1883 law class taught by Oliver Wendell Holmes. Back in southern Ohio, he was, in his advanced years, a member of the board of trustees at both the University of Cincinnati and the Cincinnati Zoo, and a member of the Cincinnati Club, the Civier Press Club, the Wednesday Club, the Masons, the Elks, the Odd Fellows, and B'nai B'rith, as well as a friend of President William Howard Taft.[22] He was even the son of the founder of the Cincinnati Southern Railroad. In short, he was a pillar of the local community.

Prosecutor Strasser did not like his chances at court with the counts regarding the books received from Cleveland and Olean—the books Smith claimed he did not want. So he dropped those, deciding instead to focus on the items stolen from the Library of Congress. With that in mind, Strasser traveled to Washington, DC, to interview employees of the library. He wanted them to testify as to the ownership of the books found in Smith's possession. He got librarians Martin Roberts and Jean Campbell to note, in a deposition, particular marks the library put in the books so that they might be later identified. These two also noted that some of the library's normal cataloguing marks had been insufficiently erased, and those, too, identified the stolen books.[23] (Because the two librarians could not come to Cincinnati, this written testimony was submitted to the court for use at trial—and immediately objected to by Victor Heintz, Smith's attorney. But Judge Mack ruled against the objection and agreed to let the depositions serve as evidence in the absence of the appearance of either Roberts or Campbell.)

Another item of evidence produced at the trial was Smith's financial ledger. This showed a number of transactions between the dealer and Wemyss—noted simply *W* in the books—all prior to 1935. Though it was known the two had done business in the twenty months since that time, on cross-examination Smith explained the discrepancy by noting that some of his payments to Wemyss might have been merely for store credit.[24] Smith also admitted meeting with Wemyss in Philadelphia in May 1936, but he claimed that no money changed hands.[25]

Aside from the depositions and physical evidence, the prosecution's case relied most heavily on the testimony of Wemyss. On the stand, he testified that Smith told him to "get books any way you can," particularly from the Library of Congress.[26] Wemyss also spoke of how the two men, together, had gotten rid of the library marks found in the books. When asked why he stole books, the thief mentioned that many "librarians haven't knowledge of the books," even less of security. Bergquist, too, was called to testify, though he had very little to say that was of practical use.

Of course, lack of having anything relevant to say was not a disqualification at the Smith trial. The great mass of the proceeding for the defense was a parade of character witnesses cobbled together from the city's most important figures, speaking on Smith's behalf—men whose main qualification for testimony seemed to be that they knew Smith from social circles. One of the men who had little of importance to say, other than that Smith was a swell guy, was Province Pogue—prominent local attorney, former president of the Cincinnati Bar Association, and, naturally, a friend of President William Howard Taft. (But not a great friend. Robert A. Taft, future Ohio senator, counseled his father in 1923 against appointing Pogue to the federal bench, noting that though he liked the man, he did not have confidence in his "complete honesty in reaching conclusions.")[27] Another legal standout testifying at the trial on Smith's behalf was former Superior Court judge Benton Oppenheimer. As evidence of what a small, tight-knit legal community Cincinnati was, former prosecutor Oppenheimer had been appointed to *his* judgeship to fill a spot vacated by Harry Hoffheimer, the law partner of Province Pogue.[28]

Still, it was not just people in the legal community who testified on Smith's account. John Shuff, a prominent national figure in the insurance industry, lined up at the trial, right next to both Davis and Roberta James of the James Bookstore, the oldest in Ohio. In addition to saying what a great guy Smith was, Davis James testified that he, too, would have bought the books Wemyss was selling.[29] And there were a dozen more people ready to testify the same way. One of them, Reverend Thomas Connell, of the Mercy Academy, a customer of Smith's, noted that he trusted the man so much that he often gave him blank checks and asked him to fill in the proper amount.

On November 21, Judge Mack agreed with the weight of popular sentiment, if not evidence, and acquitted the dealer on all counts. The judge, in an opinion that ran to seventeen pages, found that the prosecution had not proved the dealer had knowledge that the Library of Congress items were stolen.[30] He also noted that Smith had been in the book business for nearly forty years, and that his character and honesty had never before been impugned. "Bearing in mind the small volume of business transacted by Wemyss with the defendant during the last three years, a large part of which were legitimate transactions, it is almost inconceivable and certainly unbelievable that a merchant of high repute, an exemplary character in all other transactions, would risk the destruction of the reputation acquired in 38 years of activity for the acquisition of a few hundred dollars by connivance with one known to him to be a criminal."[31]

This was poor reasoning, of course. The dealings with Wemyss, which amounted to far more than a few hundred dollars and a few years' time, were more an example of than an exception to the way Smith did business. But none of that mattered. The defense's decision to let Judge Mack, instead of a jury, make the decision, had been a wise one.

After the ruling, two local newspapers ran stories whose slightly different tones could be discerned from their headlines. The *Cincinnati*

Times-Star's headline read "Acquittal and Vindication." The *Cincinnati Enquirer,* on the other hand, offered the more objective "Book Dealer Freed on Charge." Smith, who took the attitude of the *Times-Star's* headline to heart, was not gracious in victory. He had little nice to say about Wemyss, of course, but he saved his most particular criticism for William Bergquist, who he felt was bad at his job. "If I had been tracing a book thief I would have had him in 90 days," Smith said, of the special investigator's hunt for Wemyss; "it would not have taken me seven years. All Bergquist would have had to do was to have told the book trade journals; all dealers would have been warned against the thief. They [would have] caught him in Newark, wrapped him in cellophane, and handed him over to Bergquist." A preposterous charge, of course, and one made most often by book thieves and those who abetted them. In fact, the one who most loudly—and often—echoed this sentiment was Harold Clarke. For his part, Bergquist maintained that catching the thieves was not the real problem anyway. "What we have been trying to discover," he said, "is the places where they can dispose of [the books]. Wemyss declared he had been selling books he stole to Smith, and that Smith knew they were stolen."[32]

On November 19, 1936, Stanley Wemyss was let out of the Hamilton County Jail, once again a free man. He had been held in there not because of his crimes, but so that the court could be sure he would be available to testify—and the six weeks he spent inside were the longest stretch he would ever do for the thousands and thousands of books he had stolen from American libraries. Stranger still, Hamilton County paid him for his incarceration, at a rate of one dollar a day. He left jail with forty-two dollars in his pocket—honest money paid, ultimately, in the effort of a failed prosecution.[33] But Wemyss had done what he had said he would do, and was allowed to go free, a decade of looting libraries notwithstanding. It is unlikely that the habit impressed upon him those many years simply disappeared at the end of the trial, but, officially at least, he remained clean. He also remained drunk and disheveled, haunting the bookshops of many East Coast cities, particularly Philadelphia, plying whatever bookish trade presented itself. Mostly that meant hanging around in bookshops or Horn & Hardart's Restaurant, where coffee was five cents and men gathered to spend evenings gossiping about the book business.

It was in these gatherings that he told the stories of some of his exploits to an audience that sometimes included student and writer Harry Kurnitz. Kurnitz, who would write more than thirty screenplays (including the Billy Wilder classic *Witness for the Prosecution*), started his career in 1938 by penning *Fast Company*, the story of a rare book murder. One of the characters—and victims of murder—is a shady book scout named Sidney Wheeler, who regularly traveled around stealing from libraries and selling to fences. It was well known in the community of people who knew Wemyss that he was the inspiration for Wheeler.

Wemyss also put some of his own stories down on paper. In 1938, he published in a limited run with a small Baltimore press—the *only* thing the work had in common with *Al Aaraaf*—a collection of his short stories. ("Collection" might be an ambitious word for the final product. Titled "A Sky Pilot at Cactus Flat," the five stories took up only thirty-eight pages of text.) Aside from shilling his storybook door to door and being the model for a minor character in a pulp novel, Wemyss did one other notable thing. He tried to put his knowledge of rare books and Americana to good use.[34] In 1944, he published *The General Guide to Rare Americana, with auction records and prices.* The book was a survey of Americana published from 1689 to 1889, including not only the history of many imprints but their prices and, of course, locations. It was created in part from the list of valuable and theft-worthy books Wemyss carried with him—and much of the information he gathered was from the many months he spent talking to William Smith in his Cincinnati bookshop. It was not very good, or even accurate. But for a person interested in knowing exactly which libraries housed the most important and valuable rare books in America, Wemyss had written the book.

In the wake of the Wemyss episode, *Publishers Weekly* printed a recollection of a prediction from the recently deceased library legend, former Newark librarian John Cotton Dana: "The time was near at hand when librarians would have to segregate their rare and valuable books and subject their use to careful restrictions that would guard them from loss."[35] That time had come and gone.

William Smith, for his part, continued bookselling into his eighties, wholly unscathed by the Wemyss affair. When he finally retired, a living legend, in 1955, he complained, "I had to get out of the rare book business. Too many people die and leave their collections to libraries and colleges. That's the end of the rare book. It never changes hands again."[36]

In a perfect world, maybe.

Epilogue

FOR SAMUEL RAYNOR DUPREE, NEW YORK HAD ALWAYS BEEN a cold place. He had arrived as a teenager, found himself under the influence of some rather bad characters, and made the sort of poor decisions that landed him in jail time and again. But for the southern boy, being out of jail was almost worse than being in it, thanks to his parole officer, Harold Humphrey. Humphrey was in his early thirties, married, and the father of two children. At some point in his career at the Municipal Parole Commission he decided that his salary was not enough to sustain his happy home on Long Island. So he began shaking down the men he was assigned to steward into law-abiding citizenship.

The first time Dupree met his parole officer, in a church on 36th Street, the Southerner did not know what to expect. Newly out of jail—and very interested in staying that way—he certainly did not expect to be taken for the thirteen dollars he had in his pocket. Humphrey said he needed it more than the parolee: "I just bought a new car."[1]

They met again some months later, when Humphrey arrived at Dupree's room. The thief was being sent back to jail on a new charge and Humphrey told him he would keep his clothes safe while Dupree was in the joint. These clothes amounted to a "suit, hat, pair of shoes and about 10 or 15 neckties and about as many shirts and underwear, socks and topcoat."[2] The next time Dupree saw these items, he was in jail and Humphrey was wearing them—right down to the underwear.

On several occasions, Humphrey not only took the money Dupree had on him—sometimes as little as twenty-five cents—but also took the money he caused others to give Dupree. For instance, Humphrey escorted Dupree to one of his former employers at the Waldorf Astoria. The parole officer then explained to the man how well Dupree was doing—and that he only needed a little help from his friends to keep doing right. This caused the former employer to hand over five dollars for the cause. When they were back on the street, Humphrey took the money.

Humphrey ran a similar game on Metcalf and Bergquist, though without Dupree in attendance. On several occasions, after Dupree had agreed to testify against Harry Gold, Humphrey told the two that Dupree needed money to buy clothes and the like. Metcalf and Bergquist, over the course of several visits, coughed up thirty dollars. None of it made its way to Dupree.

Eventually, the parolee got sick enough of this that he decided to act. By the spring of 1934 he was an important witness for the prosecution, so in the midst of the trial, he tried to leverage the situation. He told Bergquist as well as DA Firestone about Humphrey and suggested that since he had agreed to give them Gold, they ought to do something on his behalf. On April 6, 1934, they did. Two officers from the DA's office gave Dupree two marked five-dollar bills just before he was to meet Humphrey at the NYPL. Once the two men met up at the library they traveled, as was their normal routine, to a nearby restaurant, where Humphrey took whatever he could get from Dupree in exchange for continuing to file good reports on his behalf. In this case, it was the two marked bills. When they left the restaurant and headed back to the library, Dupree signaled to the officers that Humphrey had taken the money. They came out and arrested him.[3]

Humphrey eventually pleaded guilty to "coercing a paroled person" to give him money. He was sentenced to an indefinite term not to exceed three years, and Judge John Freschi asked that Humphrey be sent to some prison "other than the city penitentiary, so that no harm could come to him from prisoners over who he formerly had supervision."[4] As it turned out, Humphrey served a term that *very much* did not exceed three years. He was inside only some six months before being paroled. And he was out just a few weeks before he had found himself another shakedown racket. Humphrey posed as an agent of the Federal Housing Administration, encouraging people in towns throughout Long Island to apply for loans. Pretending to be a man of some standing, he would promise to help the loans get through if paid three dollars for every $100 of the asked-for money.[5] Humphrey was back in jail by December 1934.

So, too, was Dupree, arrested on still another larceny charge, just in time for winter.

Ben Harris, on the other hand, was out. Thanks to his work on the Harry Gold sting, he was paroled in time for Christmas 1933. Like

Romm, he was released from jail early. Unlike Romm, however, he got right back to his book business, thanks to his brother keeping his shop alive. Like most book thieves, prison time had not soured him on the underbelly of the book trade. The man who had hated Sing Sing more than anything else began immediately to court a return visit by fencing stolen goods. The only major difference was that the Danish immigrant was smarter the second time around. For one thing, he got rid of the goods more quickly—he almost never kept stolen books in his store, selling them to other dealers as soon as he got them. He remembered how he had gotten caught the first time. And he also cultivated his own book scouts, men—especially other Danish immigrants—he thought he could trust.

One of those immigrants was a man named Knude Maisel. Pretending to be a researcher, Maisel entered the stacks of university or seminary libraries and, in the tradition of crooked Book Row scouts, slipped books and pamphlets into the hidden pockets of his clothing.[6] Using this familiar trick, Maisel stole thousands of items from places as far afield as the Harvard-Andover Theological Seminary, Princeton University, and Rutgers University. He sold most of them to Harris at his Book Row store.

Unfortunately for Harris, his precautions kept him out of trouble only for so long. In 1942, Bergquist caught Maisel stealing books. And, as he usually did, the special investigator convinced the thief to turn. (After he agreed to testify, Maisel was described as being in the DA's witness "singing school.") In this case, Maisel admitted stealing more than one thousand rare books and pamphlets over the course of four years—many on behalf of Harris. On the strength of this testimony, Harris was arrested on June 16, 1942, for the receipt of more than 200 stolen books. He eventually faced up to twenty-five years in prison for receipt of stolen goods and five more years for second-degree larceny.

Released on bail, Harris agreed to help Bergquist track down some of the books he had sold in exchange for sentencing consideration. In November 1942, Harris was sentenced to fifiteen to thirty months in Sing Sing; this time, there was not a Poe book anywhere that would spring him. The sentence, finally, marked the end of his American book theft career. At the conclusion of his time in jail he was handed over, like Maisel before him, to federal authorities for deportation back to Denmark.[7]

By that point, Harry Gold was vice president of the Fourth Avenue Booksellers Association. In 1933, in the aftermath of his first trial, the *Brooklyn Eagle* recommended that book collectors everywhere beware of the person from whom they bought rare books; if "all did so valuable books everywhere ought to be much safer from thieves" and men like Gold.[8] The newspaper also asked the dealer to make a full confession, listing all of the stolen books he had sold and to whom. But Gold, of course, never did anything of the sort—nor did he show any remorse for his actions.

His stint in prison was barely a blip in the life of the bookseller, and he returned to 95 Fourth Avenue as soon as he was out. Almost from the new beginning his business on Book Row boomed. He stayed at that location until 1940, when he moved a few blocks south to 65 Fourth Avenue. He remained there for fifteen years, becoming an outspoken advocate for booksellers' rights and an unofficial historian of the business. That no stigma attached to Harry Gold had less to do with the forgiving nature of booksellers than it did with the fact that most regarded his crimes as relatively minor. This was particularly true on post-Depression Book Row, where many of the ones who were most likely upset by Gold—the honest dealers—had gone out of business.

In 1955, Gold moved to yet another location on Book Row—a large space with a huge basement that could accommodate his enormous stock. He prospered there but, in 1961, moved out of Book Row altogether, to 308 Fifth Avenue, ten blocks south of the NYPL. This was a four-story building that was one of the original offices of IBM.[9] And for him to be able to afford an entire building on Fifth Avenue, business must have been good, indeed. His move north from Fourth Avenue was typical of the gradual dismantling of the character of the area, a fact illustrated nicely by the first sentence of a 1956 *New York Times* article: "Progress's chrome-and-concrete heel is poised now over Fourth Avenue's antiquarian book row."[10] Gold left just after the high-water mark, when the area was still packed with dozens of secondhand bookstores.[11] Over the course of the next twenty years, they all gradually disappeared as proprietors grew older and went unreplaced while rents skyrocketed. (In 1957, the Strand Bookstore on the corner of Twelfth and Broadway—a spot within throwing distance of the pool hall where Chudnowsky and Harris made their loot exchange—was paying rent of $400 per month. Forty years later the rent was $55,000 per month.)

Gold eventually sold the entire stock of the Aberdeen Book Company—some one hundred thousand books—to Penn State University, whose dean wanted to enlarge the school's library quickly for little money.[12] (The plan backfired. It cost the school a great deal of money to dispose of much of the collection that simply was not suitable.) Some forty-five years after starting the Aberdeen with a pittance, Gold had become as prosperous as any bookseller of his time could hope to be. In the mid-1970s, Gold had had enough of New York and decided to head south. He settled in North Carolina, having it on good authority that the winters were mild.[13] He continued to both collect and sell books. He also wrote a great deal of poetry. Harry Gold died there in 1990, on a warm and clear spring day, surrounded by the green smell of Carolina pine, a million miles away from the Lower East Side.

But no one, not Bergquist nor Wemyss nor Mahoney nor Smith nor Gold, was more successful, finally, than Harold Borden Clarke. In June 1932, he was released from prison in Lancaster, Massachusetts. He was promptly scooped up on a warrant for theft from the Lowell Library, put back in jail, and brought before a judge at the local court. This was done by Police Superintendent Michael Winn at the behest of federal authorities. They wanted to deport Clarke, who had never become an American citizen, back to Nova Scotia.[14] This plan was largely orchestrated by Clarke's lawyer, Boston's Robert J. Curran. Though the attorney could not keep Clarke out of jail, he knew he could help him afterward. In district court, Curran pleaded with the judge to dismiss the charges against Clarke, who had spent a year in jail already and was "mentally ill and in need of treatment," so that he could be turned over to federal agents. They would see that he was expelled from the country in lieu of further punishment. The judge agreed and, upon the strength of a warrant for illegal entry into the United States, the Canadian was taken into federal custody.

Clarke was not, of course, mentally ill. It was just another role he agreed to play so that he could get sentenced to return to Canada. His deportation allowed him to become what he had always planned on becoming: a book dealer. Over the years, he had certainly accumulated a lot of free stock and a discerning eye for quality. For the former, he immediately rented a walk-in vault in Ottawa, where he stored $10,000 worth of his best books. He was keeping them aside for the day when he had his own shop and the price of books returned to what it once had been. In the meantime, he worked at bookshop in Montreal for a couple of years. Then he opened his own place in Ottawa, telling people he had gotten his training in antiquarian books in New York and Boston, which was, technically, true.[15] By that point, he had also met the woman he would spend the rest of his life with—her name was Dorothy, and she was eighteen years old.[16] (Even many years later, when writing him letters, she sometimes referred to him as "Professor.") Like most Depression-era businesses, his struggled at first, suffering from lack of cash until, he later claimed, "an old Jewish junk dealer" came to him with a roll of papers "found in an old vault of a railway building, demolished" to make way for a post office. Clarke immediately identified them as the long-lost Rideau Canal maps, hand drawn by Col. John By, the British military engineer credited with founding Ottawa. Clarke sold them to Queen's University after erasing the British government's broad arrow from the corner of each map. Removing marks of ownership was, by that point, so uneventful for him that he did not even think to hide the fact.

What he did hide, though, was his name. There had not been a great deal of press coverage—and almost none in Canada—about his thefts or involvement in the Book Row gang. But "Harold Clarke" might, in some parts of the world, still have had a stigma attached. Not least, Clarke was afraid that some of the Romm Gang might want to settle scores. In any event, it was an inconvenient name for the aspiring bookseller. So he dropped the "Harold" altogether and reinvented himself as Borden Clarke. When he was putting on airs, he even went by H. Borden Clarke. And, just like that, he became Canada's most celebrated book dealer.

Not that he outran his past completely. Over the course of a half century in the business, he ran across people—or they across him—who either knew or discovered who he was. The trouble this caused him ranged from threats to blackmail to lost sales.[17] Of these last, one involved Harvard, where Keyes Metcalf had become the librarian after leaving the NYPL in 1937. In that capacity, he discovered, a few years later, that the library sometimes bought books from Clarke. He immediately put a stop to this.[18] Still, few enough people knew Clarke that he could continue to lie about his past, sometimes in very public ways, and fear no repercussions. For instance, by 1961 he was printing on his company letterhead that he had "40 years of honest business in Canada." Not one bit of that claim was true.

But aside from a few inconveniences, Clarke, like most book criminals, bore few scars from his earlier wounds. He continued to make trips, for business and pleasure, to the United States.[19] And he continued to have a lot of professional interaction with librarians and archivists, eventually claiming as many as five thousand among his clients. Over the course of his bookselling life in Canada, he sold to the British Museum, Oxford, Cambridge, Harvard, Yale, Illinois, Columbia, McGill, the Library of Congress, and the Smithsonian, along with an array of smaller institutions.[20]

Of course, not all of his transactions were happy ones—but this had everything to do with his personality, not his former career. Even as he got older, his interpersonal skills never improved. The regular misunderstandings of a business conducted mostly by catalogues and post routinely devolved into threats and lectures. For instance, one ninety-five word inquiry from the Canadian Department of National Revenue was met by Clarke with a five-page, 2,700-word screed in reply. At one point, on page two of this letter, Clarke offered the recipient an "apology for the long report but I know of no way to make it short. I am a fool and a trusting fool but never, and I mean never, a Liar."[21]

The Canadian tax authorities were a constant thorn in his side, but no one earned his ire more quickly than a person who questioned his book sense. Walter Roesch, English professor, librarian, and Marianist brother at the University of Dayton, wrote, upon receiving a package from Clarke, "I am quite unsatisfied with some of the items."[22] The *Britannica* "is not the original leather edition, but is a cheap reprint and I shall not accept it." Another book was "unfit for library use because the book is completely marked throughout, besides being water soaked." With another, the catalogue description did not match what was sent.

Predictably, Clarke was the picture of red-faced fury upon reading this note. He had little respect for Roman Catholics—an opinion he shared with a good number of people, except, presumably, his wife, who was one—and none at all for librarians. "At my age," Clarke replied, "I resent intensely a half formed librarian telling me my 'Description of books is FALSE.' I have handled more books than you will ever see, let alone examine and my clients accept my values or quit instantly being such."[23] Clarke then spent three paragraphs explaining to Roesch exactly why Roesch had better pay up or risk a lawsuit. (Threats of lawsuits that never quite materialized remained standard operating procedure for Clarke.)

The Marianist in this episode might well have felt like reacting to Clarke the way another disappointed customer, John H. Hilton, of Saskatoon, did. When *he* was unhappy with what he received from Clarke he wrote, "I wish you to know that I AM VERY DISAPPOINTED that you would imagine I'd be the sort of person who you can treat in this fashion."[24] Clarke had sent him items Hilton felt were significantly different from advertised (including some pages "evidently ripped from the front of some old rubbish you have picked off someone's garbage.") Hilton wrote:

> I am holding these two so called books, and if your refund is here in seven days you will have them returned BUT if you do not refund take my word for it you are surely in for a surprise—or maybe it won't be a surprise; maybe that's why you hide behind the name "Old Author's Farm" however even we in Saskatchewan have means of finding out who you are and brining you to the palce [*sic*] you seem preparing for.

You will find MY BILL enclosed and if you know what's good for you, you won't wait for any further lettrs [*sic*] from me.

Hilton, it seems, was treating Clarke the way Clarke was used to treating other people. Five days later, Clarke sent Hilton a refund via registered mail—which is the way it usually went when any recipient of his false descriptions or outright lies pushed back. In one instance, Clarke had a months-long battle with the estate of the author Louis Blake Duff, the "Samuel Johnson of Canada."[25] Duff had been a Clarke customer, and the book dealer had long coveted the author's collection, particularly of Canadiana. After Duff's death Clarke promised, in writing, to pay $1,500, plus postage, for the man's books. But when Clarke later changed his mind and wrote Duff's son a letter agreeing to pay only $1,000 for the books and $200 for postage, he explained that the material was worth, at best, $700. What the Duff estate did not know, of course, was that only ten days earlier Clarke had offered to sell a *part* of the Duff collection to the University of Texas for $5,000, noting, "I guarantee it to be worth minimum of $8,000; and closer to $10,000." He also offered Texas a separate part of the collection, at $3,000. That he was lying to either the Duff estate or the University of Texas was clear; he was probably lying to both.

In any event, he later capitulated—sort of—when the Duff estate insisted he honor the original offer. But before doing so, he wrote several letters of considerable length explaining the book business. In the middle of one fourteen-hundred-word missive, he noted, "I can't go on giving you lectures on values and why and how, as it goes on forever."[26] Clarke then continued his lecture, dropping in the names of his "colleagues" George Goodspeed and Theodore Schulte, and noting he had been in the book business for forty years.

Despite it all, Clarke ran a very successful business selling books, maps, stamps, and ephemera through the 1970s. He sold to the who's who of American and Canadian collectors: businessmen, doctors, lawyers, and many university professors, including several important academics. One of these was Henry Steele Commager, first of New York University, then Columbia, then Amherst. Over the course of several years, Commager bought books from Clarke, including a number of history books and the *Encyclopedia Britannica* (minus volume 11, which Clarke neglected to send).[27]

The former book thief was always a man who thought much of himself, and expected the same of others. One of the things bookselling did was to allow him entrée into arenas he otherwise would never have entered, and he did a great deal of business with very important people. He had a particular fondness for politicians, maybe because they could offer cover. The biggest name he dropped was that of Canadian Prime Minister ("my personal friend these many years") Mackenzie King. He and Clarke apparently had such a good relationship that the man—considered to be the most important PM in Canadian history, according to the bookseller—called Clarke the day he heard the Soviets got the H-bomb, and sobbed.[28] Clarke claimed both Winston Churchill and Franklin Roosevelt as clients as well as various governors and lieutenant governors (both American and Canadian), ambassadors, members of the US House of Representatives and Canadian Senate, and J. R. Smallwood, first premier of the Province of St. John's.

But despite all his success, and the relatively gentle treatment he had received given the enormity of his crimes against American libraries, Harold Borden Clarke never let go of a grudge—nor did he lose his fear that a whole range of people were out to do him harm. The fear he once had that emissaries of the Romm Gang were going to travel to commit violence against him did not subside so much as get replaced by fears of others. The Canadian government was always a looming specter in his life ("Three goons came in last winter, lied steadily an hour that it was just 'routine' then proceeded to snoop all over for desks and files"), and when he eventually concluded that long letters and name-dropping did not help him, he decided to leave the country altogether. As it was later for Harry Gold, the book business had been so good to Clarke that he, too, was able to move south—in his case, the Bahamas. He was "free down there of all forms of tax" and the "vast and endless paper work" and "outrageous and stupid demands" by the government.[29] Plus, the winters were much nicer. In 1959, he paid $60,000 in cash for two five-room apartments in Nassau.

But no matter where he went, he never lost his distinct and utter hatred for G. William Bergquist and his protégé, William Mahoney. Clarke rarely passed up a chance to take a shot at Bergquist, and when he did, he called it benevolence. (He took pains to note that Fiorello La Guardia was a client and, had Clarke wanted, he could have had the popular New York mayor take away Bergquist's pension.)[30] And though the menace of the Romm Gang and the Canadian government eventually receded in his mind, he never lost the idea that Bergquist would, for one reason or another, have him silenced.

But this was just the sort of weird paranoia Clarke trafficked in. There is little evidence that the genial special investigator thought at all of the Canadian in the remaining years of his life. Every decade or so, until he died in 1967, at age eighty-four, Bergquist would get a request from a reporter for some stories about his life in the world of book crime. He would usually oblige, telling tales of Joseph Cosey, a notorious forger, and of Romm, Gold, and Babyface Mahoney. But not Clarke. To his greatest antagonist, the strange and angry Canadian bookman remained the one thing he never wanted to be: forgotten.

Notes

Prologue

1. "Born in Boston," *Baltimore Sun*, January 17, 1909.
2. R. Eden Martin, "Collecting Poe," *Caxtonian*, June 2004, 1.
3. Rufus Wilmot Griswold, *Poets and Poetry of Early America, 17th ed.* (Philadelphia: Perry and McMillan, 1856), 469.
4. John Henry Ingram, *Edgar Allan Poe* (London: John Hogg, 1880), 78.
5. Arthur Hobson Quinn, *Edgar Allan Poe: A Critical Biography* (New York: Appleton-Century, 1941), 138–43.
6. Eric W. Carlson, *A Companion to Poe Studies* (Hartford, CT: Greenwood, 1996), 542; Charles Heartman and James Canny, *A Poe Bibliography* (Hattiesburg, MS: The Book Farm, 1943), 25.
7. Heartman and Canny, *A Poe Bibliography*, 25.
8. Ian Walker, ed. *Edgar Allan Poe, The Critical Heritage* (London: Routledge, 1986), 72.
9. *The Dial*, May 17, 1917; Col. Richard Gimbel, "Quoth the Raven," *Yale University Library Gazette*, April 1959, 142.
10. Edgar Allan Poe to James Russell Lowell, July 2, 1844. Reprinted in J. Gerald Kennedy, ed., *The Portable Edgar Allan Poe* (New York: Penguin, 2006), 490.
11. H. R., "Poe's Early Poems," *The Philobiblion*, March 1862.
12. Rufus Wilmot Griswold, "The Ludwig Article," originally in the October 9, 1849, *New York Tribune*. Reprinted in James Albert Harrison, *Life of Edgar Allan Poe* (New York: Thomas Crowell, 1903), 349.
13. Griswold, *Poets and Poetry of Early America, 17th ed.*, 469. Upon Poe's death, he used much of this same language to describe the 1827 publication of *Tamerlane*.

1. The Antics of the Leading Industrials

1. Marvin Mondlin and Roy Meador, *Book Row: An Anecdotal and Pictorial History of the Antiquarian Book Trade* (New York: Carroll & Graf, 2003), xv.

2. Christopher Morley, *The Haunted Bookshop* (New York: Doubleday, 1921), 240.

3. Ibid., 114.

4. Charles Cooke, "Two People," *New Yorker*, November 16, 1929, 23.

5. Ibid.

6. WPA, *Guide to New York City* (New York: Pantheon, 1982), 122.

7. Henry Roth, *Call It Sleep* (New York: Picador, 2005), 10.

8. Frederick Lewis Allen, *Since Yesterday* (New York: Harper, 1940), 2–3.

9. "The New York City Bookshops in the 1930s and 1940s," *Dictionary of Literary Biography Yearbook*, 1993, 143–49; Meyer Berger, "About New York," *New York Times*, February 1, 1956, 21.

10. Mondlin and Meador, *Book Row*, xvi.

11. Guido Bruno, *Adventures in American Bookshops, Antique Stores and Auction Rooms* (Detroit: Douglas Book Shop, 1922), 39. Bookselling was a grueling business with little room for error. Booksellers, even in the best of times, routinely went out of business. And even the most successful had to fight to stay alive. Charles Heartman notes that George D. Smith worked daily for "16, 17, 18 hours, and Sundays were required to catch up on unfinished work." Charles Heartman, *George D. Smith* (Hattiesburg, MS: The Book Farm, 1945), 7.

12. Mondlin and Meador, *Book Row*, 78.

13. Harry Gold, *The Dolphin's Path* (Chapel Hill, NC: Aberdeen Book Company, 1979), 11.

14. A. B. Shiffrin, *Mr. Pirate—A Romance* (New York: Mitchell Kennerley, 1937), 13–14. Lou Cohen had a similar experience at the Madison. "I had various duties. I took dictation, typed letters, arranged the stock, made delivieries, searched for books, did some packing, and waited on trade." Jacob Chernofsky, "Louis Cohen and the Argosy Book Store," *AB Bookman*, April 15, 1991, 1508.

15. Madeleine Stern, *Antiquarian Bookselling in the United States* (New York: Greenwood Press, 1985), ix–xv.

16. Mondlin and Meador, *Book Row*, 25.

17. Harold Borden Clarke, Unpublished remembrances of his time with book thieves in Boston and New York, 12. Archives of Ontario, F264.

18. Carolyn Wells, *Murder in the Bookshop* (Philadelphia: Lippincott, 1936), 102.

19. Walter Goldwater, "New York City Bookshops in the 1930s and 1940s," *Dictionary of Literary Biography Yearbook* (Detroit: Gale Research, 1994), 161–62.

20. Charles Everitt, *The Adventures of a Treasure Hunter* (New York: Little, Brown, 1951), 160. This story comes from the memoirs of a dealer and is probably exaggerated. But, if current textual sources are any indication, it is also at least mostly true. Yale University's Beinecke Library owns the autographed

manuscript of *The Ebb-Tide*. Housed as B6179, it contains chapters 1–9 and 11–12 on 115 folios numbered and written by Stevenson and dated at the foot of folio 108 as June 5, 1893. The missing chapter (ten) is Lloyd Osbourne's handwritten transcript, and it, too, is part of the Yale collection. So ten is likely the chapter Wells was missing; Yale, at some point, recognized it was a later creation and took it out of the original manuscript. See Peter Hinchcliffe and Catherine Kerrigan, *The Ebb-Tide* (Edinburgh: Edinburgh University Press 1995), 155–56.

21. This is a fact the author knows firsthand. But for a more weighty citation, see Charles Goodspeed, *Yankee Bookseller* (Boston: Houghton Mifflin, 1937), 240: In dealing with pitfalls of the trade—stolen and forged books—he notes, "Everyone in the trade is likely to stumble into them sometime."

22. "Rare Books Bring $8,889," *New York Times*, March 5, 1921. There is no shortage of articles tapping Romm as the ringleader of the group. See, for instance, description of Romm in John Kobler, "Trailing the Book Crooks," *Saturday Evening Post*, March 13, 1943, 18 and "Rare Book Easy to Steal but Hard to Sell," *Milwaukee Journal*, June 2, 1937.

23. Charles Romm, *The Charles Romm Collection of English and American Authors* (Arbor Press, 1921), unpaginated.

24. Goldwater, "New York City Bookshops," 150.

25. Jay Gertzman, *Bookleggers and Smuthounds: The Trade in Erotica, 1920–1940* (Philadelphia: University of Pennsylvania, 1999), 15.

26. Charles Heartman, "The Curse of Edgar Allan Poe," *The American Book Collector*, July 1933, 45.

27. Gold, *The Dolphin's Path*, 3–4, 14.

28. WPA, *Guide to New York City*, 401.

29. Ibid., 108.

30. Gold, *The Dolphin's Path*, 79–80, 119. His childhood is alluded to throughout *Dolphin's Path*, a memoir written in verse.

31. Harry Barton, "The Second Hand Book Business," *Bookseller and Stationer*, May 1922, 21.

32. Mondlin and Meador, *Book Row*, 115–16. Gold, 6, 18. There is no record of exactly how much money Gold started with, but $500 was a good entry-level sum. Lou Cohen started the Argosy Book Store in 1925 by borrowing just that much money from an uncle while Jack Biblo, of the famous Book Row store Biblo and Tannen, started his first store in 1928 with a mere $300 borrowed from his mother. Walter Goldwater started his store on Book Row in 1932 with $600. George D. Smith, the A. S. W. Rosenbach of his time, claimed he started his Fourth Avenue shop with $63. Because that was in the 1880s, it was at least possible he was telling the truth. See "Argosy Awash in Title Wave," *New York Daily News*, September 13, 1997; Obituary of Walter Goldwater, *New York Times*, June 28, 1985; Jack Biblo, "Used Book Seller for Half a Century," *New York Times*, June 18, 1998; Charles Heartman, *George D. Smith* (Hattiesburg, MS: The Book Farm, 1945), 5.

33. Shiffrin, *Mr. Pirate*, 26.

34. Marco Page, *Fast Company* (Philadelphia: Blakiston, 1928), 25.

35. Charles Goodspeed, *Yankee Bookseller*, 237.

36. Adolf Growoll, "The Profession of Bookselling," *Publishers Weekly*, 1893, 177.

37. Mondlin and Meador, *Book Row*, 115.

38. "Shops Here Linked to Library Thefts," *New York Times*, June 11, 1931; "Brains of Book Ring Thieves," *New York Herald*, June 11, 1931.

39. Gold, *The Dolphin's Path*, 11.

40. Everitt, *The Adventures of a Treasure Hunter*, 114. There are plenty of books and articles that mention book scouts, but Everitt talks about their importance to the trade as well as anyone. Another accessible account comes from David A. Randall, who describes his experiences in *Dukedom Large Enough* (New York: Random House, 1962).

41. Stanley Edgar Hyman, "Book Scout," *New Yorker*, November 8, 1952, 39. See also Calvin Trillin, "Scouting Sleepers," *New Yorker*, June 14, 1976, 86. This article gives an interesting take on more modern book scouting. In particular, Trillin learns from Larry McMurtry, one of America's great book scouts.

42. Harold Borden Clarke, Unpublished remembrances of his time with book thieves in Boston and New York, 14. Archives of Ontario, F264.

43. Ibid., 13.

44. Ibid., 17.

45. Page, *Fast Company*, 26. Page was the pen name for Harry Kurnitz. He based this book thief character on an actual thief he had met and studied. While not quite a roman à clef, this book closely follows the actions of men both Kurnitz and Bergquist knew.

46. Edwin White Gaillard, "The Book Larceny Problem, pt. II," *Library Journal*, April 1, 1921, 307.

47. Adolf Growoll, "The Profession of Bookselling," *Publishers Weekly*, 1893, 177.

48. Kenneth E. Carpenter, "Libraries," in *A History of the Book in America* (Chapel Hill: University of North Carolina Press, 2007), 301–12.

49. Everitt, *The Adventures of a Treasure Hunter*, 5.

50. Michael J. Walsh, "Adventures in Americana," in *Four Talks for Bibliophiles* (Philadelphia: Wm. Fell Co., 1958), 84.

51. Morriss H. Briggs, *Buying & Selling Rare Books* (New York: R.R. Bowker, 1927), 22.

52. John Kobler, "Trailing the Book Crooks," *Saturday Evening Post*, March 13, 1943, 18.

53. Keyes Metcalf, *Random Recollections of an Anachronism* (New York: Readex, 1980), 264–65; *Publishers Weekly*, December 1931, 2600; Plea Agreement, Charles Romm, Pen. #55681, February 10, 1932. New York City Municipal Archives. Romm's first major taste of real success was his sale of Americana, in 757 lots, with the Anderson Auction House in 1921. He continued to not only collect, but also contribute to the bibliographic collections in the field, including two relating to the works of Jack London. See "An Index to Nathan Van Patten," *Bibliographies and Bibliographical Contributions Relating to the Work*

of American and British Authors (Palo Alto, CA: Stanford University Press, 1934), 155.

54. Alfred Claghorn Potter and Edgar Huidekoper Wells, *Descriptive and Historical Notes on the Library of Harvard University* (Cambridge: Harvard University, 1911), 10.

55. "New York City Bookshops," 139–41, 151–52.

56. Bruno, *Adventures in American Bookshops, Antique Store and Auction Rooms*, 81.

57. See, generally, Metcalf's comments on this subject, along with "Buying and Selling Libraries," *New York Observer*, December 1, 1910.

58. Mondlin and Meador, *Book Row*, 64, quoting from "Review Copies," *New Yorker*, January 30, 1937, 12. See, in general, Mondlin and Meador, *Book Row*, 62–70.

59. "Indicted as Fences for Rare Book Loot," *New York Times*, December 5, 1931. Also, "Review Copies," 12.

60. Charles Goodspeed, *Yankee Bookseller*, 238.

61. Both Schwartz and Heartman mention that other book dealers knew these guys were crooked.

62. "Thieves and Forgers," *American Book Collector*, 1935, 69–70.

63. Charles Goodspeed, *Yankee Bookseller*, 238.

64. Growoll, "The Profession of Bookselling," 174.

65. These authors were constantly invoked by booksellers of the era as valuable to collect, even though the authors were alive.

66. Everitt, *The Adventures of a Treasure Hunter*, 23.

67. Clarke, Unpublished remembrances, 3.

68. Ibid., 14.

69. *New York v. Gold*, CR-68509, Statement of Samuel Dupree, January 4, 1934, 4.

70. There are any number of articles that mention the techniques for eradicating marks from books. But see, in general, "New York Library's Detective Has Unique Job," *Hartford Courant*, June 6, 1937; John Kobler, "Trailing the Book Crooks," *Saturday Evening Post*, March 13, 1943, 18; "Rare Book Easy to Steal but Hard to Sell," *Milwaukee Journal*, June 2, 1937.

71. Ric Burns and James Sanders, *New York* (New York: Knopf, 1999), 338.

72. Nicholas Basbanes, *Patience & Fortitude* (New York: HarperCollins, 2001), 191–93.

73. The address of the Anderson Galleries is well known, but see, for instance, the sale catalogue titled *Americana* from the Rhode Island Historical Society (New York: Anderson Galleries, 1921). Trump Park Avenue website http://www.trumpparkavenue.com/, accessed January 19, 2012.

74. George Goodspeed, *The Bookseller's Apprentice* (Philadelphia: Holmes Publishing, 1996), 43.

75. Gold, *The Dolphin's Path*, 11.

76. Page, *Fast Company*, 6.

77. "Demand for Rare Books Forces Prices Skyward," *New York Times*, December 16, 1923.

78. Charles Heartman, "Depression Proof," *American Book Collector*, July 1932, 6. Rare book dealers often had a close relationship with brokers and men who played the market simply because these rich men were collectors. And while this often gave dealers good insight into the market, and sound buys, it also left them vulnerable to heavy losses in 1929 and 1930. Heartman took a bath in the market because he listened to some of his broker clients. Even a decade after the event he was still sore, noting these brokers "had the souls of prostitutes. But why insult the latter, who are honest women and deliver the goods." *George D. Smith*, 15.

79. Edwin Wolf and J. F. Fleming, *Rosenbach* (Cleveland: World Publishing, 1960), 350.

80. Clarke, Unpublished remembrances, 13.

81. Harry Schwartz, *The Book Collecting Racket* (Milwaukee: Casanova Press, 1934), 20.

82. Clarke, Unpublished remembrances, 2–5.

83. James Lenox was known for his Americana collection long before this area became popular with collectors. This allowed him to get the absolute choicest pieces at relatively low prices. Add to this the donation he got from other collectors, like Evert Duyckinck, and his library, by 1931 a part of the NYPL, was arguably the best Americana library in existence. See, in general, Joel Silver, "James Lenox and His Library," *AB Bookman*, January 1, 1996, 5–11 and Henry Stevens, *Recollections of Mr. James Lenox of New York and the Formation of his Library* (London: Henry Stevens, 1886).

2. The Accumulated Wisdom

1. Christopher Gray, "Once It Held Many Pages," *New York Times*, February 10, 2002.

2. Phyllis Dain, *The New York Public Library: A History of Its Founding and Early History* (Ann Arbor: University Microfilms International, 1966), 4.

3. Gray, "Once It Held Many Pages."

4. Meyer Berger, "Public Library Here, 100 This Month," *New York Times*, February 24, 1954.

5. Gray, "Once It Held Many Pages."

6. Dain, *The New York Public Library*, 8.

7. "The Complaint of a Poor Scholar," *New York Times*, July 19, 1855.

8. "Stealing from the Astor Library," *New York Times*, August 6, 1881.

9. Allen, *Since Yesterday*, 23.

10. "CHA Bjerregaard,, Librarian, Dies," *New York Times*, January 28, 1922. Jack Richmond, *Immigrants All, Americans All* (New York: Comet Press, 1955), 4.

11. "Stole Rare Books to Sell," *The Sun*, March 6, 1893.

12. *The Critic*, March 11, 1893, 155.

13. "Is Fond of Literature," *The Daily Inter-Ocean*, March 6, 1893.

14. Travis McDade, "Frederick Lauriston Bullard: Lincoln Scholar, Pulitzer Prize Winner, Book Thief," under review and on file with the author.

15. "Divinity Student Turns out to be a Professional Book Thief," *Minneapolis Journal*, December 23, 1898.

16. "Stole Rare Books to Sell," *The New York Sun*, March 6, 1893.

17. There are several sources about bookselling in Manhattan in the nineteenth century. See, in general, W. H. Wallace, "The Booksellers of Nassau Street in the 1850s," *AB Bookman*, April 11, 1988, 1457. Edwin Hoffman, "The Bookshops of New York City," *New York History*, January 1949, 53. Jacob Chernofsky, "The Mendoza Bookstore: Surviving a Century of Change," *AB Bookman*, April 11, 1988, 1490.

18. "Valuable Book Stolen," *New York Times*, March 6, 1893. Douglas was not only broke in New York. He was wanted in Washington, DC, for seventy-five dollars he owed a local attorney. *J. S. Easby-Smith v. Theodore Olynthus Douglas*, No-33393, November 8, 1892.

19. *Publishers Weekly*, March 11, 1893, 427.

20. "Special Notices," *Publishers Weekly*, February 2, 1893, 280.

21. "Arrested for Robbing Libraries," *New York Tribune*, March 6, 1893.

22. "Douglas to Be Tried," *New York Times*, March 7, 1893.

23. "More About Brockway's Paddle," *New York Times*, December 14, 1893.

24. Charles Woodward, "About Baker and Woodward." Broadside. New York Historical Society, SY1893 #3.

25. Dain, *The New York Public Library*, 117–21.

26. Henry Hope Reed, *The New York Public Library* (New York: Norton, 1986), 6–10.

27. Ibid.

28. "Their First Day on the Bench," *New York Times*, July 13, 1895; "New Men on the Bench," *New York Tribune*, July 13, 1895.

29. "A Judicial Comparison," *New York Tribune*, August 31, 1895.

30. "Magistrate Pleads for Boy," *New York Times*, December 22, 1897.

31. Ibid.

32. "The Library Presses Its Charge," *New York Tribune*, December 22, 1897.

33. Dain, *The New York Public Library*, 113.

34. "Stealing Library Books," *New York Tribune*, January 2, 1898.

35. Dain, *The New York Public Library*, 113.

36. "The Library Book Thief," *Dallas Morning News*, June 23, 1907.

37. "Five Thousand Books Stolen Within a Year," *New York Tribune*, April 17, 1904.

38. "Hits or Misses," *Boston Globe*, January 21, 1904.

39. *The Newsman*, January, 1891, 4.

40. "Mr. Goff on the Bench," *New York Times*, January 8, 1895.

41. "Recorder John W. Goff," *Green Bag*, November 1897, 470.

42. "Mr. Goff on the Bench."

43. "Rob Libraries of Rare Books," *The Sun*, April 9, 1904.

44. "Book Thief Pleads Guilty," *New York Times*, May 5, 1904, 3; "Sketched Suspected Thief," *New York Times*, April 9, 1904.

45. "Alleged Book Thief Caught," *New York Daily Tribune*, April 4, 1904.

46. "Rob Libraries of Rare Books."

47. "Alleged Book Thief Held," *New York Tribune*, April 12, 1904.

48. "Mrs. Osborn's Page Goes Free," *New York Tribune*, May 7, 1904.

49. "Book Thief Gets a Year," *New York Times*, May 7, 1904.

50. David Gray, "A Modern Temple of Education," *Harper's*, March 1911, 562.

51. John Shaw Billings, *Book Thieves*, July 15, 1910. Circular. New York Public Library Archives, Special Investigator, Thefts & Losses.

52. *Library Journal*, October 1910, 464.

53. *Edwin White Gaillard, A Tribute* (New York: New York Public Library, 1929), 8–10.

54. Editorial, *Atlanta Medical and Surgical Journal*, March 1886, 58.

55. "New York Public Library Has Its Police Department," *New York Tribune*, October 5, 1913.

56. Edwin White, "Draft," June 20, 1928, 1. This is the draft of the synopsis of the special investigator job Gaillard was working on when he died. New York Public Library Archives, Special Investigator, 1924–1928.

57. "Book Thieves," *Library Journal*, June 1904, 308.

58. "Book Thieves," *Literary Collector*, August 1904, 89.

59. Ibid.

60. Edwin Anderson to William Kipp, December 16, 1914. New York Public Library Archives, Special Investigator, 13/17.

61. "Draft," 2.

62. "It's Becoming Harder to Steal Books in the Library," *New York Herald Tribune*, January 19, 1919.

63. *Edwin White Gaillard, A Tribute*, 10.

64. "Draft," 2–3.

65. Edwin White Gaillard, "The Book Larceny Problem, Part. II." April 1, 1921, 301–12.

66. Thomas Lannon, "A History of the Library as Seen Through Notable Reseachers," available at http://www.nypl.org/blog/2011/05/02/history-library-seen-through-notable-researchers, accessed January 27, 2012. Compare the call slip differences, between 1928 and 1939, on the examples shown here.

67. "New York Public Library Has Its Police Department."

68. Metcalf, *Random Recollections of an Anachronism*, 155–61.

69. Phyllis Dain, "Harry M. Lydenberg and American Library Resources," *The Library Quarterly*, October 1977, 456.

70. "New York Public Library Has Its Police Department."

71. Edwin White Gaillard to Edwin Anderson, July 22, 1913. New York Public Library Archives, SI, 13/17.

72. Edwin White Gaillard to Edwin Anderson, June 5, 1914. New York Public Library Archives, SI, 13/17.

73. Edwin White Gaillard to Edwin Anderson, December 31, 1924. New York Public Library Archives, SI, 23/28.

74. "Steals 4 Cab Loads of Library Books," *New York Times*, February 3, 1925.

75. "Book Thief Released," *New York Times*, February 10, 1925.
76. "Charles P. Cox Dies," *New York Times*, July 26, 1933.
77. "Book Thefts at Brentano's," *Publishers Weekly*, September 27, 1902, 576.
78. "Accused of Book Thefts," *New York Times*, September 22, 1902.
79. Edwin Gaillard to Edwin Anderson, January 21, 1916. New York Public Library Archives, SI, 13/17.
80. "It's Becoming Harder to Steal Books in the Library," *New York Herald Tribune*, January 19, 1919.
81. Edwin White Gaillard to Edwin Anderson, July 13, 1920. New York Public Library Archives, SI, 15/23.
82. Edwin White Gaillard to Edwin Anderson, August 7, 1920. New York Public Library Archives, SI, 15/23.
83. Edwin Gaillard to Edwin Anderson, December 4, 1914. New York Public Library Archives, SI, 13/17.
84. Edwin White Gaillard to Edwin Anderson, November 20, 1914. New York Public Library Archives, SI, 13/17.
85. "It's Becoming Harder to Steal Books in the Library."

3. A Purloined Poe

1. Dupree recounted various parts of his interactions with Gold, and his time in New York, in four separate documents. Three of these were statements, taken as sworn depositions, on November 15, 1933; January 4, 1934; and April 2, 1934. He also wrote a five-page letter to William Bergquist dated only "Thanksgiving," but probably written after his first deposition—at which Bergquist, like always, was present—in 1933. All are available in the *New York v. Harry Gold* file at the New York Municipal Archives. Further information on Dupree comes from Keyes Metcalf, who met with the man, and heard his story, on several occasions.
2. Stephen Crane, "An Experiment in Misery," in Kevin Kerrane and Ben Yagoda, eds., *The Art of Fact* (New York: Simon & Schuster, 1997), 63.
3. James Trager, *The New York Chronology* (New York: HarperCollins, 2003), 457.
4. Book Exchange, *New York Times*, September 21, 1930. The "gnome-like" description is from Manuel Tarshish, "The Fourth Avenue Book Trade," *Publishers Weekly*, October 20, 1969, 54. Dupree told Bergquist that Giller was like a more cautious version of Harry Gold.
5. *New York v. Harry Gold*, Statement of Samuel Dupree, November 15, 1933, 2.
6. E. W. Gaillard to W. B. Badger, February 3, 1914. New York Public Library Archives.
7. E. W. Gaillard to Edwin Anderson, December 22, 1914. New York Public Library Archives.
8. Dupree letter, 4.
9. *New York v. Gold*, Statement of Samuel Dupree, January 4, 1934.
10. Allen, *Since Yesterday*, 16.

11. J. H. Whitty, *The Complete Poems of Edgar Allan Poe* (Boston: Houghton Mifflin, 1917), 217. The description of the NYPL copy comes from author's inspection in July 2010, as well as the description in the grand jury testimony of September 7, 1932.

12. A. S. W. Rosenbach, *Books and Bidders* (Boston: Little, Brown, 1927), 4.

13. "Unique Value of Poe First Editions Among Book Collectors," *New York Times*, January 17, 1909.

14. "Scarce First Editions Appreciated," *New York Times*, November 24, 1894.

15. "The Auction Season of 1906," *Publishers Weekly*, February 16, 1907, 725.

16. "Tamerlane Brings $1,460 at Book Sale," *New York Times*, March 20, 1909.

17. "American Auction Sales, 1910," *Publishers Weekly*, January 28, 1911, 126. See also Edgar Allan Poe Society of Baltimore's fine online census. http://www.eapoe.org/works/editions/atmp.htm, accessed November 7, 2012.

18. "Few Nuggets More Highly Prized by the Collector," *Washington Post*, January 17, 1909.

19. *The Dial*, May 17, 1917, 447. An *Al Aaraaf* or two came up under less-than-ideal circumstances. One came up for sale in May 1917, while war-induced profit taxes and lack of transit between New York and London severely depressed book prices. It still brought in nearly $1,000.

20. Charles Heartman, "The Curse of Edgar Allan Poe," *American Book Collector*, January 1933, 46.

21. "Asks $2,000 for Rare Poe," *New York Times*, April 1, 1913.

22. Edwin Wolf and J. F. Fleming, *Rosenbach*, (Cleveland: World Publishing, 1960), 321.

23. Advertisement, *Baltimore Sun*, September 27, 1930.

24. J. Wynn Rousuck, "Tamerlane: 15-cent Bomb to $123,000 Gem," *The Sun*, December 1, 1974.

25. Nicholas Basbanes, *A Gentle Madness* (New York: Henry Holt, 1995), 422.

26. Chris Kaltenbach, "Poe Rarity Sells for $662,500," *Baltimore Sun*, December 4, 2009.

27. Josephine Young Case, *Owen D. Young and American Enterprise* (Boston: Godine Press, 1982), 413.

28. Charles Everitt, *The Adventures of a Treasure Hunter* (Boston: Little, Brown, 1952), 13.

29. Mondlin and Meador, *Book Row*, 49.

30. David A. Randall, *The JK Lilly Collection of Edgar Allan Poe*, (Bloomington: Indiana University Press, 1964), 11. What made this particularly valuable is that there were only two other copies known to exist. David A. Randall, *Dukedom Large Enough* (New York: Random House, 1962), 190.

31. "Rare Copy of Poe's Al Aaraaf Saves Aged Woman," *Washington Post*, March 31, 1913.

32. "Morgan Pays $3,800 for a Poe Pamphlet," *New York Times*, November 25, 1909.

33. Gold, *The Dolphin's Path*, 24.

34. Page, *Fast Company*, 77–8.

35. "Notes on Rare Books," *New York Times*, June 29, 1924. What became the Reserve Book Room was described, upon the opening of the library in 1911, this way: "On the court side, along the Fortieth street corridor...are three rooms for the shelving of the Americana, early printed books, manuscripts, and other material requiring particular attention." "The New Building of the New York Public Library," *Library Journal*, May 1911, 225.

36. Jefferson Bell, "Demand for Rare Books," *New York Times*, December 16, 1923.

37. New York Public Library Rare Book and Manuscript Division Accession Sheet. New York Public Library Archives, Wilberforce Eames Papers.

38. Joel Silver, "James Lenox and His Library," *AB Bookman*, January 1, 1996, 5. The description of the Lenox collection comes from "Notes on Special Collections Libraries in the United States," in *Bibliographical Contributions* (Cambridge: Harvard University, 1892), 44.

39. Metcalf, *Random Recollections of an Anachronism*, 112.

40. John Kobler, "Trailing the Book Crooks," *Saturday Evening Post*, March 13, 1943, 19.

41. *New York v. Gold*, Dupree statement, January 4, 1934, 1–4.

42. Harry Lydenburg to A. S. W. Rosenbach, January 11, 1931. Rosenbach Museum and Library; Joseph Moldenhauer, "Bartleby and The Custom-House," *Delta*, November, 1978, 21–23.

43. Jerry Patterson, *Fifth Avenue* (New York: Rizzoli, 1998), 94–95.

44. E. B. White, *Here is New York* (New York: The Little Bookroom, 1949), 28.

45. Metcalf, *Random Recollections of an Anachronism*, 270–71. Also, Dupree mentions his time in the NYPL in each of his statements.

46. "The New Building of the New York Public Library," *Library Journal*, May 1911, 225.

47. Metcalf, *Random Recollections of an Anachronism*, 260–65.

48. Alexander Woolcott, "Da Capo," *New Yorker*, April 6, 1929, 38.

49. Matthew Bruccoli, *The Fortunes of Mitchell Kennerley* (New York: Harcourt Brace Jovanovich, 1986), 199. Along with Bruccoli, David Randall, who was in attendance, has a long section on the Kern. There was a great deal of coverage for the Kern sale, much of which I quote. Except as otherwise noted, most of the Kern sale information comes from these two sources. For a fairly academic account of the sale (one I did not consult until after this section had been written), see Arthur Freeman, "The Jazz Age Library of Jerome Kern" in Robin Meyers, Michael Harris, and Giles Mandelbrote, eds., *Under the Hammer: Book Auctions Since the Seventeenth Century* (New Castle, DE: Oak Knoll, 2001), 209–28.

50. Wolf and Fleming, *Rosenbach*, 308.

51. John Winterich, "Dr. Rosenbach," *Harper's*, March 1956, 80.

52. Charles Heartman, *George D. Smith* (Hattiesburg, MS: The Book Farm, 1945), 10. There were three other bidders for the Gutenberg that day. A. S. W. Rosenbach, still in the nascent stages of his career, was bested early. But London's Bernard Quaritch hung around until $30,000, and Philadelphia's Joseph Widener pushed Huntington, $1,000 at a time, to the even $50,000. "Gutenberg Bible Sold for $5,000," *New York Times*, April 25, 1911.

53. "Bulls and Books," *New York Times*, January 10, 1929.

54. Randall, *Dukedom Large Enough*, 4.

55. Ibid., 12.

56. Talk of the Town, "Writ in Gold," *New Yorker*, April 28, 1928, 16. Rosenbach's biographers note that the Doctor spent $72,000 at the John Quinn sale in 1923, mostly in direct competition with Wells, who only "managed to snatch from" Rosenbach one lot. Wolf and Fleming, *Rosenbach*, 189–92. The Hoe sale excepted, George D. Smith generally discouraged collectors attending auctions precisely to avoid the situations created by the likes of the Rosenbach/Wells rivalry. "He saw at first hand the disastrous consequences resulting from collectors attending auction sales in person and bidding recklessly and sometimes spitefully against each other, to the delight of the auctioneers and the owners of the material dispersed in such a manner." Charles Heartman, *George D. Smith* (Beauvoir, MS: Book Farm, 1945), 4.

57. Robert Coates, "Books at a Million," *New Yorker*, January 19, 1929, 9.

58. Bruccoli, *The Fortunes of Mitchell Kennerley*, 203–7.

59. Randall, *Dukedom Large Enough*, 197. Also, Freeman, "The Jazz Age Library of Jerome Kern," 223.

60. Talk of the Town, "Da Capo," *New Yorker*, April 6, 1929. See also Randall, *Dukedom Large Enough*, 12.

61. "Talk of the Town," *New Yorker*, April 26, 1928. This story is almost certainly apocryphal, at least as recounted. The collector, Harry Widener, died on the *Titanic* in 1912, before Rosenbach could likely mark his stock up by $1 million with any hope of selling it. So, too, in the years before 1912, it was far less common for a man to make $1 million in a single day in the stock market. In the late 1920s, however, both parts of the story would have been believable. In any event, Rosenbach absolutely marked up his stock—as did most other dealers—with some regularity in the 1920s, as prices soared.

62. Randall, *Dukedom Large Enough*, xiv.

63. "The Weather," *New York Times*, January 10, 1931; David Gray, "A Modern Temple of Education," *Harper's*, March 1911, 564.

64. Marion K. Sanders, "A Slight Case of Library Fever," *Harper's*, April 1962, 68.

65. *Handbook of The New York Public Library* (New York: New York Public Library, 1916), 51; Edwin White Gaillard, "The Book Larceny Problem," *Library Journal*, March 15, 1920, 254.

66. New York Public Library Report, 1920, 22.

67. "J.P. Morgan Shows Noted Manuscripts at Public Library," *New York Times*, December 8, 1924, 1; Malcolm Ross, "Scholar's Paradise," *New Yorker*, April 9, 1932, 50.

67. "Exhibition," *Bulletin of the NYPL*, January 1931, 19.

69. "Dealer Is Indicted in Rare Book Theft," *New York Times*, September 9, 1932; Dupree, statements and letter.

70. Metcalf, *Random Recollections of an Anachronism*, 261–62.

71. E.B.White, *Here Is New York*, 16.

72. Carolyn Wells, *Murder in the Bookshop* (Philadelphia: Lippincott, 1936), 55.

4. Scholarship and Investigation

1. "Books and Crooks Are His Specialty," *New York Times*, January 25, 1949. There are various sources detailing Bergquist's early life, including Keyes Metcalf's recollections and John Kolber, "Trailing the Book Crooks," *Saturday Evening Post*, March 13, 1943.

2. *Illinois in the World War, An Illustrated History of the Thirty-Third Division* (Chicago: States Publication Society, 1921), 659.

3. Metcalf, *Random Recollections of an Anachronism*, 257.

4. Ibid.

5. Dain, *The New York Public Library*, 741.

6. Ernest J. Reece, "The New York Public Library School," *Library Journal*, March 1, 1922, 215.

7. Metcalf, *Random Recollections of an Anachronism*, 73.

8. Wally Pipp was the popular starting first baseman for the New York Yankees from 1915 to 1925. Still in his prime, he was replaced for one game in the starting lineup by a young Lou Gehrig—a legend who never gave the starting position back.

9. Metcalf, *Random Recollections of an Anachronism*, 262.

10. Kobler, "Trailing the Book Crooks," *Saturday Evening Post*, March 13, 1943, 18.

11. Edgar Allan Poe, "The Purloined Letter," in *The Works of Edgar Allan Poe in Ten Volumes* (Chicago: Stone & Kimball, 1894), 168.

12. The other two books, while valuable, were not nearly as rare as the Poe. It is a universal fact of the book theft business that thieves need to steal valuable, but not too valuable, books. If everyone in the business knows where all the copies are, it is not a book worth stealing. Regarding these two books in particular, Bergquist made the point several years later. "The favored class runs between $400 and $1,000. The 'Moby Dicks' and 'Scarlet Letters' are among the dangerous things [to protect], for the discovery of a new book in this class doesn't immediately set every bibliophile on the trail to prove or disprove." "Rare Book Easy to Steal but Hard to Sell," *Milwaukee Journal*, June 2, 1937.

13. John Kobler, "Yrs. Truly, A. Lincoln," *New Yorker*, February 25, 1956, 38.

14. G. William Bergquist, "Rare Book Easy to Steal."

15. Harry Lydenburg to A. S. W. Rosenbach, January 11, 1931. Rosenbach Museum and Library.

16. Metcalf, *Random Recollections of an Anachronism*, 261.

17. Terrance Greenwood, "Arthur Swann, Lover of Books," *The American Book Collector*, October 1932, 215–16. Anderson hardly noticed his absence. It remained one of the biggest auction houses for books in the world. Along with the Kern sale of 1929, it also sold off Charles Romm's first batch of American and English firsts, in some 757 lots, in March 1921.

18. Donald Dickinson, *Dictionary of American Antiquarian Bookdealers* (Westport, CT: Greenwood Press, 1998), 214.

19. Advertisement, *New York Times*, April 27, 1924.

20. "Notes on Rare Books," *New York Times*, April 26, 1931.

21. "Notes on Rare Books," *New York Times*, October 13, 1929.

22. Percy Hutchinson, "Mr. Pirate and other Recent Works," *New York Times*, July 11, 1937.

23. Lisa Jo Sagola, *The Girl Who Fell Down* (Boston: Northeastern University Press, 2003), 486.

24. "New Plays in Manhattan," *Time Magazine*, January 29, 1951, 53.

25. Miles Jefferson, "An Empty Season on Broadway," *Phylon*, 1951, 129.

26. Everitt, *The Adventures of a Treasure Hunter*, 120.

27. A. B. Shiffrin, *Mr. Pirate*, 24.

28. Gold, *The Dolphin's Path*, 14–15.

29. *New York v. Gold*, Statement of Abraham Shiffran [*sic*], January 8, 1934.

30. Jack Tannen of the long-running Book Row shop Biblo and Tannen noted that when someone requested pornography, he was forced to go to Harry Gold to find out what the customer was talking about. Gold then supplied, "at what I felt were outrageous prices," as many pornographic books as the store could take. Jacob L. Chernofsky, "Biblo and Tannen: A Fourth Avenue Landmark," *AB Bookman*, April 14, 1986, 1669. Tannen's partner, Jack Biblo, in a later interview, noted word of mouth between dealers was key to knowing who could be trusted with illicit material. See Jay Gertzman, *Bookleggers and Smuthounds: The Trade in Erotica, 1920–1940* (Philadelphia: University of Pennsylvania Press, 1999), 61.

31. Charles Heartman, "The Curse of Edgar Allan Poe," *American Book Collector*, January 1933, 47.

32. *New York v. Gold*, Grand Jury Testimony, September 7, 1932, 1–4.

33. Talk of the Town, "Mezzotint," *New Yorker*, November 4, 1928, 17.

34. "Books Wanted," *Publishers Weekly*, February 4, 1922, 302; *New York Tribune*, January 29, 1922.

35. Randall, *Dukedom Large Enough*, 198–99.

36. *New York v. Gold*, Grand Jury, 3.

37. A remarkable number of the memoirs of booksellers are basically anecdote delivery devices. Rosbenbach's *Books and Bidders* and *A Bookhunter's Holiday* are rich with stories of acquisitions and near misses; Kraus's *A Rare Book Saga* is more like a proper biography, though it, too, deals largely with triumphs and accomplishments. This is true of most of these types of books simply because that is what people want to read about. The idea of possessing fantastic books for a short while and then willingly passing them on is a trait shared, as a necessity of the business, by all successful dealers—indeed, it is what separates them from collectors. And it continues to this day. The magazine *Fine Books & Collections* has a series on its *Fine Books Notes* blog called "Bright Young Booksellers." On December 22, 2011, it interviewed David

Eilenberger, a new antiquarian bookseller in Chapel Hill, North Carolina. When asked what he personally collects, he noted that he buys almost nothing for himself. "I do not have much desire to collect. My craving for books is satisfied by having interesting volumes in my possession for a period of time and moving on to other things once they sell."

38. *New York v. Gold*, Grand Jury, 4.

39. Arthur Swann to Harry Gold, 1927. Grolier Club Archives.

40. Norman Hall, "Polonius was Right," *Publishers Weekly*, October 31, 1931, 2013.

41. Malcolm Ross, "Scholar's Paradise," *New Yorker*, April 9, 1932, 50.

42. Nicholas Basbanes, *A Gentle Madness* (New York: Henry Holt & Co., 1995), 211.

43. Mondlin and Meador, *Book Row*, 53.

44. "Cheap," *New Yorker*, April 13, 1946, 25. Ironically, in a result that would have irritated him if he had not been its ringleader, Rosenbach then conspired to get the *Alice* purchased by a consortium of collectors with the express intent that it be donated to the Library of Congress and then, on behalf of the United States, to the British Museum, where it remains today.

45. Randall, *Dukedom Large Enough*, 29.

46. John Carter, "Playing the Rare Book Market," *Harper's*, April 1960, 74.

47. William Targ, *Indecent Pleasures* (New York: Macmillan, 1975), 371.

48. See, for instance, *1933 Bulletin of the NYPL* for examples both of collections purchased for and items donated to the NYPL collection.

49. Everitt, *The Adventures of a Treasure Hunter*, 87.

50. John Crichton, The American Antiquarian Book Trade, in *Book Talk*, Robert Jackson and Carol Rothkopf, eds. (New Castle, DE: Oak Knoll Press, 2006), 95.

51. Leona Rostenberg and Madeleine Stern, "The Changing Rare Book Trade, 1950–2000," *Rare Books and Manuscripts*, 2004, 15.

52. Heartman, "The Curse of Edgar Allan Poe," 47.

53. Randall, *The JK Lilly Collection*, 7.

54. Ibid., 24.

55. Edward Anderson to Edwin White Gaillard, October 3, 1928, New York Public Library Archives, Draper Employment Fund File.

56. Edwin White Gaillard to Edward Anderson, June 20, 1928, New York Public Library Archives, Special Investigator, 1924–8.

57. Kobler, "Trailing the Book Crooks."

58. *New York v. Gold*, Additional Grand Jury, September 7, 1932, 6.

59. Kobler, "Trailing the Book Crooks," 101.

60. Robert Hallett, "Private Eye in a Public Library," *Christian Science Monitor*, December 15, 1950.

61. *Report of the New York Public Library for 1931* (New York: New York Public Library, 1932), 294.

62. Edwin White Gaillard, "Tentative List of Regulations." New York Public Library Archives, Special Investigator, 1931.

5. *The Boston Scene*

1. *Annual Report of the Trustees of the Public Library of the Town of Brookline, 1878–1879* (Brookline, MA: Chronicle Press, 1879), 182.

2. "Crimes and Casualties," *Boston Globe*, November 27, 1879.

3. *Annual Report*, 182.

4. W. B. Clarke, "Book Thieving and Mutilation," *Library Journal*, September 1879, 249.

5. "Conviction for Book Thieving," *Library Journal*, October 1879, 377.

6. Samuel Green, "Capture of a Notorious Book Thief," *Library Journal*, January 1880, 48.

7. Ibid.

8. Harold Borden Clarke, Unpublished remembrances of his time with book thieves in Boston and New York, 10, Archives of Ontario, F264.

9. "Looting of Libraries is Charged," *Boston Post*, June 9, 1931; Fred Inglis, "Huge Collection of Rare Books and Old Papers," *Ottawa Citizen*, January 4, 1956.

10. Christopher Redmond, *Welcome to America, Mr. Sherlock Holmes* (Toronto: Simon & Pierre, 1987), 214.

11. Clarke, Unpublished remembrances, 29.

12. Ibid., 1–2.

13. Perry Duis, *The Saloon: Public Drinking in Chicago and Boston* (Urbana: University of Illinois Press, 1999), 92.

14. Clarke, Unpublished remembrances, 29–35.

15. Buckley to Charles Belden, April 18, 1929. Boston Public Library Archives, Harold Clarke file.

16. Travis McDade, *The Book Thief: The True Crimes of Daniel Spiegelman* (New York: Praeger, 2006).

17. Charles Goodspeed, *Yankee Bookseller*, 239.

18. George Goodspeed, *The Bookseller's Apprentice*, 50.

19. Charles Belden, "Urgent," February 7, 1930. Circular. Boston Public Library Archives, HC.

20. H. Langevin to Louis Ranlett, March 11, 1930. Boston Public Library Archives, HC.

21. Oscar Wegelin to Charles Belden, February 8, 1930. Boston Public Library archives, HC.

22. Mondlin and Meador, *Book Row*, 46.

23. Ibid., 111–12.

24. Oscar Wegelin to Charles Belden, February 8, 1930. Boston Public Library archives, HC.

25. Everitt, *The Adventures of a Treasure Hunter*, 48.

26. "L. Felix Ranlett, Retired Librarian," *Boston Globe*, October 15, 1989.

27. *Annual Report of the Trustees of the Public Library of the City of Boston, 1928–1929* (Boston: Boston Public Library, 1929), 41.

28. Felix Ranlett to William Bergquist, April 8, 1930. Boston Public Library Archives, HC.

29. "Book Racket Thefts Total $500,000," *Boston Evening Transcript*, June 9, 1931.
30. Felix Ranlett to Charles Belden, May 28, 1930. Boston Public Library Archives, HC.
31. Dierdorff to Felix Ranlett, March 3, 1930. Boston Public Library Archives, HC.
32. Michael Crowley, "Record of Events," March 3, 1930. Boston Public Library Archives, HC.
33. Borden Clarke to Charles Belden, May 25, 1930. Boston Public Library Archives, HC.
34. Felix Ranlett to Charles Belden, June 16, 1930. Boston Public Library Archives, HC.
35. William Bergquist to Charles Belden, April 5, 1930. Boston Public Library Archives, HC.
36. "Sherlock Holmes of the Library," *The Pentwater News*, December 14, 1945.
37. "Indict Book Thief on Twenty Counts," *Harvard Crimson*, November 4, 1931.
38. "Cambridge Court Drops Books Larceny Charge," *Boston Globe*, November 14, 1931.
39. Robert Blake in *Harvard University, Report of the President, 1929–1930*, (Cambridge: Harvard University, 1930), 221.
40. *Annual Report of the Trustees of the Public Library*.
41. "Lampy Artists Not Allowed to Sketch Widener Stiles," *Harvard Crimson*, October 9, 1930.
42. Clarke, Unpublished remembrances, 29.
43. Kobler, "Trailing the Book Crooks," 18.
44. "Clarke Unable to Get $5000 Bail," *Boston Globe*, June 10, 1931.
45. Felix Ranlett to William Bergquist, June 26, 1930. Boston Public Library Archives, HC.
46. Blake in *Harvard University*, 230.

6. *Someone Qualified as a Bookman*

1. Charles Goodspeed, *Yankee Bookseller*, 26.
2. "Looting of Libraries is Charged," *Boston Post*, June 9, 1931.
3. "Gave University Rare Books," *New York Times*, June 11, 1931.
4. Clarke, Unpublished remembrances, 30.
5. "Dr. Clarke Held For Hearing on Saturday," *Clinton Courant*, June 13, 1931.
6. Ibid.; "Withdrew Not Guilty Plea," *Clinton Courant*, November 20, 1931. Even in Clinton, this news was not exactly burning up the presses. This single-column article appeared next to a two-column article telling the box scores of the town's three bowling leagues. The "Men's club bowlers of the Church of the good Shepherd performed on the lanes on the holiday night and as a result the Israelites vanquished the Canaanites by taking four points and the [J]ebusites took three from the Moabites." Also, the "Heaters took four points from the Percolators and the Toasters three from the Washers in the Clinton Gas Light Co. league bowled on Tuesday night."

7. "Clarke in Lowell Two Days Last Week," *Lowell Sun*, June 9, 1931; "Poe's Conchologist's First Book," *New York Times*, June 18, 1898.
8. Clarke, Unpublished remembrances, 29.
9. This is covered in various documents and publications. See "Story Stirs Library Here," *New York Times*, June 11, 1931; "Book Thief Changes His Plea to Guilty," *Boston Globe*, November 11, 1931; Plea Agreement, Ben Harris, Pen. #55760, March 9, 1932. New York City Municipal Archives, *Gold* file.
10. "Harold Clarke Goes to Grand Jury," *Clinton Daily Courant*, June 13, 1931. See also, Kobler, "Trailing the Book Crooks," 18.
11. Kobler, "Trailing the Book Crooks," 18; "Looting of Libraries"; Clarke, Unpublished remembrances, 30; "Dr. Clarke Held"; "Book Thief Changes His Plea."
12. Metcalf, *Random Recollections of an Anachronism*, 262–65.
13. Sanka Knox, "Rare Book Sleuth to End Library Job," *New York Times*, December 15, 1960.
14. A. S. W. Rosenbach, *The Unpublishable Memoirs* (New York: Mitchell Kennerly, 1917), 115.
15. Gaillard, "Book Larceny," 247.
16. Rosenbach, *The Unpublishable Memoirs*, 317.
17. E. V. Lucas, "Notes on an American Visit," *Harper's*, August 1934, 330.
18. Rosenbach, *The Unpublishable Memoirs*, 105.
19. He represented himself as a doctor, but almost immediately reporters doubted his credentials. On June 13, he was described in *Publishers Weekly* as "Dr. Clarke, thus self-styled on the strength of a diploma from a Chicago school of chiropractice..." and by the *New York Times* with "Doctor" in quotations. By August, the *Times* dropped the title altogether.
20. "Accused of Book Thefts," *New York Times*, June 9, 1931; "Allege Wholesale Book Loot by Ruse," *Boston Daily Globe*, June 9, 1931; "The Weather," *Boston Daily Globe*, June 8, 1931. Other *Globe* editions before and after this date mention a particularly hot early summer; "Brains of Book Ring Thieves," *New York Herald*, June 11, 1931; Clarke, Unpublished remembrances, 30.
21. "Rare Book Thief Caught," *Publishers Weekly*, June 13, 1931, 2791; "Robs Libraries of Rare Books," *Boston Herald*, June 9, 1931. Clarke, 3; "Allege Wholesale."
22. "Book Racket Thefts Total $500,000," *Boston Evening Transcript*, June 9, 1931.
23. "Identifies 28 Books," *Lowell Sun*, June 10, 1931.
24. Clarke, Unpublished remembrances, 29–30.
25. "Book Racket."
26. *Boston Daily Post*, June 8, 1931.
27. "Rare Book Thief Caught."
28. "Shops Here Linked to Library Thefts," *New York Times*, June 11, 1931; "Brains of Book;" "Accused of Book Thefts."
29. "Police Find Three New Lots of Stolen Books." Also, "Dr. Clarke Held," 4.

30. "Says Big Ring Steals Books," *Worcester Telegram*, June 10, 1931; "Thefts of Rare Books Widespread," *Boston Post*, June 10, 1931.

31. "Dr. Clarke Held"; "Shop Here Linked to Library Thefts," *New York Times*, June 11, 1931.

32. Miscellany, *Time*, December 17, 1945, 46.

33. "Clarke Unable to get $5,000 Bail," *Boston Globe*, June 10, 1931.

34. "Brains of Book."

35. Clarke, Unpublished remembrances, 30.

36. "Book Dealer Sentenced as Fence," *New York Evening Post*, January 5, 1932.

37. William Bergquist to Charles Belden, June 16th, 1931. Boston Public Library Archives, HC.

38. "Dr. Clarke Held"; "Clarke Goes to Grand Jury."

39. Clarke, Unpublished remembrances, 2.

40. "Clarke in Lowell."

41. "Clarke to Grand Jury," *Clinton Courant*, June 12, 1931.

42. Ibid.

43. "Dr. Clarke to Hospital," *Clinton Courant*, August 28, 1931.

44. Enoch Callaway, *Asylum: A Midcentury Madhouse* (Westport, CT: Praeger, 2007), 4–5.

45. Robert Curran to Felix Ranlett, September 11, 1931. Boston Public Library Archives, HC.

46. Felix Ranlett to Robert Curran, September 14, 1931. Boston Public Library Archives, HC.

47. "Book Thief Changes His Plea," "Withdrew Not Guilty Plea," *Clinton Courant*, November 20, 1931; and "Clarke Pleads Guilty to Book Larceny," *Lowell Sun*, November 12, 1931.

48. Clarke, Unpublished remembrances, 30.

49. "Dr. Clarke Held."

7. *The People of the State of New York and Their Dignity*

1. Harris plea. For information on Panger see, in general, "Magistrates Facing Inquiry in 2 Counties," *New York Times*, January 22, 1930; "Crain is Sworn In," *New York Times*, December 13, 1929; "MA Panger Named Swann's Aid," *New York Times*, January 25, 1920.

2. Cedric Larson, "New York Library's Book Detective," *American Swedish Monthly*, October 1955, 6–7; Arthur Strawn, "Racketeers in the Rare Book Market," *The Sun*, May 22, 1932.

3. *The Bookshelf of Brander Matthews* (New York: Columbia University Press, 1931).

4. See, in general, "Scott Exhibition Opens," *New York Times*, October 9, 1932; "Morgan Manuscript by Scott is Stolen," *New York Times*, November 23, 1932; "$500 Reward Offered for Lost Morgan MS," *New York Times*, November 24, 1932; "Priceless Scott MS. Mysteriously Restored to Morgan Library," *New York Times*, April 19, 1933; Kobler, "Trailing the Book Crooks," 19. In another article alluding the theft, an author suggests that the same thief

should steal two hundred pages of many modern manuscripts, making them a more manageable size.

5. Selling stolen books is one thing. But selling what was deemed pornography was a dangerous profession. New York Vice enforcers routinely prosecuted booksellers for violating obscenity laws, closing stores and sending their proprietors to prison. Harry Gold made a great deal of money operating an illicit business; it is likely he had at least some member of the police force on his payroll. For the issue of vice prosecutions in the bookselling business, see, in general, Gertzman, *Bookleggers and Smuthounds*.

6. "Dealer Is Indicted As Rare Book Thief," *New York Times*, November 26, 1931.

7. "Romm Sent to Jail in Rare Book Thefts," *New York Times*, January 6, 1932.

8. *New York v. Charles J. Romm*, CR-62417, December 4, 1931.

9. "Indicted as Fences for Rare Book Loot," *New York Times*, December 5, 1931; also *New York v. Ben Harris*, CR-62485, December 2, 1931.

10. "Such Thievery is Serious," *Publishers Weekly*, December 26, 1931, 2718.

11. "Romm Sent to Jail in Rare Book Thefts," *New York Times*, January 6, 1932.

12. "Sing Sing Inmate Stabbed to Death," *Boston Globe*, November 13, 1931.

13. "Sing Sing Jobs Spurned," *New York Times*, January 5, 1931.

14. "New York Public Library Has Its Police Department."

15. *New York v. Gold*, testimony, September 7, 1932, 10.

16. "Jailed in Rare Book Theft," *New York Times* January 20, 1932.

17. Death Certificate # 5536, Manhattan. NYC Municipal Archives.

18. The story of Ed Harris, Oscar Chudnowsky, and Charles Shaw as they attempted to get the book back from Harry Gold was recounted in the testimony of them and others, before the grand jury, on September 7, 1932. Most of the men were re-interviewed for Harry Gold's second trial, telling the same basic story. To the extent that those interviews add anything new, they are separately noted.

19. Metcalf, *Random Recollections of an Anachronism*, 268; "Dealer Is Indicted in Rare Book Theft," *New York Times*, September 9, 1932. Metcalf claims that Harris sent his brother-in-law, Chudnowsky, to the NYPL. The contemporaneous, and more believable, account is from Heartman, who claims it was Eddie Harris that was sent. While, overall, Metcalf's account of the incident it interesting and mostly accurate, he incorrectly states many small details (some of which he admits), simply because he wrote his account some thirty years after the fact.

20. See, for instance, "Check Frauds Laid to 13 Held as Ring," *New York Times*, August 23, 1931; "Palmer Canfield Indicted as Forger," *New York Times*, September 26, 1931.

21. *New York v Gold*, Statement of Gaughran, January 8, 1934.

22. Charles Heartman, *American Book Collector*, January 1, 1933, 48; "Guilty in Book Theft," *New York Times*, May 24, 1933, 19.

23. Grand jury, 9.
24. Frank Polk to Thomas Crain, September 19, 1932. New York Municipal Archives, *Gold* file.
25. Richard Tofel, *Vanishing Point* (Chicago: Ivan R. Dee, 2004), 112.
26. *New York v. Gold*, Gold deposition, September 28, 1932, 3.
27. Ibid.
28. "Corrigan Named to Succeed Bertini," *New York Times*, April 2, 1931.
29. "Corrigan in New Post," *New York Times*, April 10, 1931.
30. "End of Parole Board Urged by Corrigan," *New York Times*, April 13, 1933.
31. "Jurist Disputes Warden on Crime," *New York Times* April 1, 1933.
32. "Buchler Win Stay," *New York Times*, May 20, 1932.
33. "Prosecutor's Coat Stolen," *New York Times*, May 10, 1933.
34. Thomas Crain to Oscar Chudnowsky, May 15, 1933. New York Municipal Archives, *Gold* file.
35. Charles Heartman, *American Book Collector*, January 1, 1933, 48.
36. *New York v. Gold*, CR-68509, Affidavit and Notice of Motion, March 5, 1934.
37. "Rare Book Fence Gets Prison Term," *New York Times*, June 7, 1933.
38. *New York v. Gold*, 239 AD 368, 372–3 (NY AD 1933).
39. Ibid., 369.
40. Frank Polk to Irving Mendelson, January 15, 1934. New York Municipal Archives, *Gold* file.
41. "Jay Rothschild, 83, Dead," *New York Times*, August 27, 1976; Jay Leo Rothschild, *The Students' Work Product and the Profession's Free Press*, 25 Brook. L. Rev. 187 (1958–1959).
42. *New York v. Gold*, affidavit and notice of motion, March 5, 1934.
43. *New York v. Gold*, "Harry Gold Case Witnesses."
44. Anonymous to Ben Harris, November 6, 1933. New York Municipal Archives, *Gold* file.
45. Dupree statement, November 15th, 1933; Dupree statement, January 4, 1934.
46. "Bookseller Again Guilty," *New York Times*, June 28, 1934; "Book Fence Sentenced," *New York Times*, July 16, 1934.
47. Note, appended to the NYPL's copy of *Al Aaraaf*.

8. That's the End of the Rare Book

1. "Rare Book Theft Bared by Bargain," *New York Times*, February 14, 1937. "Theft Revealed as Five Rare Books are Sold for $1.15," *Washington Post*, February 14, 1937.
2. "Stolen Books," *Publishers Weekly*, 1937, 1406.
3. "Seven Volumes Stolen From Widener," *Harvard Crimson*, March 22, 1937.
4. George Allen, "Stanley Wemyss, Biblioklept, Bibliophile, Bibliographer," a talk given at the Philobiblion Club, March 14, 1989; George Allen, *History of*

William H. Allen Bookseller, 1917–97 (Bethlehem, PA: Lehigh University Information Services, 1997).

5. *Ohio v. Smith*, Hamilton County No. 42567, October 8, 1936. Deposition of Jean Campbell, November 11, 1936.

6. *Ohio v. Smith*, Deposition of Martin Roberts, November 11, 1936.

7. "Book Thief," *Cincinnati Enquirer*, November 17, 1936. "Dealer Seized in Nation Wide Book Theft Plot," *Washington Post*, October 9, 1936.

8. "Readers' Open Forum," *Library Journal*, November 15, 1936, 859; "Book Thief Jailed, Wide Plot Is Seen," *New York Times*, September 26, 1936. "Man Held in Newark for Rare Book Thefts," *The Sun*, September 26, 1936.

9. "Cincinnatian Bought Stolen Books," *Cincinnati Times Star*, October 8, 1936.

10. "Readers' Open Forum."

11. Madeleine Stern, *Antiquarian Bookselling in the United States* (New York: Greenwood Press, 1985), 65–8.

12. Ibid., 77.

13. *Annual Report to the Secretary State, Ohio* (Springfield, OH: Springfield Publishing Company, 1920), 71.

14. See, for instance, *The Evening-Gazette*, April 25, 1918.

15. *Pharos-Tribune*, July 14, 1923.

16. *Vidette-Messenger*, November 15, 1929.

17. *Evening Independent*, April 10, 1929; *Antiques*, July 1922, 95.

18. William C. Smith, *Queen City Yesterdays* (Crawfordsville, IN: RE Banta, 1959). Thomas D. Clark, *My Century in History* (Lexington, KY: University of Kentucky Press, 2006), 206. Donald C. Dickinson, *Dictionary of American Antiquarian Booksellers* (Westport, CT: Greenwood Press, 1998), 206.

19. "Alleged Fence in Book Thefts Held," *Times Recorder*, October 9, 1936.

20. *Ohio v. Smith*, Hamilton County CR- 42567, October 8, 1936.

21. "Counsel to be Heard Today," *Cincinnati Enquirer*, November 19, 1936.

22. "Judge Alfred Mack Is Dead," *Youngstown Vindicator*, April 21, 1950. Also, "Judge Alfred Mack," *New York Times*, April 24, 1950.

23. Jean Campbell and Martin Roberts depositions.

24. "Counsel to be Heard."

25. "Smith Denies Testimony of State Witness," *Cincinnati Times-Star*, November 18, 1936.

26. "Book Thief."

27. Clarence Wunderlin, ed., *The Papers of Robert A. Taft* (Kent, OH: Kent State University Press, 1997), 276.

28. *Law Notes*, February 1913, 214.

29. "Defends Buying of Old Books," *Cincinnati Times-Star*, November 17, 1936.

30. "Smith Acquitted in Book Suit," *New York Times*, November 22, 1936; "Book Dealer Freed on Charge," *Cincinnati Enquirer*, November 22, 1936.

31. "Book Dealer Freed."

32. Ibid.

33. *Ohio v. Smith*, Entry Releasing Material Witness, November 19, 1936.
34. Allen, "Stanley Wemyss, Biblioklept, Bibliophile, Bibliographer."
35. "Ohio Book Dealer Arrested," *Publishers Weekly*, 1936, 1630.
36. Stern, 77.

Epilogue

 1. *New York v. Gold*, Statement of Raynor Dupree, April 2, 1934.
 2. Ibid.
 3. "Parole Agent Seized in Extortion Trap," *New York Times*, April 7, 1934, 32.
 4. "Ex Prison Aide is Jailed," *New York Times*, January 18, 1935, 3.
 5. "Home Loan Racket," *New York Times*, December 21, 1935, 1
 6. "Book Dealer Seized in Library Thefts," *New York Times*, June 17, 1942.
 7. "Book Fence Sentenced," *New York Times*, November 25, 1942.
 8. "Why Do Men Steal Rare Books?," *Brooklyn Daily Eagle*, June 12, 1933, 14.
 9. "Publisher Buys Building," *New York Times*, October 7, 1960, 57.
10. Meyer Berger, "About New York," *New York Times*, February 1, 1956, 21.
11. Nicholas Basbanes, *Patience & Fortitude* (New York: HarperCollins, 2001), 182.
12. Jacob Chernofsky, "Louis Cohen and the Argosy Book Store," *AB Bookman*, April 15, 1991, 1511. Cohen indicated that he brokered this sale, along with another sale of the O'Malley Bookshop. There is no substantial record of this in the Penn State archives, but Sandra Stelts, curator of rare books and manuscripts at PSU, talked to some retired colleagues on my behalf. What she discovered was that the dean of the libraries wanted to increase the library's holdings but that the bookstore purchases brought in a lot of material that was simply not suitable for a library. Some made it into the general stacks, some into special collections, and much was simply thrown away. Sandra Stults to Travis McDade, March 10, 2011. On file with author.
13. Meador and Mondlin, *Book Row*, 115–17.
14. "Book Racketeer to be Deported to Halifax," *Lowell Sun*, June 4, 1932, 1.
15. Fred Inglis, "Huge Collection of Rare Books and Old Papers," *Ottawa Citizen*, January 4, 1956, 25; Borden Clarke to F. A. Humphreys, January 14, 1954. Archives of Ontario, F264.
16. Dorothy "Dot" Clarke to Borden Clarke, January 6, 1961. Clarke to Humphreys. Archives of Ontario, F264; 1974 Individual Income Tax Return, Dorothy Clarke, Account 3290604.
17. Clarke, Unpublished remembrances, 1–2.
18. Metcalf, *Random Recollections of an Anachronism*, 264–65. Clarke's claims of forty honest years in the business appear on his letterhead and his mailings. He also mentions it in letters and even in a 1960 interview with a Bahamian newspaper. "New for Bookworms," *Nassau Guardian*, January 27, 1960, 1.
19. See, for instance, Pen Points, *Utica Observer-Dispatch*, November 13, 1951, 6. For the rest of his life, Clarke made almost yearly trips to Boston and, in particular, New York.

20. Clarke, Unpublished remembrances, 18.
21. Clarke to Humphreys.
22. Walter A. Roesch to Borden Clarke, April 27, 1957. Archives of Ontario, F264.
23. Borden Clarke to Walter A. Roesch, May 1st, 1957. Archives of Ontario, F264.
24. John Hilton to Borden Clarke, March 14, 1951. Archives of Ontario, F264
25. Borden Clarke to Mr. Carroll, June 4, 1960. Archives of Ontario, F264.
26. Borden Clarke to G.S. Duff, June 24, 1960. Archives of Ontario, F264.
27. HSC to Borden Clarke, August 10, 1944. Harold Borden Clarke to Hayward, March 6, 1961. Archives of Ontario, F264.
28. Clarke, Unpublished remembrances, 3.
29. Harold Borden Clarke to Cyril and Mary, August 8, 1959. Archives of Ontario, F264. To this day, Clarke's most long-lasting contribution to the world of books is the *Lucayos Cookbook*, a self-published work said to be based on an Elizabethan-era manuscript he found in the Bahamas. Among others, he sent copies of this book to Presidents Truman and Eisenhower, the Duke of Edinburgh, and Prime Minister John Diefenbaker.
30. Clarke, Unpublished remembrances, 31.

Index